Empowering the Community College
First-Year Composition Teacher

Empowering the Community College First-Year Composition Teacher

PEDAGOGIES AND POLICIES

Meryl Siegal
Laney College

and

Betsy Gilliland
University of Hawai'i, Mānoa

University of Michigan Press
Ann Arbor

Published in the United States of America
The University of Michigan Press
Manufactured in the United States of America

∞ Printed on acid-free paper

ISBN-13: 978-0-472-03791-9 (print)
ISBN-13: 978-0-472-12900-3 (ebook)

2024   2023   2022   2021   4   3   2   1

Contents

Introduction: Why FYC Teachers' Perspectives Are Important

First-year math and English courses at community colleges have become sites of contestation. Community colleges in the United States are the first (or the last) point of entry for the majority of students to access higher education, a career, a new start, and new skills. Community colleges have also become the entry point for many international students into U.S. higher education. Since the 1960s, a focus on higher education access for the traditionally disenfranchised has been paramount in the mission of community colleges (Shaughnessy, 1977). Today, community colleges are seeing a shift in emphasis from access to completion. In efforts to ameliorate what has come to be known as a "leaky" pipeline—the path from remedial and developmental courses to first-year composition (FYC) and degree, transfer, or certificate completion—colleges have trimmed their remedial and developmental education curriculum, combining FYC courses with separate but concurrent support courses or increasing class time to add support components to the traditional FYC. In many community colleges, FYC serves as the last English course students take toward the associate's degree; this same course is often articulated (see Glossary) with university and four-year college FYC classes. This book explores teacher, researcher, and curricular responses to changes in the traditional FYC course.

Community College FYC Trends: Eliminating Remedial Pre-Requisites

Current higher educational policy, often introduced as educational reform, has made radical changes in student placement protocols, college funding schemes, and course delivery mechanisms. Where community colleges once held the goal of providing educational access to

1

students with a wide range of goals, the focus now is on having students complete a course of study, accelerating students through English and math requirements.

The rise of big data and advanced statistical analysis has, in some ways, led the charge that community colleges could do things differently, accelerate course-taking patterns, and get better results for students. Here, results, or "student success," are typically understood as students: (1) getting through (passing) a course and (2) transferring or finishing a program, certificate, or degree. Much of the data collected on completion of higher education considers a six-year cycle. By 2017, 31.5 percent of students who first enrolled in a community college in the United States in 2011 had transferred to a four-year college or university; of those, 42 percent completed a bachelor's degree in the six-year span (Shapiro et al., 2017). It is assumed that students who neither transferred nor completed an associate's degree had dropped out, but little information is available to track students' actual reasons for dropping out.

Jaggars and Stacey (2014) have re-characterized the remediation problem as one of students leaving the community college:

> Only 28 percent of community college students who take a developmental education course go on to earn a degree within eight years [while for non-remedial students the figure is 43 percent] and many students assigned to developmental courses drop out before completing their sequence and enrolling in college-level courses. (p. 1)

Current research suggests that it is not necessary to know the exact reasons for dropping out, however, since data shows that in colleges where remedial classes have been removed and replaced with accelerated FYC and Math sequences, student success rates (getting students through English and math classes) are compelling (Kolodner 2017; Mejia, Rodriguez, & Johnson, 2019).

This movement has further been justified by a concern with increasing equity for all students. Researchers note that remedial education affects the poor and traditionally disenfranchised groups, including ethno-racially minoritized students, more egregiously:

> Underrepresented student groups are overrepresented in developmental courses. Eighty-seven percent of both Latino and African American students enroll in developmental education, compared to 70 percent of Asian American and 74 percent of white students. Among low-income students, 86 percent enroll in developmental coursework. (Mejia, Rodriguez, & Johnson, 2019, p. 3)

In community colleges, success toward equity means closing the "leaky pipeline" from which low-income students and students of color are more likely to be lost.

Statistical data show that students are less apt to drop out and more likely to stay in school if the trajectory to college-level courses is immediate (Mejia, Rodriguez, & Johnson 2019). In other words, eliminating courses that are not at the college level can shorten the time it takes to transfer or get an associate's degree because students get through their required courses for transfer more expediently. An example of the new wave of thinking in community colleges is California, where in 2017 the California State Legislature passed a bill, AB 705, that has nearly eliminated English placement testing for incoming students (a noted exception is in English for Speakers of Other Languages) and mandates that students who want to transfer to a four-year institution finish FYC within the first year of their arrival at the community college (California Community Colleges, 2018).

One question is how English departments decide which model is the best for their department. Several models have been put forth (e.g., Adams et al., 2009; California Acceleration Project, n.d.), and colleges have latitude as to which method they choose to implement to accelerate their students. The main models include having a support class, either credit or non-credit, attached to a FYC course designated for learners who need the support or offering a single FYC class with more unit hours for those learners who need support.

There is to date little information on how faculty collaborate to change pedagogy and make informed curricular decisions. In our experience, most departments do not have a set method to work through the difficult decisions of curricular change, something we hope will change. Furthermore, because of the differential ability or differential will for colleges to accomplish research and collaborate with faculty on areas of common concern, institutional research might not give the whole picture of what is happening at a particular college or in a particular department. Anecdotally, more students seem to fail and have to retake FYC now that remedial and developmental education classes have been removed. Yet, because of how data is collected, reported, and used, in some schools the view is that if the student finishes FYC successfully within a year, failing the first time can be viewed as successful through the lens of "one-year throughput." Still many questions remain to be answered about the effects of placement and FYC reforms on both students and faculty:

- ○ Are those students who actually need support taking the appropriate class?
- ○ How does being in a class where they are struggling affect students?
- ○ When a department is recognized as successful at accelerating students, what are the curriculum and student learning outcomes that the department agrees upon?
- ○ Are students assessed equitably or just passed on?
- ○ How do students feel about the expectations that are set for them?

Many states are decreasing funding to higher education and seeking ways to get more economic "value" from public higher education (Selingo, 2018). One way they are doing this is through curriculum and placement reforms. Although the curriculum at community colleges is perceived as the purview of faculty, state legislatures and college chancellors' offices have mandated curriculum reforms and offered financial incentives to colleges to get more students through a course of study (transfer, certificate, or degree) more quickly. Furthermore, additional funding can influence how well-positioned a department is to implement successful curricular changes. A recent webinar hosted by the RP Group (2020) on acceleration and co-requisite models described one college's accelerated FYC program as adding a credit unit to its core FYC course and mandating a two-credit unit for-credit support course; the amenities allotted by the FYC accelerated curriculum also included embedded note-takers (a person in the class taking notes for those students who are unable to do so), embedded tutoring (one or more tutors who assist students during the class), and embedded counseling staff (a counselor who is associated with the class and provides academic counseling for students), as well as faculty support groups that focused not only on creating and continuing collaborative work on new pedagogy but also collective support for faculty emotional health. All of these support structures add to the cost of running the course and require additional preparation and time on the part of instructional faculty. We suspect there is a new burden on faculty teaching accelerated FYC and wonder how this kind of teaching differs from teaching other FYC courses.

College for All: Ramifications for FYC

All of these reforms are occurring alongside changes in the student population enrolled in community college FYC courses. At the same time that there has been a sharp decline in the numbers of students going to college (Hechinger Report, 2018), especially in urban areas with record (pre-pandemic) low unemployment rates such as the San Francisco Bay Area (Johnson, Mejia, & Bohn, 2015), and a drive for a more educated populace in the face of a future robotized workforce and stagnant wages (Lennon, 2018), there has been a push for English faculty to make curricular changes in their FYC courses to accommodate a wider range of students, including those whose placement test scores, in the past, might have placed them in remedial or developmental education. Faculty, therefore, find themselves faced with changing their curriculum to accommodate a broader range of students but still mandated to achieve the same student learning outcomes and the demand that the course follow articulation agreements with four-year institutions.

Indeed, it is not clear just how diverse the community college student body is. At the 2019 California Association for Postsecondary Education and Disability meetings, statewide professionals expressed concern over the California Community Colleges Chancellor's Office reported data on the AB705 accelerated curriculum as it relates to students with disabilities: The student data was not disaggregated by disability category, thus ignoring the range of disabilities that include students who may only need accessible furniture to those with intellectual disabilities and autism spectrum disorders, as well as students who are blind/partially sighted, deaf, or hard of hearing. It was noted that data that is not disaggregated for specific disabilities gives an incomplete picture as it does not consider the differing needs and supports of students in divergent disability categories, which, if appropriately referenced, could, at the very least, mandate more funding and differentiated funding across districts (Rachel Goodwin, personal communication, 2019). In a prescient warning on how changes in remedial education—that is, ending remedial education—can affect community college instruction, W. Norton Grubb (2013) writes: "...the heterogeneity of students, which is one of the unique aspects of community colleges, may be too much for instructors in basic skills courses to handle. Accordingly, developmental education programs need to provide additional diagnostic and support mechanisms for students with learning disabilities and mental health problems" (p. 213). This would also affect the new accelerated FYC classes.

Community College FYC in Society

Despite many campuses' ongoing struggle to fulfill their missions, U.S. community colleges continue to be places of personal transformation and, ultimately, societal transformation. Increasingly, this transformation is occurring within what some see as a neoliberal perspective—one goes to college to become trained, find a career, and make money from that career (Kroll, 2012). The student is a customer focused on getting in, getting through, and getting out. Colleges actually recommend websites where students can look into annual salaries for particular career choices (for example: https://salarysurfer.cccco.edu/SalarySurfer.aspx). Community colleges are increasingly seen as a direct way to train young adults to be part of the new economy. However, in a society where the new economy is more uncertain when it comes to jobs that have been the focus of a typical community college curriculum, how can ongoing change be incorporated into the curriculum, particularly for FYC and English?

We note that community college FYC is a place of complex ideological disagreement. Discussing how student knowledge gained from a community college FYC course transfers to other courses across the curriculum, Howard Tinberg (2015) writes that

> beyond the stated purpose of offering students instruction in generalized writing skills (essentially a command of grammar and mechanics and mastery of the essay form, as well as some experience in writing with sources), the first-year composition course, some have argued, should give students a localized knowledge set that transfers to, and can be repurposed for different contexts, whether in history, sociology, chemistry, criminal justice, and so forth. (pp. 7–8)

Considering the current multiple purposes of transferable FYC courses, students' various purposes in taking the course, and the increasingly diverse student body that attends community colleges, is it still appropriate or possible to consider a cohesive set of skills that transfer to different contexts? Many of us are teaching FYC within departments that offer limited English course offerings focused primarily on teaching students to write coherently, cohesively, and engagingly without the benefit of writing across the curriculum courses (WAC) in other departments. We continue to wonder about the outcomes of these program structures: What actual skills do students learn in FYC courses? Will they be competitive if a four-year degree is their ultimate college goal? Will they be able to succeed in completing a job application and writing a convincing and coherent cover letter?

The community college system is unique in that it provides various pathways for students to gain job skills: "In an era when a college credential seems necessary for middle-class jobs and achieving the American Dream, increasing numbers of students are being pushed, or counseled, toward college as the only route to individual advancement" (Grubb, 2013, p. 1). However, for many students, the road for college advancement has been blocked because of "the remediation problem" (Grubb, 2013, p. 1) that starts in primary and secondary education; this is a problem that has evolved, according to Grubb, because of "passing along students who are not ready for the next level of schooling—something that generates the high numbers of students requiring remediation at every level" (p. 214), including the community college. The accelerated movement is thought by some to provide a more equitable pathway for ethno-racially minoritized students to pursue a college degree precisely because of the importance of that degree in U.S. discourse. We cannot underestimate the statistical evidence that those who have a college degree in the U.S. lead a better life, not just due to salary, but in part, due to health care benefits (Case & Deaton, 2020). Case and Deaton also note the changing workplace and economy, suggesting that higher education needs to be nimble and innovative as "there is obviously nothing in a bachelor's degree that insulates the holder against being replaced by a machine or outcompeted by cheaper labor in the rest of the world" (p. 258). Certainly, curricular innovation should be continuously occurring in the community college, and we believe that the chapters in the book provide both the steps and vision toward innovation and how FYC faculty could be the foundation and source for change.

Among the 1,047 public community colleges in the United States (U.S. Department of Education, 2017), there is wide variability from state to state as to how they are run, what kinds of classes and programs they offer, and whether their courses articulate to four-year degree programs. Since the 1960s, following closely on the heels of the civil rights movement, a focus on access for the traditionally disenfranchised has been paramount in community colleges' missions. Today, for many of these schools, the focus is on equity through retention and transfer (Bailey, Jaggars, & Jenkins, 2015), and FYC plays a key role in that effort. As Bailey, Jaggars, and Jenkins (2015) see it, changing the face of FYC is a way to improve student retention rates.

With this focus on student completion, the FYC course has been the subject of FYC faculty meetings, curricular and funding changes, grant projects, and policy changes. California made a major change to its community college FYC policy in 2009, requiring all students who wanted an associate's degree in any subject, including career and technical education, to take and pass the FYC course rather than a course one level below FYC but still transferable for college credit (Morse, 2019). Despite that change, there seems to be no research on how the change in the sequence for an associate's degree affected the way the course is taught or the number of students getting a degree, or even how it may have affected teacher burnout or attrition. Considering the aims of FYC and its articulation with four-year colleges, many FYC faculty were alarmed at the 2009 change, which Morse noted sparked a "contentious debate" (2019, p. 1). These teachers saw the move as a reification of one form of academic literacy, rather than a change to help students complete career technology education degrees where other types of literacies might be more appropriate. In 2009, many FYC faculty wondered how it would be possible to teach a FYC course that was both articulated with the four-year university system and useful to students in career and technical education. How could a single course address all students' diverse goals and needs? Why should students who wanted an associate's degree in a subject such as culinary arts, welding, or carpentry need to complete FYC?

Curricular changes in English programs have left some community college faculty wondering if education is no longer the primary goal for community college English classes (Kroll, 2012). Questioning the role that community colleges will play in the future, Kroll notes the difficulties of a neoliberal approach to education and quotes humanist philosopher Martha Nussbaum: "Distracted by the pursuit of wealth, we increasingly ask our schools to turn out useful profit-makers rather than thoughtful citizens. Under pressure to cut costs, we prune away just those parts of the educational endeavor that are crucial to preserving a healthy society" (quoted in Kroll, 2012, p. 119). Still, faculty are

innovating and radically transforming their pedagogies and the ways
that students learn, hoping that their course is not "pruned" because of
budget restrictions and lack of student enrollment.

Why This Book Now?

Although common sense (and actual community college policy) dic-
tates that faculty are at the heart of the curriculum and that changes
made to the curriculum should emanate from faculty, recent reforms
at U.S. community colleges have in many ways bypassed full faculty
involvement. The reasons why FYC faculty are not always the first to
be consulted and included fully in FYC curriculum changes are complex and unique to each state and college. The reasons why they might
not respond even when a call for a broader consultation is issued are
also complex. Changes in class offerings and curriculum are often made
without any documented qualitative data such as close examination of
student writing, observations of classroom instruction (or a comparison
of FYC instruction before acceleration and after the implementation of
accelerated sections), teacher and student interviews about the quality
of student work, teacher interviews about how they are changing their
curriculum, or even interviews with transfer institutions that accept the
new FYC classes as equal to previous ones. Often, college administrators
and state legislatures focus on accountability through college completion rates and student pass rates rather than the learning that occurs in
the classroom.

This book was born when we were each working in different sectors in public education and thinking about the changes in FYC in our
respective contexts. It is an effort to bring grassroots faculty perspectives back to the curriculum, showcasing faculty knowledge, expertise,
and creativity in designing and implementing excellent instruction in
FYC. The range of topics grew out of an open call for manuscripts on
community college FYC; we also invited authors working in this area.
The book covers themes integral to current FYC teaching: faculty-
driven innovative curriculum and creative programs that change the
face of FYC, faculty expertise in literacy and in teaching a broad range of

students, and current research on community college policy and practice. We believe that faculty creativity and innovation must be part of all curricular change, and we hope that this book fosters a creative, collaborative dialogue among English faculty and other disciplines in the community college, focusing on student success and needs while also allowing faculty across disciplines full discretion toward creating programs of excellence.

In honoring teachers' creativity, experience, and knowledge, this book is an inquiry with teachers into community college FYC pedagogy and policy at a time when change has not only been called for but also mandated by state lawmakers (in some cases, backed by philanthropic foundations with interests in community college education, cf. Harklau et al., 2019) who hold the purse strings for public education.

Overview of the Book

The chapters in this volume, organized into four areas of concern for FYC teachers, are authored by a diverse group of community college instructors and researchers across the United States. Their range of perspectives provides a broad look at contemporary community college FYC that inspires teaching and learning and, at the same time, endeavors to present the complexity of community college FYC in higher education. The book focuses on pedagogy and policy/research, both of which are essential to the work of today's community college faculty.

Part 1: Refining Our Pedagogy

The four chapters in this part offer teachers new lenses through which to view their current pedagogy and provide sound practices for teaching FYC in traditional or accelerated formats. In "Negotiating Writing Identities Online and in Person: The Growth of Metacognition and Writing Awareness in FYC" (Chapter 1), Brenda Refaei and Ruth Benander focus on student agency and the construction of a writer's identity as crucial to FYC students and their writing development. Refaei and

Benander provide reflective writing activities for students that support students' agency and efficacy within the writing classroom and beyond.

Considering the importance of reading skills for academic writing development is next as Michael Larkin outlines the ways in which technology can both help and hinder student learning in "They Are Reading from Screens, But (How) Are They Reading from Screens?" (Chapter 2). Although 21st century youth may be glued to their smartphones, they have not necessarily developed strategies for understanding and retaining what they read in electronic modes. Larkin provides creative approaches to help students identify their purposes and processes for reading in the FYC classroom and outlines pedagogy for different approaches to reading on screens versus print reading.

In "The Socio-Cognitive Approach in Academic ESL Composition Classes" (Chapter 3), Barbara A. Auris uses a socio-cognitive framework for student dialogue about writing that acts to empower English language students while also focusing on the basics of good instruction such as modeling, metalinguistic conversations, and practice to ensure student success in FYC.

Concluding this part, Miriam Moore presents an approach for engaging with student writers at any level through texts that focus on writing in "Using 'Writing about Writing' Pedagogy with L2 and Developmental Readers and Writers at the Community College" (Chapter 4). Through this approach, FYC teachers can provide a framework to help students develop metalinguistic knowledge and an academic writing practice that includes key threshold concepts such as the writing process, revision, and literacy practices.

Part 2: Teaching Toward Acceleration

The three chapters in this part focus on pedagogical practices currently playing a role in many accelerated classrooms. In "Contract Grading as Anti-Racist Praxis in the Community College Context" (Chapter 5), Sarah Klotz and Carl Whithaus describe the practice of contract grading and provide evidence for its transformative value in the FYC classroom.

Traditional student success is re-examined through the lens of the grading contract, a change that allows student agency; students consider their course responsibilities with competing demands on their time outside of school and also develop a sense of themselves as responsible for their efforts in the class.

Next, Andrew Kranzman and Chandra Howard focus on how FYC instructors can incorporate community-building activities to engage students in the classroom learning community. Their chapter, "First-Year Composition: Building Relationships to Teach Emerging Writers" (Chapter 6), provides ways for teachers to build trust within the classroom while supporting cognition and developing academic literacy.

Caroline Torres brings her expertise in learning disabilities and working with English learner community college students to "Supporting English Learners with Disabilities in College Composition Courses" (Chapter 7). Torres's work clarifies how scaffolding writing assignments can be both engaging and efficacious. Her chapter reminds faculty that the reasons why students are struggling are complex and that planned, clear instruction can make the curriculum accessible for all.

Part 3: Considering Programmatic Change

In many community colleges, programs have been created to address students' personal and career needs. The chapters in this part examine ways that three colleges have developed FYC programs and pedagogy to meet specific student goals. Two chapters focus on technical writing and literacy pedagogy, and the third describes a distance learning program that allows high school students in remote locations to access college FYC before completing their secondary school degrees.

In "Teaching Writing in a STEM Learning Community: The Heart and Science of Communication" (Chapter 8), Gonzalo Arrizon presents a structured approach to teaching FYC with a STEM (Science, Technology, Engineering, and Math) focus. Because he recognizes that FYC students need more than a science- and mathematics-based FYC curriculum to succeed in a STEM learning community, he created a supportive curriculum that provides a humanities perspective on how STEM concepts fit into students' lives and dreams.

Next, Kellyanne Ure, Kade Parry, and David A. Allred highlight a distance learning program with an innovative approach to dual (concurrent) enrollment that they designed and taught. Their chapter, "Motivating Students from Afar: Teaching English in a Live Broadcast Concurrent Enrollment Program" (Chapter 9), features a model for student success from "afar" that includes synchronous video instruction assisted by onsite class facilitators with regularly scheduled teacher visits to the rural schools. Key to the success of the program was the work faculty put into the design, reworking, and assessment of the program.

This part closes with an in-depth look at how an English class can provide students with the writing curriculum necessary to respond to the demands of CTE (Career and Technical Education) professional writing and can motivate and invigorate students and teachers toward a CTE degree and certification completion. "Contextualized FYC Courses for Career Technical Education" (Chapter 10), by Erin B. Jensen, Jennifer Stieger, and Whitney Zulim, focuses on the ways that CTE English courses act as a reminder that the rigor of college writing is not just for students intent on transfer, but also for those following through with career and technical education.

Part 4: Considering Curriculum: Research and Policy

The six chapters in this part present different approaches to researching issues in FYC instruction, student success, and educational policy. Two chapters (11 and 16) focus on large-scale statistical research to better understand the needs of diverse student populations and suggest ways to achieve more equitable outcomes for community college students. Chapter 12 uses a case study ethnographic approach to understand Korean international students in FYC while Chapter 13, using a similar approach, focuses on educational reform undertaken in one English department. Chapters 15 and 16 analyze teacher interview data to understand how educational reforms affect the teachers as well as the curriculum.

Rebecca M. Callahan, Catherine E. Hartman, and Hongwei Yu, in "Heterogeneity among Community College English Learners: Who Are Our ELs in FYC and How Do They Compare?" (Chapter 11), present new analyses of how students who use English as an additional language engage both academically and socially in community colleges. Their work shows that the English learner population is not monolithic and points to the importance of engagement in college persistence rates.

Drawing on ethnographic fieldwork focused on Korean international students at a community college in Utah, Justin G. Whitney points out the significance of community colleges for middle-class international students who have been shut out of four-year universities at home and in the U.S. His chapter is titled "Avoiding the 'Cliffs': Korean International Community College Students and Rhetorical Flexibility" (Chapter 12).

George C. Bunch, Ann Edris, and Kylie Alisa Kenner, in "First-Year Composition Faculty in a Changing Community College Policy Landscape: Engagement, Agency, and Leadership in the Midst of Reform" (Chapter 13), address ways that an English department faculty responded to educational reform directives affecting their programs. The chapter details the steps that faculty took to create instructional change.

Heather B. Finn and Sharon Avni based their chapter, "Combining Developmental Writing and First-Year Composition Classes: Faculty Perspectives on How Co-Requisite Teaching Affects Curriculum and Pedagogy" (Chapter 14), on interviews of faculty in New York teaching an accelerated FYC class. The authors show how the faculty negotiate reform while teaching the new models of FYC, becoming what Finn and Avni term "educational policy brokers."

In "Valuing Teacher Knowledge, Valuing Local Knowledge: FYC in Hawai'i Community Colleges" (Chapter 15), Meryl Siegal focuses on FYC change seen through the lens of community college faculty perspectives. The research analyzes interviews with teachers in FYC programs that were undergoing both curriculum reform and changes in student placement protocols. The faculty responses demonstrate that despite a curriculum in flux and questions on how changes were made, teachers remain engaged, creative, and visionary.

The final chapter in Part 4, "Institutional Research (IR) and Remediation Reform: A Contextualized Exploration for Faculty" (Chapter 16), is authored by Terrence Willett, Mallory Newall, and Craig Hayward, all of whom are currently engaged in community college institutional research. Their chapter allows English instructors an inside look at what campus Institutional Research (IR) offices do and how institutional researchers can effectively work alongside and with faculty on policy and pedagogical issues.

The volume concludes with our reflections and thoughts for future work, followed by questions for discussion and reflection and a glossary. We hope that the research and pedagogical recommendations in this volume serve as a springboard for our readers' continued growth as teachers, researchers, and teacher-educators for community college first-year composition and beyond.

REFERENCES

Adams, P., Gearhart, S., Miller, R., & Roberts, A. (2009). The accelerated learning program: Throwing open the gates. *Journal of Basic Writing, 28*(2), 50–69.

Bailey, T.R., Jaggars, S.S., & Jenkins, D. (2015). *Redesigning America's community colleges: A clearer path to student success.* Cambridge, MA: Harvard University Press.

California Acceleration Project. (n.d.). The California Acceleration Project. Retrieved from www.accelerationproject.org

California Community Colleges. (2018). What is AB 705? Retrieved from https://assessment.cccco.edu/ab-705-implementation

Case, A., & Deaton, A. (2020). *Deaths of despair and the future of capitalism.* Princeton, NJ: Princeton University Press.

Grubb, W.N. (with Gabriner, R.). (2013). *Basic skills education in community colleges.* New York: Routledge.

Harklau, L., Batson, K., & McGovern, K. (2019, March). Eliminating college ESL courses, services, & programs: Teacher perspectives. Paper presented at the American Association of Applied Linguistics Annual Conference, Atlanta, Georgia.

Hechinger Report. (2018, Sept. 10). Colleges set to fight for fewer students. *U.S. News & World Report.* Retrieved from www.usnews.com

Jaggars, S.S., & Stacey, G.W. (2014, January). What we know about developmental education outcomes. New York: Community College Research Center. Retrieved from https://ccrc.tc.columbia.edu/media/k2/attachments/what-we-know-about-developmental-education-outcomes.pdf

Johnson, H., Mejia, M.C., & Bohn, S. (2015). *Will California run out of college graduates?* San Francisco: Public Policy Institute of California.

Kolodner, M. (2017, May 11). California's new effort to fix remedial education. *Hechinger Report.* https://hechingerreport.org/californias-new-effort-fix-remedial-education/

Kroll, K. (2012). The end of the community college English profession. *Teaching English at the Two-Year College, 40*(2), 118–129.

Lennon, M. (2018, Sept. 14). Benefits of an educated workforce in the fourth industrial revolution. *Digitalist.* Retrieved from www.digitalistmag.com

Mejia, M.C., Rodriguez, O., & Johnson, H. (2019). *What happens when colleges broaden access to transfer courses? Evidence from California's community colleges.* San Francisco: Public Policy Institute of California.

Morse, D. (2019). A historical and historic success for the ASCCC 2007: Raising English and math requirements. Academic Senate for California Community Colleges. Retrieved from https://www.asccc.org/content/historical-and-historic-success-asccc-2007-raising-english-and-math-requirements

RP Group (Producer). (2020, April 30). Corequisite support models for English and math [webinar]. https://rpgroup.org/RP-Projects/All-Projects/Multiple-Measures/Publications

Selingo, J.J. (2018, Sept. 8). States' decision to reduce support for higher education comes at a cost. *Washington Post.* Retrieved from www.washingtonpost.com

Shapiro, D., Dundar, A., Huie, F., Wakhungu, P.K., Yuan, X., Nathan, A. & Hwang, Y. (2017). *Tracking transfer: Measures of effectiveness in helping community college students to complete bachelor's degrees* (Signature Report No. 13). Herndon, VA: National Student Clearinghouse Research Center.

Shaughnessy, M. P. (1977). *Errors and expectations: A guide for the teacher of basic writing.* New York: Oxford University Press.

Tinberg, H. (2015). Reconsidering transfer knowledge at the community college: Challenges and opportunities. *Teaching English at the Two-Year College, 43*(1), 7–31.

U.S. Department of Education. (2017). Community college facts at a glance. Washington, DC: DOE Office of Career, Technical, and Adult Education. Retrieved from https://www2.ed.gov/about/offices/list/ovae/pi/cclo/ccfacts.html

Part 1

Refining Our Pedagogy

1

Negotiating Writing Identities Online and in Person: The Growth of Metacognition and Writing Awareness in FYC

Brenda Refaei and Ruth Benander
UNIVERSITY OF CINCINNATI BLUE ASH COLLEGE

Students at our two-year, open-access college are often unsure if they are prepared for the reading and writing activities they will encounter at college and in their composition courses. Many students do not feel their past experiences have prepared them for the increased reading and writing demands they expect to encounter. In two-year colleges responsible for supporting diverse students who may not have strong identification as college writers, instructors must understand the difficult journey that FYC can be for uncertain, unprepared students. This chapter discusses how structured reflection journals specifically focused on the learning experience of becoming writers can support students from diverse backgrounds as they make sense of college writing, begin to feel confident in their skills, and learn to be proud of their accomplishments.

Located in Blue Ash, Ohio, a northeast suburb of Cincinnati, University of Cincinnati Blue Ash College is the largest regional college in Ohio offering primarily associate's degrees, with an enrollment of approximately 5,900 students, most of whom are enrolled full-time. Our students reflect the local diversity of the area with 21 percent Black or African American, 5 percent Hispanic or Latino, and 8 percent registered with Accessibility Resources. Multilingual students are Ohio residents who may speak a language other than English at home. (Our college has been unable to track the number of multilingual students enrolled because it is not part of the demographic data students supply with admission.) On the semester system, our required composition sequence is divided into one semester of FYC and a second-year composition course. The FYC course outcomes are derived from the Council of Writing Program Administrators' Outcomes Statement for First-Year Composition (2014).

Due to growth of online programs at our college, our department offers a one-semester online FYC course. The online courses and in-person courses are available to all students in the university system. As a result, students in our in-person and online FYC courses have mixed in-person and online schedules. We note that the pass rate for the in-person FYC courses is higher than the rate for online FYC. The online intermediate composition course, however, has a slightly higher completion rate than the in-person FYC.

Reflective Journals for a Diverse Community of Students

Reflective journals work for any student demographic since they ask writers to become more self-aware regardless of their circumstances. However, for students who are new to reflective practice, this approach to thinking about learning can be a critical step in gaining a sense of agency in their own learning experiences. Our students come from a wide variety of ethnic backgrounds, socioeconomic statuses, and academic preparation. What this means is that FYC is a diverse community of students with a high variety of experiences related to writing, from very little experience to high school Advanced Placement classes.

Given the range of students we serve in FYC, these reflective journal assignments work well for all students. We scaffold experiences for students who do not have the cultural capital expected in college classrooms and whose families do not have the insider knowledge to help them navigate higher education. The journal assignments provide guiding questions that support students as they grapple with metacognition and focused reflection on how their experience in the course relates to their identity as writers.

Scaffolding Reflective Journals to Promote Reflective Practice

We designed this series of journal prompts to help students reflect on their development as college writers. Bower (2003) has suggested, "Like writing, reflective metacognition is a process with components such as review, reflexivity, and cognitive analysis, which require practice throughout the semester in order to maximize a learner's potential for growth and change" (p. 64). We address this challenge by distributing the journal assignments throughout the term, and we ask students to reflect on their own beliefs, their interactions with others, and how their writing skills transfer to their further course work and, later, their professions. Each of the journal prompts focuses students' attention on a specific literate behavior and asks them to consider how they use that behavior in a reflection of how they perceive themselves. Points are associated with the journals to encourage completion, elaboration, and editing, but the points are not related to content. These journal assignments are timed to appear at key junctures in the course so that students reflect critically on recent experiences. The journal prompts ask them to consider these points:

- ○ Journal 1: How they see themselves as writers at the start of the course
- ○ Journal 2: How they arrive at their writing topic
- ○ Journal 3: How interactions with others influence their development as writers
- ○ Journal 4: How they deal with conflicting opinions and information in their writing
- ○ Journal 5: How the course structure supports their writing development

○ Journal 6: How they change their identity based on the rhetorical situation

○ Journal 7: How they have experimented as writers in the course

○ Journal 8: How their overall development as a writer has changed since the beginning of the semester based on going back and reading Journal 1.

The journal prompts support students as they build their meta-cognitive skills. The journal prompts were posted through the "Journals" function in Blackboard, the learning management system used at our institution. As a way to synthesize the information collected in the journals and encourage students to analyze their own development, we asked for a final paper for which the journal entries could be used as content as they discussed their personal development as a writer and the principles that now guide their choices as writers.

Rationale for the Pedagogy

Developing an identity as a writer is essential if students are to be able to transfer writing knowledge across situations as Tinberg (2015) suggested, but how do these writing identities develop? Gee (2015) described how individuals create understanding through an alignment of linguistic, social, and cultural interaction. He argued that when we communicate with others, we are interacting with created identities. This raises the question: What identities are our students enacting in the writing classroom?

Examining social theories of the development of the self, Ivanič (1998) claimed that "writing is an act of identity in which people align themselves with socio-culturally shaped possibilities for self-hood, playing their part in reproducing or challenging dominant practices and discourses, and the values, beliefs and interests which they embody" (p. 32). It is through discourse that learners come to know who they are. Writing provides special affordances to learners to capture their thoughts for inspection over time. McAdams (2013), in his development of a framework of the self, suggested that the self develops over a person's life, first as an actor defined by traits and roles, then as an agent with personal goals, and finally as an "autobiographic author" (p. 273). McAdams argued that this final stage of identifying as the author of one's life emerges in late childhood/ early adolescence and continues into early adulthood. This development means that many of our students are just learning to use their personal actions, goals, and personality traits to explain who they are to themselves and others. Adopting this developmental perspective on identity formation may help explain why first-year college students struggle with reflective writing activities, since they are still learning to assign meaning to the events in their lives and see their own agency in their identity.

This developmental approach to identity, from actor to agent to author, is clear in students' reflective work. Explicitly structuring the reflective journals to guide students through their writing journey and then asking them to reflect on that very journey helps students begin to see how the "self of yesterday becomes the self of today, and how [that will] all lead to the anticipated self of tomorrow" (McAdams, 2013, p. 274). Being aware of one's own thinking, metacognition, is integral to academic writing development (Negretti, 2012). Students need opportunities to become aware of their writing awareness, such as declarative, procedural, and conditional knowledge about writing. When Negretti used journal assignments to help students engage in these metacognitive activities, she found that "metacognitive awareness also seems to have a reciprocal relationship with self-regulation and students' development of individual writing approaches" (p. 143). The journal assignments that we have incorporated are a systematic scaffolding of student metacognition to support them in understanding their own efficacy and agency in owning their identity as writers.

Student Identity as Reflected in Journals

We have collected journal entries from students enrolled in both online (N=21) and in-person (N=20) FYC, as well as an online second-year composition course (N=20) to assess if the mode of instruction influences a student's development of a writing identity. These numbers reflect the number of students who completed all the journals, not necessarily those who completed the course.

Following Huckin (2004), we used content analysis to examine the journals, "identifying, quantifying, and analyzing ... specific words, phrases, concepts, or other observable semantic data in a text or body of texts with the aim of uncovering some underlying thematic or rhetorical pattern running through these texts" (p. 14). The thematic patterns in the students' writing illuminate the development of their writing identity.

How Students See Themselves as Writers

Journal 1 asks students to reflect on their writing identity and Journal 8 asks students to look back at Journal 1 to discuss how their identity has changed over the course of the term. In McAdams' (2013) discussion of the self, many of our students would be classified as "emerging adults" who are negotiating the "construction of an integrative life story" (p. 273), which integrates past experiences and future experiences. This life story appears as very short narratives of, perhaps, one sentence in Journal 1 for the FYC students. These students are still identifying themselves through traits such as "I am a hard worker," or they are able to identify a specific personal goal such as "I want to be successful in this class." When they reach the end of FYC, they are all beginning to construct more sophisticated identities that demonstrate their integration of their past, present, and future selves as writers. One student illustrates this development well:

- ◯ Journal 1: *I have constant issues with doubting myself. I think this course will benefit me and push me in college.*

- ◯ Journal 8: *As I went back to read journal 1, I have grown tremendously not only as a writer but as a student. Seeing how I can deliver a thesis with no problem amazes me so much! I am very proud of my work in my portfolio... . Seeing how I am able to portray my writings to an audience and give valid details made me feel so good about myself.*

In Journal 1, this student's narrative expresses anxiety about her writing ability, and she vaguely refers to her self-doubt as motivation to grow. By Journal 8, benefitting from looking back at all her previous work, she creates a coherent narrative of how her past self informs her present self through mastery of specific skills.

This theme of increased confidence and pride in accomplishment appeared frequently in FYC final narratives of writing identity. Both online and in-person courses cited pride and confidence, with 35 out of 41 students explicitly referencing these aspects of their writing identity. In contrast, of the 20 second-year students, only 8 referenced increased confidence. Possibly, the students in the second-year composition course already felt good about their abilities and so did not need to discuss newfound confidence. These second-year students, sufficiently confident in their identity as academic writers, emphasized their identity as writers in their professions more than the first-year students. In their final writing, 13 of the 20 second-year students included narratives of how they planned to use their writing in professional contexts. This identity was established in Journal 1, where all 20 of the second-year students referenced their professions as a context for their writing, while only half of the first-year students referenced their professions, usually in the context of mentioning their academic major.

How Students Perceive Transferring Writing Knowledge

FYC students did not differ in how they applied the writing concepts and processes they had learned in the course to their professional lives. They described a nebulous future need to write professionally, such as this student's reflection: "The healthcare field requires a lot of writing that must be clear and accurate and this class has prepared me for that." By the end of FYC, many students identified being able to write in a more professional style as an element of good writing. Students in intermediate composition had a much firmer grasp of the writing used in their profession. Six explained how they use the course concepts in their professional lives. As one student wrote, "My genre analysis helped me to write professional emails and business memos and I've already used that experience and practice in my internship."

First-year students were more likely than most intermediate students to connect the writing concepts from English composition to their other courses. Students in FYC mentioned planning and organizing writing, utilizing peer review, and developing an appropriate topic as strategies they could use in other courses. Students in the in-person classes were more likely to identify specific strategies they would apply such as considering audience, identifying genre, rough drafting, and quoting, while online students referred vaguely to strategies of using sources, eportfolio, and applying the concepts to other courses. Four of the 20 intermediate students listed four or five writing concepts each, such as researching, peer revising, analyzing genres, and analyzing language used in discourse communities that they could use in other courses.

A few students in FYC and intermediate composition described how they would use what they learned in the composition course in other writing situations. When first-year students described this general transfer, they identified specific strategies such as revising, developing "a deeper thought process," and identifying if a source is reliable. Intermediate students described how they applied the writing concepts and practices to their lives as in, "I apply it to everyday life and how I approach different people." In describing how they can apply writing concepts to their lives, intermediate students were engaging in authoring their own identities as writers beyond the composition classroom.

In conclusion, scaffolding the journal prompts allowed students to reflect on their writing identity as actors, agents, and authors. For instance, as actors, students identified their social roles and skills as writers. They conveyed an agent role when they acted as their own assessors as they examined their personal writing goals. Some students expressed an author role as they began developing a coherent narrative of their writing identity. Students in FYC engaged in these reflective journals to increase their self-confidence in writing. The writing concepts and processes introduced in the course helped students meet assignment requirements, while the journals provided an avenue for them to reflect on the processes that were the most productive for them. In considering how they could apply writing processes to other contexts, students began to construct a life narrative for themselves as college writers.

Without prompting, students commented on how this sequential approach to reflection helped them develop as writers. One student wrote, "Journals are also very interesting and helpful. Looking back in Journal 2 where I did sort of a reflection of why I chose my research project topic, it made me to [sic] realize more about myself and what I did not know about myself." It is possible that if we had not asked the students to reflect on their writing, they might not have done so. For example, Bharuthram (2018) and Page and Benander (2011) note that reflection is a difficult practice that students may be reluctant to pursue. While they may be able to reflect on personal feelings or describe experiences, more critical reflection analyzing and assessing academic performance may need to be learned practices. However, by scaffolding the reflection process for them, the students responded with growth. The increase in confidence in the FYC course was clear. The students frequently commented on their qualities as hard workers and the fact that writing was hard work. The optimistic result of the FYC is that they conclude, "Writing is hard work, and I can do it."

Through journaling, FYC students can begin constructing authorship narratives as college/professional writers. They perceive their skills as transferring to other courses and to workplaces, they can see how their early writing contributes to their development in the course, and they can recognize the elements of good writing. This approach to iterative journaling throughout the course, paired with an eportfolio that allows students to review their writing progress, is successful. Since it is personalized, and specific to the individual's experience, this approach can be used in any composition course. In the case of FYC, tailoring journaling to the progress of the course enhances the opportunity for students to begin to see themselves as the authors of their own experiences.

REFERENCES

Bharuthram, S. (2018). Reflecting on the process of teaching reflection in higher education. *Reflective Practice, 19*(6), 806–817.

Bower, L. (2003). Student reflection and critical thinking: A rhetorical analysis of 88 portfolio cover letters. *Journal of Basic Writing, 22*(2), 47–66.

Council of Writing Program Administrators. (2014). WPA outcomes statement for first-year composition (3.0). Retrieved from http://wpacouncil.org/positions/outcomes.html

Gee, J. P. (2015). Reflections on understanding, alignment, the social mind, and language of interaction. *Language and Dialogue, 5*(2), 300–311. doi: 10.1075/ld.5.2.06gee

Huckin, T. (2004). Content analysis: What texts talk about. In C. Bazerman (Ed.), *What writing does and how it does it* (pp. 13–32). Mahwah NJ: Lawrence Erlbaum.

Ivanič, R. (1998). *Writing and identity: The discoursal construction of identity in academic writing.* Philadelphia: John Benjamins.

McAdams, D. (2013). The psychological self as actor, agent, and author. *Perspectives on Psychological Science, 8*(3), 272–295. doi: 10.1177/1745691612464657

Negretti, R. (2012). Metacognition in student academic writing: A longitudinal study of metacognitive awareness and its relation to task perception, self-regulation, and evaluation of performance. *Written Communication, 29*(2), 142–179. doi: 10.1177/0741088312438529

Page, D., & Benander, R. (2011). Promoting cultural proficiency through reflective assignments in study abroad. *International Journal of Arts and Sciences, 4*(25), 205–216.

Tinberg, H. (2015). Reconsidering transfer knowledge: Challenges and opportunities. *Teaching English in the Two-Year College, 43*(1), 7–31.

2

They Are Reading from Screens, But (How) Are They Reading from Screens?

Michael Larkin
UNIVERSITY OF CALIFORNIA, BERKELEY

A scene in the modern college composition classroom: A novel is up for discussion at the start of a session, and the students spring into action in a manner that is long familiar, though with some digital twists. One brings out a paperback she ordered from Amazon; another cracks open the one hardback copy that was available in the school's library; one pulls out pages they have printed from a PDF; still another goes to their laptop for an html version broken up by pulsing online advertisements as 20 other tabs open alongside it. One student makes the presto-change-o conjuring gestures at his smartphone as he tries to enlarge the words on his tiny screen; an ongoing group text buzzes at him again and again with messages insisting there are much more important things than what the novel's protagonist is up to that are happening right now.

And then there are the students who make no move at all. They stare at the instructor or their notebooks, perhaps blankly, perhaps with embarrassment. They have done the reading (or not), but they do not have it at hand because they have only been able to access it when they are using one of the college's computers. Maybe they do not have a laptop or WiFi at home; maybe the text is not available in a responsive design that resizes for their smartphones.

Scenes like this play out every day on college campuses, where readings increasingly come to be illuminated by the backlit, blue light screens our students carry. In the community college classroom, where initiatives such as the Community College Consortium for Open Educational Resources (n.d.) seek to use electronic tools to improve access to education, the era of extensive (if not yet peak) screen reading is already here. Despite this reality, and despite two-plus decades of research into the distinctions between screen and print reading, not enough attention has been given to how instructors should teach their students to read from screens. This becomes ever more important when students at community college may well be doing little reading for school outside their composition classes (Del Principe & Ihara, 2017) and when many of them are being placed in remedial reading classes—33 percent in one study of 250,000 students at 57 community colleges (Bailey, Jeong, & Cho, 2010). Unguided reading on screens, in and out of class, is likely to exacerbate these reading deficiencies.

In her book *Reader, Come Home* (2018a), Maryanne Wolf, the leading explicator of the reading brain, suggests that as vigorous investigation of screen reading continues and informs practice, K–12 schools must design effective curricula to help children develop a "biliterate brain": one that can leverage the respective virtues of reading in print and on screens. As we wait to see if such curricula can be developed, millions of students with widely varying aptitudes and experiences with reading will continue to come to college needing our help. It's my contention that composition instructors—whatever their preferences for print or screen readings—must teach their students to read well from screens just as they have been carefully teaching critical reading for years. Our students (and we) are reading more and more texts—for school, for work, for pleasure—on screens, and so it behooves us to squarely face that reality. At the risk of sounding overdramatic, I believe our students' futures and our country's future depend on us doing so.

What We "Know" about Screen Reading

Screen reading has been studied from many angles with findings that have been variously confounding, discouraging, and promising. Part of what makes it difficult to study are the multifarious screen reading devices and scenarios one can imagine. And yet, as Naomi Baron notes in her book *Words Onscreen* (2015), "Studies have probed everything from proofreading skills and reading speed to comprehension and eye movement. Nearly all recent investigations are reporting essentially no differences" between printed and digital texts (p. 12). However, Baron acknowledges that these findings tend to derive from studies carried out in artificial laboratory conditions using brief texts. She says, "What we don't have—but sorely need—are data on what happens when people are asked to do close reading of continuous text . . . . onscreen versus in print" (p. 171).

We still don't have much of that data, but what we do have is Singer and Alexander's (2017) excellent review of the literature on digital/screen reading, covering more than 800 studies conducted between 1992 and 2017. Their survey makes it eminently clear that it is difficult to generalize about the way people read on screens. Even so, in the studies Singer and Alexander examined, one general finding was that when texts were 500 words or shorter, there was either no significant difference in reading comprehension of digital versus printed texts (as Baron noted) or else better reading comprehension of digital texts. In contrast, for texts longer than 500 words, "comprehension scores were significantly better for print than for digital reading" (Singer & Alexander, 2017, p. 1028). Getting student readers to overcome the distractions inherent in digital devices and to successfully attend to readings longer than one computer screen is perhaps *the* central challenge for teachers of critical screen reading.

This difficulty is often reinforced by student attitudes toward reading in the two media. When I ask my first-year composition students what they notice about their own print and screen reading, their responses track very closely with what Baron (2015) reports in her surveys of American, German, and Japanese college students: Much as undergraduates like the affordances, convenience, lower cost, and perceived environmental friendliness of digital texts, most of them still tend to associate reading on paper with better learning outcomes. Particularly with longer texts on digital devices, students are more easily distracted; they experience eye fatigue from the backlit screens most of them use; they are less inclined to read deeply; they have a harder time remembering or comprehending what they have read; and they have a harder time getting a holistic sense of the text. How much of these attitudes is rooted in the student's experience and how much in values inculcated by educators and parents is unclear.

Student attitudes can have a profound effect on educational performance, of course. A student who believes they cannot read as effectively on screens as they can in print may create a self-fulfilling prophecy. Conversely, a student believing they can read better on digital devices than in print may be expressing overconfidence that does not acknowledge the obstacles to be overcome if one is to do more than "efficient" scrolling and reading for gist. As such, it's likely our students' attitudes toward screen reading are the first things we need to address.

Overcoming "Too Long; Didn't Read": Creating a Screen Reading Mindset

How much does a computer, a tablet, or, especially, a smartphone act as a powerful deterministic tool as opposed to a neutral instrument that the student reader has more agency in choosing how to use? Short texts, quick responses, skimming and skipping—this is what most of us do when reading on screens. The design of these devices—coupled with the fact that a good portion of a student's time on electronics is likely spent on entertainment or personal communication rather than an intellectual endeavor—works profoundly against anything other than "quick-hit" reading. However, there are indications that reader attitude, experience, and rigorous practice may well be key to reading successfully on machines.

Some studies have suggested that if students perceive that reading on screens must be as "effortful" as reading in print, then they may well be able to achieve success in the former (Ackerman & Goldsmith, 2011).

Further, if students have more experience seeking information and not just being entertained on screens, they may have more success while screen reading (Naumann, 2015); this effect may be more pronounced among those who are also skillful at print reading (Coiro, 2011; Naumann, 2015). (For more resources, see also Larkin & Flash, 2017.)

As I digested these and other studies over a period of several years, I had informal discussions of the matter with my students and occasionally had them write short reflections on their practices, but these were sporadic approaches. Then I decided to get more purposeful.

Two years ago, I conducted a simple "experiment" of sorts with 33 students of varying aptitudes in their second semester of first-year composition. About three-quarters of the students were from the U.S. and came from several different states, although most were Californians as is typical at UC–Berkeley; one-quarter were international (from Burkina Faso, China, Dubai, England, India, Korea, and Nepal). About a third of the students had taken my department's accelerated first-semester composition course for students who have not passed the University of California's Analytical Writing Placement Exam; another third of the students had some (or significant) markers of second language speakers in their writing. (This latter group was not a precise overlap with the third who had taken the accelerated composition course.) I asked them to read Nicholas Carr's article "Is Google Making Us Stupid?" (2008), gave them a link to the online article (which was ringed with flashing advertisements on *The Atlantic*'s website), and told them they could either read the article there, print it out to read, or look up a PDF copy in an academic database. Their choice of medium was the experimental part of the assignment.

Separately, as one in a series of library research assignments (since the course culminates in students completing independent research projects), they also looked up two articles in databases about subjects prompted by Carr's article that piqued their interest. Some of them looked into screen reading studies, while others looked up material about online distraction, artificial intelligence, digital advertising, and other topics raised by Carr. I then asked them to write a two- to three-page summary of Carr's article followed by a one-page response with their initial assessments of his arguments. (The sources found in the research assignment were not intended for use in the writing assignment, but instead to help further stimulate their thinking and to be potentially employed later in an optional, more detailed revision of their assessment of Carr's piece.) Finally, I also asked them to write a reflective note describing in what form they had read the article and what they noticed about the way they read it.

Of the 33 students, 13 immediately printed the article and worked with that version, 11 read it entirely online, and the other 9 did some mixture of online, PDF, or print reading that made it tougher to discern which medium they had used most prominently. Once I had graded the assignment using the standard essay rubric for my course, I looked at the scores of the purely online and print readers, and here's what emerged: Of the 13 who printed the article, the average grade on the paper was about a B-minus. (This group tended to include my weaker readers and writers.) Of the 11 who read Carr's article online, the average grade was an A-minus. (This group generally included the stronger readers and writers, as the grades would indicate.) While acknowledging that this sample size is not remotely statistically significant, I found this result intriguing and wondered how things had turned out this way—both what had dictated the students' choices of medium as well as how the respective groups performed on the assignment. Though there are other possible interpretations, it seemed from their reflections that the weaker readers had chosen print looking for those better learning outcomes, while the stronger readers had chosen the expediency of the online version, relying on their previously developed aptitudes at careful critical reading to carry them through. Carr's article is not short, but it is not terribly long either (it runs about 4,000 words). Given the choice, would those same students have chosen to read a much longer text on screen if they could have had it in print? One of the students who earned an A (and who had looked up a research study on screen reading) put it this way:

> I ended up reading [Carr's article] online.... I read during my research... that we can condition our mind not to be affected by the fact that we are reading online. In a sense, that if we approach... [what] we are reading [in this way], we can get as much out of it as

if we [were] read[ing it] in print. So I wanted to try. I told myself that I was [going to] focus on the reading, and read it as if I was doing so in print so that I [could write] an accurate summary....

It took me much longer just to plot...[Carr's] main ideas, and even when I thought I had them, I still had to go back to the article continuously. I did not make annotations [on the text itself], which I [always] do [when I read] in print. But it was interesting to see...what changed when I approach[ed] an online article with the mindset that I [was] reading it [as if it were in] print. I definitely know now that no matter what, reading [in print works] better for me when doing assignments [like this one].

That kind of self-awareness—doing the work of reflective writing that we ask of our first-year composition students—is just the kind of thing we need them to do with their screen reading so they can achieve success.

The Screen Reading "Phenotype": Guiding and Learning from Students

In many ways, the practice of teaching composition students to read critically is much the same as it ever was (mine is, anyway). The difference is that now first-year composition teachers should account for screen reading methods *in addition* to the traditional ones they teach students to employ with print. This is where the students' expertise and immersion in the digital world can potentially prove a help rather than a hindrance.

In subsequent terms since that first experiment (which I have not repeated), I have tried a few different approaches to raising my students' awareness of this issue—sometimes testing them on their recall of a digital text or asking them to compare the experience of reading a text online versus reading it in print—but, for the last year, I have started my courses by asking students to write an introductory reflection on their experiences with reading. I first ask them to write in detail about their reading history and practice—what they have read, what sorts of things they read on a regular basis (not just for school), what kinds of media they use for their reading, how they take notes, and whether they notice anything about how they read on paper versus on screens. I also ask them to read several articles: most commonly one by Maria Konnikova (2014) about the difficulty of reading online texts, another by the novelist Paul La Farge (2016) questioning whether concerns about screen reading are overblown and arguing for the virtues of digital texts, and a short essay by Maryanne Wolf (2010) discussing what might be happening to our brains when we read on screens (reflecting the early questions that led to her 2018 book) or a more recent one by Wolf (2018b) about skim reading. Sometimes I have had them read one of two articles by N. Katherine Hayles (2007, 2010) about, respectively, generational shifts in attention spans or the distinctions between "close, hyper, [and] machine" reading in the academy. I also give them a short handout I developed with some basic tips for good screen reading practices. Finally, I ask them to comment on whatever strikes them about each of these articles and then to conclude with an overview of what they think their own peronal best screen reading practices are.

In many cases, the students teach me about hacks—technological and otherwise—that they employ to read successfully on their distraction machines. Some report doing serious e-reading only on their laptops, turning their phones off and putting them out of sight when they read. Most students use ad blockers on their web browsers and apps like NightShift on their phones to reduce strain on their eyes as bedtime approaches. Others report using applications like Be Focused Pro, a digital variation of the Pomodoro technique that gives users 25-minute undistracted work segments on their computers broken up by five-minute breaks. Often, the students' methods are charmingly idiosyncratic. One student reported that when he prepares to read carefully on screens, he always uses a website-blocking app such as SelfControl (to keep him off Facebook) and sets his browser to Reader View; it is not until he does this and then performs the move of pushing his glasses up the bridge of his nose that he feels ready to read. Another student described how she reads better away from her computer and bent over a book because it always makes her feel she is fitting into the studious "phenotype": "I like to appear studious as it makes me think that I actually am and therefore I try even harder to be so. It's a weird mental state, but it works for helping me really learn."

The final move I have students make when we come together in class is to discuss the readings and what they have written in their reflections and then to brainstorm in small groups what they think are the most effective ways of reading on screens, augmenting and specifying the basics I have suggested to them. That many of my initial suggestions are obvious (and applicable to reading in print) does not make them any less important to impart to help students develop that screen reading mindset:

- ○ Vigilantly reduce distractions when you read.
- ○ Take active steps to manage eye fatigue (including taking regular breaks).
- ○ Take notes on what you read (or just slow down).
- ○ "Reading" means more than one thing. Recognize your purpose for reading.
- ○ Practice reflective writing. Write about what and how you read.

All of this reading, reflecting, writing, and discussion of screen reading takes place for my students in the space of that one homework assignment and one class session. I follow it with frequent reminders to reinforce their best screen reading practices as we go, including encouraging students to take notes on paper when they are reading on screens, an approach that has been shown to significantly mitigate the negative effects of being on the internet while reading (Subrahmanyam et al., 2013). It's not enough—I'm looking for ways to expand and improve my approach to this challenge—but it's a start. Returning to and refining these reminders with students is for me akin to what Julie Coiro has said about the differences in print and online reading: "In reading on paper, you may have to monitor yourself once, to actually pick up the book.... On the Internet, that monitoring and self-regulation cycle happens again and again" (as cited in Konnikova, 2014, para. 8). So it is with my students—we cover it early and I return to it over and over, the pedagogical equivalent of regularly pushing my glasses up the bridge of my nose.

Students come into our classrooms with different, sometimes radically different, levels of preparation for college-level reading and writing. This often maps onto larger societal divisions between the haves and have-nots: those who come from wealthier communities with better equipped schools and those who do not; those who have had good training and practice at reading and those who do not; those who have better access to and familiarity with digital technologies and those who do not. College—and community college especially—is a place where we try to help close these gaps and reduce the divisions that plague our country. Focusing on reading well is ever more important now in a time of rising inequality, of difficulty at discerning facts from falsehoods, and of divisiveness in a political landscape in which empathy is on the decline and misunderstanding is ascendant. Teaching students of all backgrounds to read well on screens is a democratizing practice. It ensures that such pursuits—and the very real individual and societal benefits that flow from them—keep reading from becoming a gentrified activity whose advantages are available only to a privileged few. It ensures that all of us will not simply spend more and more of our time "reading" (and talking and watching and living) on screens, further cordoned off into shrinking electronic worlds of our own making.

References

Ackerman, R., & Goldsmith, M. (2011). Metacognitive regulation of text learning: On screen versus on paper. *Journal of Experimental Psychology: Applied, 17(1)*, 18–32.

Bailey, T., Jeong, D.W., & Cho, S-W. (2010). Referral, enrollment, and completion in developmental education sequences in community colleges. *Economics of Education Review, 29(2)*, 255–270.

Baron, N. (2015). *Words onscreen: The fate of reading in a digital world.* New York: Oxford University Press.

Carr, N. (2008, July/Aug.). Is Google making us stupid? *The Atlantic.* Retrieved from https://www.theatlantic.com

Coiro, J. (2011). Predicting reading comprehension on the internet: Contributions of offline reading skills, online reading skills, and prior knowledge. *Journal of Literacy Research, 43(4)*, 352–392.

Community College Consortium for Open Educational Resources. (n.d.). Retrieved from https://www.cccoer.org/

Del Principe, A., & Ihara, R. (2017). A long look at reading in the community college: A longitudinal analysis of student reading experiences. *Teaching English in the Two-Year College, 45(2)*, 183–206.

Hayles, N.K. (2007). Hyper and deep attention: The generational divide in cognitive modes. *Profession*, 187–199.

Hayles, N.K. (2010). How we read: Close, hyper, machine. *ADE Bulletin, 150*, 62–79.

Konnikova, M. (2014, July 16). Being a better online reader. *The New Yorker*. Retrieved from https://www.newyorker.com/

La Farge, P. (2016, Jan. 7) The deep space of digital reading. *Nautilus, 32*. Retrieved from nautil.us.

Larkin, M., & Flash, D. (2017, April 9). Digital reading: Challenges and opportunities. *College Writing Programs, UC Berkeley*. Retrieved from writing.berkeley.edu/resources.

Naumann, J. (2015). A model of online reading engagement: Linking engagement, navigation, and performance in digital reading. *Computers in Human Behavior, 53*, 263–277.

Singer, L.M., & Alexander, P.A. (2017). Reading on paper and digitally: What the past decades of empirical research reveal. *Review of Educational Research, 87(6)*, 1007–1041.

Subrahmanyam, K., Michikyan, M., Clemmons, C., Carillo, R., Uhls, Y.T., & Greenfield, P.M. (2013). Learning from paper, learning from screens: Impact of screen reading and multitasking conditions on reading and writing among college students. *International Journal of Cyber Behavior, Psychology & Learning, 3(4)*, 1–27.

Wolf, M. (2010, June 29). Our 'deep reading' brain: Its digital evolution poses questions. *Nieman Reports*. Retrieved from https://niemanreports.org

Wolf, M. (2018a). *Reader come home: The reading brain in a digital world*. New York: Harper Collins.

Wolf, M. (2018b, August 25). Skim reading is the new normal. The effect on society is profound. *The Guardian*. Retrieved from https://www.theguardian.com

3

The Socio-Cognitive Approach in Academic ESL Composition Classes

Barbara A. Auris
MONTGOMERY COUNTY COMMUNITY COLLEGE

Advanced academic composition classes for English learners (ELs) can be challenging for both students and teachers due to the skills and conventions that must be mastered to become members of a discourse community (Giridharan, 2012). One of the goals of the course is to prepare them for the gate keeper first-year composition (FYC) course, which can be high stakes and intellectually demanding (Eagan & Jaeger, 2008). Many students perceive the academic composition experience as pressurized and isolating as they attempt to wrestle with a series of academic conventions (Thonney, 2011) and specialized lexicon (Hyland & Tse, 2007) that they have little familiarity with. As a result, many ELs enter advanced academic composition classes feeling nervous and fearful with low self-esteem (Choi, 2013). In my experience, some students seem to have already given up on the process on the first day (Cave, Evans, & Dewey, 2018).

A strong, flexible pedagogical framework is needed to help second language writers overcome their preconceptions and fears of the composition process, thereby taking the isolation out of that process, and should include the practice of cognitive skills needed to be a strong communicator in academic discourse. The socio-cognitive approach

41

is a viable answer. This theory posits that students learn through observation, imitation, and modeling (Bandura, Grusec & Menlove, 1966).

The Community College Context

Any composition classroom for ELs will have students from a wide variety of educational backgrounds. Preparing diverse students for college-level writing within limited time frames can add pressure to an ESL composition classroom. International students may come to the classroom with very different educational experiences than recent immigrants, who may greatly differ from long-term immigrants who have attended public school in the United States. With students coming to advanced ESL composition class with different understandings of composition and of college-level work, the socio-cognitive framework offers the flexibility that an instructor may need in modeling and teaching academic discourse for a diversity of learners in the same classroom.

This framework also supports the acceleration model of ESL classes that is taking place at many community colleges. While there are various models including the Accelerated Learning Program (Anderst, Maloy & Shahar, 2016) and learning communities (Booth, 2009), some community colleges like mine are simply opening doors to more introductory classes that have no language prerequisites. This allows ELs to take a college-level class at the same time as an advanced ESL composition class. The result is that students need to learn, practice, and transfer academic composition skills more quickly to their content classes as they are often required to write research papers in their content classes while still mastering the organization of a paragraph or short essay in the advanced ESL composition class.

Socio-Cognitive Pedagogy in the Classroom

The socio-cognitive framework is one way to provide flexible learning for students of various levels and educational backgrounds in a limited time frame within a simple pedagogy focused on observational learning (Bandura, Grusec & Menlove, 1966). Simply put, people learn by watching what others do. I incorporate this approach in my advanced ESL composition classroom to prepare them for writing academic assignments in all disciplines in three ways: analysis of model paragraphs, guided practice, and analysis of errors.

In a composition classroom, students can learn from observing a model paragraph and discussing the decisions the author made regarding organization, grammar, and lexicon. In each unit, I present three to five examples of academic discourse either exemplifying a particular genre, such as comparison/contrast, or discussing a theme similar to what the students are discussing in class, such as immigration issues. Students use these model paragraphs to create a list of characteristics of academic discourse. Through this observation, students begin to "discover" the conventions of academic composition. In one classroom activity, "Thinking and Linking," students are directed to analyze the connections between sentences in a paragraph, which focuses them on cohesion, a characteristic of successful academic prose. Instead of talking about cohesion, students learn to recognize how cohesion works in writing. For example, students are asked to find the connection between these two sentences: "I find that homework can be boring" and "This makes it hard to concentrate." Students recognize that these two sentences are linked by the idea that one result of a boring class is difficulty in concentration. From making this connection, students begin to see how writers create cohesion in their writing.

A short class discussion leads students to understand that sentences need to be logically connected, and one way to do this is to answer questions. Students can often state that the second sentence answers the question "What is the result of boring homework?" They can begin to see how an author thinks and links ideas in a paragraph. They can also begin to predict what other questions the author might answer in a paragraph or essay. They start to understand the mind of the writer. The goal of this activity is to help students begin to see the thinking behind and organization of a paragraph objectively and recognize where logical gaps may exist in their own writing.

Kim and Bowie, two international students in an advanced ESL composition course, used socio-cognitive techniques in revision. Kim was working on a revision of a paragraph about a job interview after receiving feedback that there were some sentences with no clear logical connections. In small groups, peers wrote potential questions to be answered and shared them with the class. The teacher led a discussion to choose the most salient questions. In this example, the writer and her peers chose two key questions for Kim to answer to make the writing more clear to a potential reader. The questions were: "What is an example of a crazy interview question?" and "Where can you find some help in preparing for a crazy interview question?" As a result of this interaction, Kim's revision demonstrated the depth of her argument.

Bowie used the technique of thinking and linking to recognize an illogical leap in her writing. She was writing a paragraph arguing that it was useless to purchase textbooks with so many other options. The point of her paragraph was unclear. When she was asked to connect her paragraph to her thesis, she realized that she had unrelated sentences in her paragraph and removed them.

Ilham, an immigrant L2 student, used the socio-cognitive technique to develop her argument about students being so tired in class due to work issues that they sometimes fall asleep. Her first draft was weak. She wrote, "First of all, sometimes the student is tired probably because he has more than one job, or he had to work all night. When he comes in class, he is tired; therefore, he sleeps in class." Through discussion, she recognized that she was just repeating herself. We also discussed questions she could answer to strengthen her argument, such as "What kind of jobs are very tiring?" Her final draft was changed to: "First of all, sometimes the student is tired probably because he has more than one job, or he had to work all night. Also, he can have a job that needs a lot of effort. For example, he can be a painter or roofer. This kind of job needs a lot of physical effort, so his body is physically tired in class."

The second aspect of the socio-cognitive approach that I use in my class is to offer students a chance to do some guided practice to imitate the conventions of academic discourse in a safe environment. They generally do this in small groups because knowing about academic discourse is not enough. It is a series of skills that must be practiced. In the classroom, after a discussion of the characteristics of a model paragraph, students might be put into small groups to work on an assignment I call "Make It Academic." Students read a portion of a model paragraph that does not exhibit academic sentence structure, grammar, or vocabulary and then read that same paragraph written in an academic style. They list the difference between the two versions of the paragraph and then practice with other models. They can observe what other students are doing to complete the activity. An example of a portion of a process paragraph is presented in the two forms:

Model 1: It is easy to write a process paragraph if you follow these directions. First of all, you must select a topic.

Model 1 Made Academic: Students in colleges and universities may need to write paragraphs and essays that describe a process. By following some clear yet simple directions, this activity can be made less complicated. The initial step is topic selection. It is important to choose a topic which the author has some experience or expertise with.

In small groups, students first made a list of characteristics seen in the academic model and then were given other portions of the paragraph to re-write in a more academic manner including use of passive voice, adjective clauses, more formal sentence subjects, and discourse specific vocabulary. Individual students used their knowledge of grammar and vocabulary to enhance the final group product. The goal of this kind of activity is to help students change simplistic informal writing to a more academic register. The small group environment provides a bit of support and safety in making choices. It also requires students to share and support their ideas. In anonymous online course evaluations, some students have said about this activity that "[it] helps to learn from each other's [sic]" or "from my classmates, it is always good to see how they work differently to improve my work." As a result of this small group work in guided practice, students can begin to build a support community for writing. Another anonymous comment stated, "Ask your friends for help because sometimes you will understand better a friend than an instructor."

After the analysis of model paragraphs and the guided practice, students will need to do some individual practice. Often for assessment purposes, there is assistance through Writing Centers and instructors' office hours. Students need not do this in isolation; however, there is some personal accountability. Once a student has completed a written assessment, the final aspect of the socio-cognitive framework can be taught in my classroom—error analysis. There is nothing more frustrating for instructors and students than to have the same mistake made over and over again. Using observation techniques for error correction can potentially make students more aware of their repeated errors and plan ways to avoid and/or correct them.

In my advanced ESL composition classroom, test paragraphs are written and re-written in class in a one-hour timed environment meant to prepare the students for the realities of college-level writing and testing. The first draft is assessed for organization, cohesion, sentence structure, and support. Students receive a comment page on which they might read: "The first and third reason in your paragraph about immigration seem to overlap and even repeat themselves. Can you think of a way to clearly define the two ideas? Consider reviewing the model paragraph on Syria that we analyzed." They have a second hour to re-write the paragraph with the teacher in the room. General questions are acceptable, but the instructor needs to avoid just correcting the writing. The second draft is now assessed for grammar, vocabulary, punctuation and mechanics. Students receive a grade, but further re-writes are possible to improve that grade. The goal of this activity is to show students how and why an author drafts and edits.

Some anonymous comments about this aspect of the class include: "I love how the teacher give [sic] us second chances" and "Analyzing mistakes help [sic] me to improve writing."

Ben, a long-term immigrant who tested into the advanced ESL composition class, stated that this activity particularly has helped him be successful in college-level writing classes including FYC. He recognized that analyzing mistakes "was actually a good thing for me cause [sic] I actually understand how to fix the grammar."

When my students have completed a number of written assignments, they are asked to analyze the comments they received to find the top three areas of improvement. This gives them some control over and responsibility for their own learning.

Measuring Success

The measure of success for these students is not just in their grades, but in their ability to succeed in other college-level classes, particularly those like FYC. One of my goals is to raise their level of self-efficacy and confidence. In my 2017 study, five community college students were interviewed over a semester that were taking FYC after successfully completing advanced ESL composition (Auris, 2017). They were asked about the skills they felt they had learned and transferred from the advanced ESL composition class to the FYC class. All five participants spoke about composition skills such as planning, drafting, and editing, which wasn't surprising. However, what was a little surprising was how often three of the students (Ana, Debbie, and Emily) spoke about transferring the skill of talking about their writing into their success in FYC. Ana, a non-traditional student, spoke about talking to the instructor often and meeting native speakers to help her. She specifically set out to create a support system. Debbie used tutors and built a support team, stating that "she [the tutor] helped me and she give me more ideas for write more. She asks me questions and I answer." Debbie and Emily spoke about meeting outside of class regularly to talk about the writing assignments and support each other. The social skills they learned in the ESL academic writing classroom were being used in other classes.

In conclusion, using the socio-cognitive approach in my advanced ESL composition class has given me the flexibility to work with students from diverse educational backgrounds, the confidence to let the students build social networks for support, and the knowledge that I am helping students become self-confident writers who can be successful in college-level classes. It has helped me with the realities of teaching in a very limited time frame, usually seven-week classes, and still see some changes. Teaching explicit cognitive skills in a social environment has led to positive results for students by empowering them to be strong writers with social and cognitive skills for success in college classes of all disciplines.

REFERENCES

Anderst, L., Maloy, J., & Shahar, J. (2016). Assessing the accelerated learning program model for linguistically diverse developmental writing students. *Teaching English in the Two-Year College, 44*(1), 11–31.

Auris, B.A. (2017). From English as a second language composition to first-year English composition: The perceived transferability of writing skills of second language students. Unpublished PhD diss. Immaculata University, Immaculata, PA.

Bandura, A., Grusec, J.E., & Menlove, F.L. (1966). Observational learning as a function of symbolization and incentive set. *Child Development, 37*(3), 499–506.

Booth, N.B. (2009). ESL learning communities: An approach to retaining ESL students in a community college. Unpublished PhD diss. Rutgers University, New Brunswick, NJ.

Cave, P.N., Evans, N.W., & Dewey, D.P. (2018). Motivational partnerships increasing ESL student self-efficacy. *ELT Journal, 72*(1), 83–96.

Choi, S. (2013). Language anxiety in second language writing: Is it really a stumbling block? *Second Language Studies, 31*(2), 1–42.

Eagan, M. K. Jr., & Jaeger. A. J. (2008). Closing the gate: Part-time faculty instruction in gatekeeper courses and first-year persistence. *New Directions for Teaching and Learning, 115*, 39–53.

Giridharan, B. (2012). Identifying gaps in academic writing of ESL students. *US-China Education Review*, 578–587.

Hyland, K., & Tse, P. (2007). Is there an "academic vocabulary"? *TESOL Quarterly, 41*(2), 235–253.

Thonney, T. (2011). Teaching the conventions of academic discourse. *Teaching English in the Two-Year College, 38*(4), 347–362.

4

Using "Writing about Writing" Pedagogy with L2 and Developmental Readers and Writers at the Community College

Miriam Moore

UNIVERSITY OF NORTH GEORGIA, GAINESVILLE CAMPUS

What sorts of topics should students in first-year composition (FYC) and basic writing courses write about? Writing about Writing (WAW) pedagogy as set forth by Downs and Wardle (2007) proposes a straightforward answer—ask students to write (and read) about writing. The authors claim that despite research indicating that a "unified academic discourse" (writing that is suitable for all academic writing situations) does not exist, practitioners in FYC have continued to teach as though it does. The result not only leaves students ill-equipped for examining writing contexts critically and strategically but also makes the discipline "complicit in reinforcing outsiders' views of writing studies as a trivial, skill-teaching nondiscipline" (p. 553). The authors argue for a pedagogy that conceives of FYC as an "Introduction to Writing Studies," in which students read writing-focused research and theory, especially texts addressing problems that student writers understand all too well—writer's block, editing, revision, etc. Bird (2008) sums up the approach this way: "Students learn more about reading-thinking-writing by studying, discussing, and writing about these processes than by simply practicing them" (pp. 166–167).

A Context for WAW Pedagogy

Downs and Wardle (2007) anticipated objections to the approach, including the concern that it would be too difficult for students; they recognized that scholarly articles in composition studies and a focus on primary research would be "demanding and different" for student writers (p. 574). Therefore, I had to address this concern before I first implemented the approach with developmental and multilingual students in the Virginia Community College System (VCCS). If the approach is perceived as demanding in a university context, why should community college (CC) instructors working with basic writers even consider it? Given the expectations of developmental courses at community colleges, it might seem counterintuitive to ask students to read and write about scholarly texts from composition studies that arguably are disconnected from their lives and previous experiences.

I would suggest, however, that one current trend in FYC for basic writers invites serious consideration of the WAW model: co-requisite courses paired with traditional composition classes, sometimes referred to as the Accelerated Learning Program model, or ALP (see Adams et al., 2009). In the co-requisite model, developmental students are placed into FYC with an additional course for support, thereby granting them access to challenging material and affirming their place in the university community. The extended time allotted for instruction in the co-requisite model was a critical factor in my decision to pilot WAW tenets with developmental and multilingual writers. In the VCCS, for example, students in the co-requisite course have two additional credit hours (a total of five) for FYC; the pace of instruction can thus slow a little, allowing more time to address reading content, grammar, and vocabulary, all of which may challenge multilingual and developmental writers (Anderst, Maloy, & Shahar, 2016; Polio & Park, 2016; Scordoras, 2009).

WAW Pedagogy in the Classroom

WAW pedagogy as I have applied it has three distinct components: (1) course content delineated as conceptual knowledge (not just skills); (2) writing-focused readings; and (3) writing assignments that address literacy, composing, and language.

Typically, CC composition courses list student learning outcomes in the form of skills to be mastered. WAW pedagogy, however, situates skills practice in discussions of content related to writing, literacy, and language. In my course, therefore, I begin with eight "threshold concepts" about writing, not just the mandated skill set. (See Adler-Kassner & Wardle, 2015, for a discussion of threshold concepts for composition classes.)

Mastery of skills and the development of content knowledge are related but different goals for the course. To talk about the conceptual base with colleagues (and interested administrators), I have tried to articulate the relationship between concepts and skills. For example, when course learning outcomes ask students to develop mature or sophisticated sentence structures with few mechanical and usage errors (skills), I focus on these three concepts:

1. All writing involves **choices** that affect meaning: words, structures, details, punctuation, and organization.

2. Good writing pays attention to the needs and the knowledge of a **reader**.

3. Specific writing tasks require us to follow the **conventions of a discourse community**.

Framing the course in terms of knowledge about writing—not just writing skills—is critical for the WAW approach. The features of sophisticated prose will differ in different contexts, so rather than emphasizing the features that fit most readily in the humanities or social sciences, I highlight an underlying concept that translates to any writing situation: Lexical, stylistic, and grammatical choices are made for rhetorical purposes. I also frame the course with these concepts quite literally: They appear in my assignments, handouts, and written feedback throughout the term.

The next key component of a WAW course is the selection of readings (what I call the "anchor texts"). When I began to use the approach, the department assigned an anthology, so I supplemented the given text with articles by authors such as Peter Elbow, Toby Fulwiler, James Gee, Rebecca Howard, Ken Hyland, and Donald Murray. Since then, I have generally chosen four to eight readings, each of which illustrates a course concept and gives students conceptual tools—what Bird (2009–2010) calls "meaning-making concepts"—to analyze and interpret their own writing experiences. I link students to the articles via the library's databases.

These anchor texts invite students to enter unfamiliar reading territory. Part of WAW pedagogy thus requires coaching students as they approach the readings for the first time. In my classes, this scaffolding comes in the form of previewing vocabulary, offering reading guides, and re-visiting texts multiple times. The reading guides are particularly important: I may provide annotations and comments directly on a PDF of the article or on a handout; either way, the students have a tour guide leading them to notice certain things ("Take a look at what Gee is doing here"), providing background information ("Fulwiler is writing in response to so and so"), and inviting them to explore and connect ("Where have you seen something like this before? Would you say this is true in your experience?"). When we revisit the texts, I ask them to consider how recent reading or writing experiences confirm, change, or complicate their initial readings.

The readings (anchor texts and selections from the anthology viewed through the lens of anchor texts) serve as the basis for all course writing assignments, which are the final distinctive component of a WAW course. In my classes, students write a literacy narrative framed by at least one anchor text and one additional reading, as well as an argument analysis with references to a textbook reading, an anchor text, and one or more additional readings. I also assign a research project in accordance with departmental parameters. For this assignment, I have used an exploration of a discourse community (see Wardle & Downs,

2017), but recently I have asked students to select a chapter from *Bad Ideas about Writing* (Ball & Loewe, 2017) and investigate that idea in the context of their own writing or major. For the research project, students work on a progressive annotated bibliography during the semester. As they identify each new source, students complete a works cited entry, a summary, and a PQ paragraph—a paragraph that connects an idea in the text to a previous source or course reading, using either a paraphrase (P) or quote (Q), properly cited. These paragraphs engage students early in the process of connecting and synthesizing concepts from readings. Finally, I assign a reflection, usually a letter in which students reinterpret at least three of the course concepts, explaining how their understanding of that concept has changed and illustrating from their own writing and course readings.

The distinct features of WAW pedagogy—threshold concepts and literacy-focused texts and assignments—are coupled with composition classroom activities that most instructors will recognize—collaborative writing and revision, peer review, small and large group discussion, examination of citation mechanics, and close reading of texts. With the extended time allotted for the co-requisite course, we cover other familiar territory, including brainstorming, drafting, editing for surface-level grammar and mechanics, and reflective writing. See Appendix 4A for a sample schedule of possible readings and topics in both the FYC and co-requisite courses.

A Rationale for WAW in the Community College

The WAW approach positions students as college writers and offers the "rich intellectual environment" Blaauw-Hara (2016) suggests best supports skill-building. In addition, WAW's focus on writing-centered readings offers a natural integration of reading and writing and supports a content-rich environment for literacy development (Ferris, 2015; Holschuh & Paulson, 2013; Smith, 2012; Stoller & Robinson 2015; Sullivan, 2010). In scaffolding and revisiting authentic texts about writing, students build "real levels of expertise in topics of readings," a feature that Grabe (2014, p. 16) suggests is particularly helpful for second language readers, whose frames of lexical, linguistic, and cultural knowledge often differ from those of the instructor or academic community. The WAW course foregrounds these challenges for students and grants them a vocabulary for talking and writing about them. The difficult readings provide multiple "contact zones" for integration of reading and writing (see Marsh, 2015).

Measuring Success

In more than two years of using WAW pedagogy with basic and multilingual writers, I have measured the success of the pedagogy by looking at how students think and engage with course content and how they conceptualize and talk about their writing after taking the course. Are students theorizing, revising, and applying course concepts to their own reading and writing processes? With WAW pedagogy, the answer has been yes. The excerpts that follow illustrate this view of success in the course. The first sample is an unedited and unrevised midterm reflection by a Palestinian student—a student who began the course without using any sentence final punctuation. Note the extent of her engagement with an anchor text, as well as clear evidence of sentence and paragraph structure, despite persistent surface errors:

> One of my favourite essays along with Gee's was "Looking and Listening for my voice," by Toby Fulwiler. I followed his states that a writer must write his/her real authentic voice in writing and revising the writings to make sure the reader is going to be conscious about the writer's own presents in his/her writing. I test it out with my husband as I made him read an essay I wrote and asked him if he hears my voice and identity while reading it. The first thing he said it is nice and asked who wrote it? I remembered that I never wrote in english, maybe that is why my husband did not recognize my voice through my writings. Along with Fulwiler's advice, I followed Anne Lamott's advice of how writing does

not happen from the first attempt, and a good writer goes through a lot of crummy drafts at first until he/she reaches the best idea and circle it to start from that point.

The next excerpt is from a Chinese student's course project. Note how she develops and applies Gee's (1989) concept of "Discourse" to the world of nursing, as well as how she structures the paragraph, using a question that she answers by quoting, paraphrasing, and applying the anchor text.

Does nursing knowledge acquisition make a person an RN? Gee says, "Discourses are not mastered by overt instruction, but by enculturation into social practices through scaffolded and supported interaction with people who have already mastered the Discourse" (7). In other words, it is not enough to study nursing knowledge in class. To acquire this secondary Discourse, RNs need follow experienced RNs to practice. They can have their practice in schools, laboratories, clinics, hospitals, and so forth.... .

Engaging with readings and making connections between them is a hallmark of success in my course. In the next extract, note how the student ties a personal reflection to an interview and her course reading:

I began thinking that in that case, and I feel like in every other academic field as well, there are two areas: the one that involves knowledge and the one that involves being. Knowledge will never be fully mastered by someone because new things come up all the time, but the being is something that forms with the passion you have for what you do, and how involved you are with your community. As Mr. L mentioned, being a Conservation Biologist is a matter of passion, and passion cannot be taught in a school, no matter how hard you try. As linguist James Gee puts it, "ironically, while you can overtly teach someone linguistics, a body of knowledge, you can't teach someone to be a linguist, that is, to use a Discourse. The most you can do is to let them practice being a linguist with you" (7).

In conclusion, I do not claim that WAW pedagogy is for everyone, but I suggest it offers potential and great possibility in working with often-marginalized writers in CC classrooms. I concur with Bird's (2008) eloquent conclusion:

> The primary goal of freshman composition is to improve all student writers—both the texts that students produce and the processes and knowledge that students use to produce their texts. A writing studies approach is highly successful with this goal because it goes beyond teaching writing processes and deeply engages students with the issues and concepts of writing, significantly expanding their understanding of writing and themselves as writers. (p. 169)

WAW pedagogy does not ensure improved persistence, pass rates, or retention. But I have seen evidence that it helps basic writers perceive themselves as writers, and that is why I will continue using the approach.

Acknowledgments

I would like to thank Frost McLaughlin and Jennifer Schaefer for helpful comments on an earlier draft of this chapter. I am also indebted to my colleague Ruth Holmes of Lord Fairfax Community College for introducing me to a progressive annotated bibliography.

References

Adams, P., Gearhart, S., Miller, R., & Roberts, A. (2009). The accelerated learning program: Throwing open the gates. *Journal of Basic Writing, 28*(2), 50–69.

Adler-Kassner, L., & Wardle, E. (Eds.). (2015). *Naming what we know: Threshold concepts of writing studies.* Logan: Utah State University Press.

Anderst, L., Maloy, J., & Shahar, J. (2016). Assessing the Accelerated Learning Program Model for linguistically diverse developmental writing students. *Teaching English in the Two-Year College, 44*(1), 11–31.

Ball, C., & Loewe, D. (Eds.) (2017). *Bad ideas about writing.* Morgantown, WV: Open Access Textbooks. Retrieved from https://textbooks.lib.wvu.edu/badideas/

Bird, B. (2008). Writing about writing as the heart of a writing studies approach to FYC: Response to Douglas Downs and Elizabeth Wardle, "Teaching about writing, righting misconceptions" and to Libby Miles et al., "Thinking vertically." *College Composition and Communication, 60*(1), 165–171.

Bird, B. (2009–2010). Meaning-making concepts: Basic writer's access to verbal culture. *The Basic Writing E-Journal, 8–9.* Retrieved from https://bwe.ccny.cuny.edu/

Blaauw-Hara, M. (2016, October 26). Teaching writing about writing in the two-year college [Blog]. Retrieved from https://community.macmillan.com/community/the-english-community/bedford-bits/blog/2016/10/26/teaching-writing-about-writing-in-the-two-year-college

Downs, D., & Wardle, E. (2007). Teaching about writing, righting misconceptions: (Re)envisioning "First-Year Composition" as "Introduction to Writing Studies." *College Composition and Communication, 58*(4), 552–584.

Ferris, D. (2015). Supporting multilingual writers through the challenges of academic literacy: Principles of English for academic purposes and composition instruction. In N. Evans, N. Anderson, & W. Eggington (Eds.), *ESL readers and writers in higher education: Understanding challenges, providing support* (pp. 147–163). New York: Routledge.

Gee, J. (1989). Literacy, discourse, and linguistics: Introduction. *Journal of Education, 171*(1), 5–14.

Grabe, W. (2014). Key issues in L2 reading development. *Center for English Language Communication Symposium,* National University of Singapore, 8–18. Retrieved from http://www.nus.edu.sg/celc/symposium/4thsymposium.html

Holschuh, J., & Paulson, E. (2013). *The terrain of college developmental reading: Executive summary and paper commissioned by the College Reading and Learning Association.* Retrieved from https://www.crla.net/images/whitepaper/TheTerrainofCollege91913.pdf

Marsh, B. (2015). Reading-writing integration in developmental and first-year composition. *Teaching English in the Two-Year College, 43*(1), 58–70.

Polio, C., & Park, J. (2016). Language development in second language writing. In R. Manchón & P. Matsuda (Eds.), *Handbook of second and foreign language writing* (pp. 287–306). Boston: De Gruyter.

Scordoras, M. (2009). Just not enough time: Accelerated composition courses and struggling ESL writers. *Teaching English in the Two-Year College, 36*(3), 270–279.

Smith, C. (2012). Interrogating texts: From deferent to efferent and aesthetic reading practices. *Journal of Basic Writing, 31*(1), 59–79.

Stoller, F., & Robinson, M. (2015). Assisting ESP students in reading and writing disciplinary genres. In N. Evans, N. Anderson, & W. Eggington (Eds.), *ESL readers and writers in higher education: Understanding challenges, providing support* (pp. 164–179). New York: Routledge.

Sullivan, P. (2010). What can we learn about "college-level" writing from basic writing students? The importance of reading. In P. Sullivan, H. Tinberg, & S. Blau (Eds.), *What is "college-level" writing? Vol. 2* (pp. 233–253). Urbana, IL: NCTE.

Wardle, E. & Downs, D. (2017). *Writing about writing: A college reader* (3rd ed.). Boston: Bedford/St. Martin's.

ANCHOR TEXTS

Elbow, P. (1991). Reflections on academic discourse: How it relates to freshmen and colleagues. *College English, 53*(2), 135–155.

Emig, J. (1977). Writing as a mode of learning. *College Composition and Communication, 28*(2), 122–128.

Fulwiler, T. (1990). Looking and listening for my voice. *College Composition and Communication, 41*(2), 214–220.

Howard, R., Serviss, T., & Rodrigue, R. (2010). Writing from sources, writing from sentences. *Writing and Pedagogy, 2*(2), 177–192. doi: 10.1558/wap.v2i2.177

Hyland, K. (2008). Disciplinary voices: Interactions in research writing. *English Text Construction, 1*(1), 5–22. doi: 10.1075/etc.1.1.03hyl

Murray, D. (2000). The maker's eye: Revising your own manuscripts. In P. Escholz, A. Rosa & V. Clark (Eds.), *Language awareness: Readings for college writers* (8th ed.) (pp. 161–165). Boston: Bedford/St. Martin's. (Original work published 1973.)

Penrose, A., & Geisler, C. (1994). Reading and writing without authority. *College Composition and Communication, 45*(4), 505–520.

APPENDIX 4A
Sample Syllabus

Week	Readings and Course Topics	Assignments	Co-Requisite Topics and Assignments
1	-Course overview -Introduction to Literacy Narratives -Alexie, "Superman and Me" -Sante, "Living in Tongues"	---	Strategies for active and critical reading
2	-James Gee, "Literacy, Discourse, and -Linguistics: Introduction" -Quoting and paraphrasing -Introduction to Course Project	Group paraphrase/quote practice Course project proposal	Brainstorming and drafting Draft of literacy narrative for workshop week
3	-Workshop/Conference week -Donald Murray, "The Logic of Revision"	First complete revision to literacy narrative	
4	-Recognizing genres, purpose, audience -Writing summaries -Jolliffe and Harl, "Studying the "Reading Transition from High School to College: What Are Our Students Reading and Why?"	Progressive Annotated Bibliography (PAB) #1	Reading summaries: audience, one-sentence overviews, rhetorical-choice verbs, author tags, and paragraph cohesion
5	-Works cited lists - Library overview -Elbow: "The Believing Game—Methodological Believing"	Final revisions to literacy narrative	Editing concerns: sensing sentences boundaries and pauses
6	-PQ paragraphs -Argumentation: Arguing about language -Lutz, "The World of Doublespeak" -Tannen, "But What Do You Mean?"	PAB 2, with PQ paragraph	Practicing the believing/doubting game in reading
7	-Argumentation -Hyland, "Disciplinary Voices: Interactions in Research Writing"	PAB 3, with PQ paragraph Believing, doubting, stance, and engagement	Stance/engagement as revision tools
8	Midterm review	In-class reflection/connections piece	
9	Evaluating arguments: Believing and doubting in arguments	PAB #4, with PQ paragraph Draft of argument analysis for peer review	The vocabulary of argument
10	Workshop Week	First complete revision of argument analysis essay	

Week	Readings and Course Topics	Assignments	Co-Requisite Topics and Assignments
11	-Interviewing for a source -"Writing from Sources, Writing from Sentences" by Howard, Serviss, and Rodrigue (Synthesizing sources)	PAB #5	Practice interviews and summaries
12	-Synthesizing and reviewing sources	PAB #6 Final draft of argument analysis essay	Editing concerns
13	-Preparing the final draft: PAB -Planning and organizing the course project	Final draft, PAB	Editing concerns
14	Workshop week	Drafting the course project	
15	Workshop week	Peer review and revision: course project	
16	Presentations (course project) Final "exam" (reflections on a personal theory of writing)		

Note: This is a sample syllabus and does not align with the Anchor Texts presented in the chapter.

Part 2

Teaching Toward Acceleration

5

Contract Grading as Anti-Racist Praxis in the Community College Context

Sarah Klotz

COLLEGE OF THE HOLY CROSS

Carl Whithaus

UNIVERSITY OF CALIFORNIA, DAVIS

Contract grading is an established practice that has reemerged in the past decade as a promising method for anti-racist praxis in first-year writing. While there are many approaches to contract grading, it generally involves a negotiation regarding the amount of labor students will complete to earn a course grade. Contract grading departs from more common assessment methods in which all students complete the same writing tasks and earn A-F grades based on their professor's judgment of their written products. Drawing on recent work in anti-racist writing assessment (Poe, Inoue, & Eliot, 2018), the history and theory of contract grading in open-access institutions (Blackstock & Exton, 2014; Davidson, 2011; Kohn, 2011), and research on equity in higher education (Dowd & Bensimon, 2015), this chapter presents a method for contract grading tailored to community colleges. This method emerges from the California Community College (CCC) system. Conversations around equity gained momentum in 2014 after the Chancellor's office allocated funding to close gaps in degree, certificate, and basic skills completion with an explicit focus on racial/ethnic groups, as well as veterans, foster youth, students with disabilities, and economically disadvantaged students.

Benefiting from financial resources and a policy climate attentive to addressing race and racism, writing faculty began to think about assessment as a lever for addressing racial inequities. This chapter's method for contract grading emerges from work with those faculty as they considered how to reform assessment practices ranging from placement to classroom and programmatic ecologies. We acknowledge and account for the complexity of teaching in today's community colleges; some of this complexity emerges from the open access philosophy, the significant gap between faculty racial demographics and the racial/ethnic makeup of the student body (Campaign for College Opportunity, 2018), and the many demands and vulnerabilities that students balance, such as childcare, jobs, military service, and basic needs insecurity. We consider how contract grading supports equity when approached through a lens of student agency and reflection. This chapter focuses on contract grading as a means of developing anti-racist writing assessments and fostering more options for anti-racist writing pedagogies. We approach the assessment of student writing as a site of race-based oppression *and* a potentially transformative practice. We put forward a method that centers student agency and critical capacity while mitigating the potential for racial bias (implicit or explicit) to affect faculty decisions around the quality of students' written work.

How Does Race Impact the Assessment of Student Writing?

In the community college context, contract grading can be particularly effective in achieving equitable outcomes for students across racial groups. Community college students are the most racially diverse population in U.S. higher education, but providing broader access has not resulted in equal opportunity or outcomes for Black, Latinx, Native American, and other racially minoritized student groups (Dowd & Bensimon, 2015). Scholars such as Dowd and Bensimon continue to identify persistent forms of structural racism that add up to inequity in degree completion and transfer rates for students of color. As faculty, we may be tempted to view these structural trends as beyond the scope of our day-to-day decisions and practices but, in fact, classroom assessments and approaches to writing are racialized. As Poe (2016) argues, "Both teachers and students bring raced expectations to educational contexts, and those expectations shape the ways that teachers respond to student writing and the ways that students respond to teacher feedback" (p. 98). Other research relevant to the question of how racial stereotypes affect assessment ecologies include Claude Steele's (1997) work on stereotype threat showing how student performance can be hindered by fear of confirming a negative stereotype about one's group and Bulinski et al.'s 2009 study (cited in Asao Inoue's *Antiracist Writing Assessment Ecologies* [2015, p. 306]. For more, see the video the graduate students produced based on their study: https://www.youtube.com/watch?v=-LA6nBFkNb8). The Bulinski et al. research found that white teachers provided more comments to white students than to students of color while Latinx students received more comments on grammar than their peers. In placement assessments, community colleges continue to scrutinize students' literacy through standardized tests such as ACCUPLACER® that direct students from minoritized racial groups disproportionately into remediation (Chen, 2016). At public two-year colleges, 78 percent of Black students, 75 percent of Hispanic students, and 64 percent of white students take remedial courses. Of students in the lowest income group, 76 percent take remedial courses, compared with 59 percent in the highest income group (Chen, 2016). Due to reforms in remedial education, this is changing, but as the reforms are largely structural, it is worthwhile to consider how classroom practice is influencing racialized outcomes in community colleges as well.

Each of these findings provide tangible evidence for what sociologists and critical race theorists have long argued—that race is not a biological reality but a social one that creates fundamentally different learning conditions for students of color. There is a growing body of research showing that our assessment practices are racialized (Inoue, 2015; Lederman & Warwick 2018; Poe & Cogan 2016). The question for faculty committed to anti-racist praxis is: How can we construct classroom assessments and pedagogies that address these inequities?

Inoue (2015) has shown that contract grading provides a space for students to negotiate the evaluation of their writing within the context of an overwhelming white racial habitus—a "set of linguistic codes and textual markers that are often not a part of the discourses of many students of color, working class students, and multilingual students, but are a part of many white, middle-class students' discourses" (p. 17). Inoue draws on Bourdieu's (1974, 1977, 1984) concept of *habitus* as the basis for his systemic critique of institutional racism in U.S. higher education, particularly in writing assessment. Inoue describes how a white racial habitus informs writing assessment systems ranging from college-level placement exams to individual classroom instructors' grading practices. In "High-Performing English Learners' Limited Access to Four-Year College," Kanno (2018) links Bourdieu's concept of habitus and the related concept of institutional habitus to empirical data about students' paths into higher education. One of the three major factors Kanno identifies as impacting students' access to a four-year college is their linguistic insecurity about proficiency with English, particularly written English. Kanno sees the students' habitus intersecting with the school's institutional habitus in a way that highlights the students' linguistic deficits for teachers, advisors, and the students themselves. In Kanno's (2018) study, "The students themselves internalized the deficit orientation and came to view community college as the only possible college choice for them" (p. 1). The two case studies in that work revealed that the students' insecurity was reinforced by an institutional habitus of writing assessment that had a deficit orientation. Inoue's (2015) work suggests that a deficit orientation toward writing assessment is connected to an institutionalized white racial habitus.

In community college writing classrooms, however, teachers are engaged not only in the ideological struggles that Inoue has identified, but they are also responding to—and shaping—a habitus that they partially share with students. Atkinson (2011) and Reay (2004) trace some of the ways in which Bourdieu-inspired notions of habitus have been used in educational research. They remind us that Bourdieu saw a complex interplay between identity and habitus. Reay (2004) makes the case for habitus being used in educational research in ways that reflect the dynamic movements among individuals and the environments they inhabit. We are making a similar case, but one related to pedagogical practice rather than educational research. Contract grading provides a technique that can allow community college faculty the freedom to reshape expectations around the grading of writing.

While Inoue (2015) and Poe (2016) argue that the linguistic codes and textual markers privileged in most postsecondary writing assessment tasks tend to be white and middle class, empirical studies similar to those described in Kanno (2018) or Reay (2004) could be designed to interrogate this claim. They could examine how the habitus at a particular site is—or is not—shifting as faculty in community college situations become more diverse and use a variety of pedagogies and texts in their classrooms. Contract grading is one tool, among many, that could be used to foster a wider range of attitudes toward writing and language use in community college settings.

As a particular technique, contract grading is a promising approach for community college faculty committed to anti-racist teaching practices. By taking the question of an essay's quality out of the assessment protocol—out of an institutional habitus that may embody racist approaches to language—contract grading de-centers a teacher's judgment that may be subject to racial stereotypes while relieving students' fears that they will confirm negative stereotypes about their group. A contract grading pedagogy that focuses on reflection also encourages students to think critically about how power, privilege, and language intersect in their educational experiences, both in and beyond their first-year writing course.

A Pedagogy for Contract Grading

The most important thing is not the contract itself, which is infinitely customizable, but the ways that a contract assessment methodology grounded in values of anti-racism and equity can help students build their critical capacity to understand how assessment structures power and privilege in academia, both in and beyond their first-year writing courses. To re-orient the feedback and assessment process in such a way that students are building this critical capacity, we present a simple grading contract to include on the syllabus and discuss with students on the first day of the semester (see Figure 5.1). Again, the particular content of the contract is not the issue—the contract is an artifact of a broader pedagogy of critical questioning and linguistic agency for students. In our experience, faculty can use grading contracts such as the one shown to structure conversations with students about their writing and the evaluation of their learning.

A detailed annotation of how to interpret, present, and discuss the contract, both on the first day and throughout the semester, based on Sarah's classroom experience at Butte College, is presented. For reference, the use of *I* in the next section denotes Sarah speaking from her experiential perspective. Syllabus language regarding contract grading that is a touchstone for ongoing reflection and planning is also pre-

FIGURE 5.1. Syllabus Language around Contract Grading

We will use a method called contract grading in which your final grade in the course is determined by how fully you engage with the opportunities to read, analyze, and write. To receive the grade listed on the left in the table, you must do all of the items listed in that row; failing to complete the requirements in any category will drop you to the next row. At any time, your essays may not be considered passing. You will need to revise them to a passing grade to succeed in your final portfolio.

Grade	Homework	Portfolio	Presentation
A	86–100%	Cover Letter; Essays 1, 2, 3, 4 revised to a passing level	Yes
B	75–85%	Cover Letter; Essays 1, 2, 3 revised to a passing level	Essay 4 or Presentation
C	65–74%	Cover Letter; Essays 1, 2, 3 revised to a passing level	No

*Receiving a D or F in English 101 is not considered passing.

sented. We encourage faculty to adapt it for their own contexts. For us, it works as a dialogic moment about shared classroom practice, behavior, expectations, and inquiry with students.

The first day of the semester is not one where the instructor presents the syllabus and students passively receive course requirements. Because contract grading is unfamiliar to many students, this is an opportunity for students to react and become curious. Through a first-day writing prompt, students plan their semester and begin to consider their choices. This prompt can include questions like:

- What is your ideal grade in this course?
- What are your educational goals, both short-term and long-term?
- What competing demands are you balancing with learning in first-year writing (such as childcare, work, other courses)?
- What questions do you have about this grading method?
- How do you think contract grading may affect your motivation and learning?

Students may know, for example, that they can do their school work at night when their kids are sleeping, but convening outside of class for a group project is not going to be feasible. They may, as a result, plan for a B in the course, knowing how to be successful to keep their GPAs up for their goal of entering a nursing program at a local state university.

On Day 1, students write about the grade they plan to work toward and ask questions about how this grading system works. When distributing learning contracts, Shor (1992) notes that he asks students not only to discuss them in class but also to take them home, consider the contract, and possibly amend or revise it before returning for the next class meeting. Grading contracts provide an opportunity for shared strategic planning around learning that is attentive to the many ways that a faculty member may not foresee the choices that students are making to access and complete their educational goals. This approach humanizes the classroom and allows for students to be present as people as well as learners.

The criteria within the contract can change based on an instructor's needs, values, and context. For example, students in this class receive ten points per homework and classwork assignment, which adds up to hundreds of points over the semester. Based on the first column of the contract, students can see that there is flexibility around attendance, which is rewarded through classwork points. There is also flexibility around how much out-of-class time they spend on homework (i.e., an 86 percent on homework and classwork can still be an A in the course). The second column shows that this particular contract emphasizes regular engagement both in and out of class because these are the values of the instructor. It also leaves room for students to make mistakes and deal with the challenges that life presents because homework and classwork requirements are not overly strict. The specific criteria in the columns is based on the instructor's values and experiential knowledge. In other environments, those values or needs may change. For example, in a large research university where I struggled with students attending and prioritizing class, I changed the contract to include a column just for attendance. Presence for writing workshops and daily activities thus becomes a more significant part of the grade and students can see that in-class engagement is a crucial part of learning in first-year writing.

After discussing the grading system and writing informally in response to the Day 1 prompt, students write a letter to the instructor about their plans to fulfill the contract. This plan is not set in stone; students who show up and say, "I just need a C. I just need to pass. I always struggle in English" can revise their goal and bump up to a B or an A. That is, if students become excited about their writing and see themselves growing—if they see that they understand the norms and expectations of the classroom and that their hard work is paying off—then they can revise the contract to meet a higher level of performance. The opposite happens as well. Students can recognize that they had aimed for an A but cannot complete all that they had originally intended and can then revise their contract to earn a lower grade.

Students initially have many reactions: confusion, skepticism, excitement. Many express confidence that they know they can pass with at least at C from Day 1, and this is crucial—the grading contract emphasizes completing the work to become better writers, not aiming for an A, which can often feel like performing for the teacher's particular standards. Students who have the experience of working extremely hard on an essay only to receive a low grade heave a sigh of relief. This is not a class about appealing to the professor's tastes or preferences, both of which are culturally and racially mediated, but rather about writing and revising to produce a product one can feel proud of.

The combination of contract grading with portfolio assessment is particularly effective in reorienting students and teachers away from the instructor's preferences above all other audience concerns. In this model, revision is required to pass the course. By necessity, a draft is not passing until it has been through the requisite round of revisions (see Inoue, 2019). Usually that means one revision in response to peer feedback and one revision in response to instructor feedback. To facilitate the revision process, I provide a pass/no pass rubric based on some key competencies that I want students to think about, although qualitative commenting on drafts can be just as effective without a rubric. Figure 5.2 is a sample rubric that I use in addition to commenting with my thoughts throughout the essay.

The benefit of a rubric is to help students prioritize where to focus their revisions, but the rubric does not work without substantial in-class time thinking through key terms such as *evidence, analysis, claim,* and *audience.* You will notice that this rubric does not evaluate language correctness, grammar, or any sentence-level concern, and this is very deliberate. My main purposes are to orient students toward rhetorical thinking and to reinforce their growing conceptual knowledge around audience, claim, and evidence. As Asao Inoue (2019) has so eloquently put it, "All grading and assessment exist within systems that uphold singular, dominant, standards that are racist, and White supremacist when used uniformly. This problem is present in any grading system that incorporates a standard, no matter who is judging, no matter the particulars of the standard" (p. 3). If a rubric becomes involved in the counter-productive work of enforcing standards, it has ceased to be useful. Formative comments such as "I had trouble understanding this sentence. I wonder if you could re-word?" substitute for any blanket statements about the so-called "correctness" of students' language, leav-

FIGURE 5.2. Sample Rubric for Summarizing Instructor Feedback

Learning Criteria	Pass/No Pass
An **Opener** that includes a compelling title and introduction that make the audience want to continue reading.	
A **Claim** that makes a clear argument that is specific, manageable, and interesting to the audience.	
Topic and concluding sentences that connect back to the thesis and transition between paragraphs so your audience can follow your thinking.	
Evidence that supports your claim (personal experience, readings, research).	
Analysis of this evidence that advances your claim and helps your audience make sense of the relationships between the different voices you are in conversation with.	
A **Closer** that summarizes and points to larger implications of your ideas.	

ing room for students to make choices that balance their communicative purposes with the needs of their readers.

This system offers a different choice than what often happens when students become overwhelmed with workload or struggle with writing. Here a student can adjust their work based on the grade they want to earn rather than giving up on the course when things get overwhelming. With this new level of flexibility, instructors and students may feel adrift, and this calls for regular class time devoted to revisiting the grading contract. Check-ins can involve brief one-on-one conversations with students as the class works on an independent activity. During these check-ins, teachers can update students on their classwork/homework grade and ask students to revisit their grading contract to refresh their memories about upcoming choices and responsibilities.

As in all first-year writing courses, some students may disappear for a few weeks and come back having missed crucial writing and revision opportunities. I have made it a habit to intervene early and often when students miss class. I email students about where they are in relation to the grading contract and encourage students to make the choices that still remain even late into the semester. For example, students can always bow out of the presentation assignment if they have gotten behind on writing and thereby pass the course. For those students who maintain regular attendance and engagement, the contract grading environment facilitates authentic learning opportunities to seek ongoing feedback from peers, professor, and self to write the most compelling text possible in the 16-week semester. Because revision is the primary criteria of bringing an essay to a passing level, students are rewarded for engaging in the hardest part of writing—rethinking and rewriting their work.

Elbow (2011) has long advocated for a similarly pragmatic and reflective approach to writing assessment. For Elbow, this advocacy is tied directly into students' distrust of teachers' grades:

> It's not surprising that so many students are suspicious and even hostile about the grades they get on their pieces of writing. Almost every citizen of the U.S. has gotten more grades on pieces of writing than on any other school performance in their lives. Understandably, most of these citizens have had experiences that led to resentment and distrust. ("That was really a good paper but she gave me a C-plus on it!" "This was a hurried piece of crap where I just told him what he wanted to hear, but he gave me an A.") (2011, p. 4)

Elbow sees this student attitude as a "pervasive and justified distrust of invalid teacher grades on writing" (2011, p. 4), which he believes is tied to our attempts as teachers to place a single, quantitative score on a piece of student writing. Elbow (2011) argues that pieces of student writing are always complex, multidimensional performances and as authors of the pieces, students are close to and knowledgeable about the pieces' successes and failures. In fact, Elbow (1996) suggests that a student writer's agency and reflection are key elements in both the writing and learning processes.

Like other pedagogies based around portfolio assessment, contract grading emphasizes reflection and revision. In fact, contract grading operationalizes Elbow's (2011) ideal process by including the grade as part of the dialogic process between teacher and student rather than hoping that grading will just go away. Contract grading adds new levels of student participation in all aspects of the writing process, including the assessment of writing to see if course goals have been achieved. Asking writers to set their own goals, work toward those goals, and then reflect on how well a piece meets their goals creates the opportunity for a deeper and more engaged learning experience than one where students try to guess what a teacher wants by reading a rubric and writing toward that.

Each decision point in the contract becomes a reflective opportunity. For example, when introducing Essay 4, the teacher reminds the class about their options and the grades associated with each. Students revisit their initial contract/plan and reflect on whether they want to spend their time revising the first three essays for the portfolio or moving on to the new assignment because the previous revisions have gone well thus far. This takes some flexibility on the part of the instructor, as she or he will be juggling students in different stages of process. It is important to plan for the late-semester divergence in options and ensure that part of each class period allows students to engage in reflection, planning, or group time as needed. Students gain new areas on which to reflect on learning as well: How did their plans change? How did they address struggles and failure? How did they make choices and how did those choices work out? What would they do differently if given another chance? All of these questions can appear in a portfolio cover letter and provide both instructor and student with another opportunity to reflect and build powerful dispositional knowledge and critical thinking for future writing situations.

What do these reflections and dispositions look like in actual community college classrooms? When we have seen faculty combine portfolios with contract grading, students show an increased interest in assessment—how it works, who has the power to assess writing, and what it means to become a better writer based on one's own values and reflections. Students build the critical capacity to challenge even the most seemingly unassailable assessment decisions, including the placement tests they have experienced so far and the standardized tests they may experience in the future. This is the most crucial aspect of contract grading for transformative, anti-racist praxis: Students become the arbiters of their own learning in first-year writing and now have tools to self-assess and push back against unfair assessments of their writing. Grading contracts allow teachers a way to embrace an approach that may be consistent with the ideas described in the CCCC's (1975) "Students' Right to Their Own Language" position statement. When we depart from traditional grading, we are no longer focused on enforcing a particular linguistic standard in our writing classrooms; instead we are engaged in the critical work of partnering with students to build awareness around language and power in our institutions. Teachers also experience a disposition shift when using grading contracts. Now we find ourselves reading papers with an authentic desire to respond, ask questions, and engage with students' ideas as they develop. Most crucially, contract grading can create a relational shift between teachers and students. Students can take more intellectual risks without fear of failure and inquire more deeply into their topics because they do not need to identify their professor's culturally specific standards and/or stylistic preferences. Students and professors are partners in learning with a shared understanding of their roles and responsibilities thanks to the ongoing development and negotiation of the contract document.

We would be remiss if we did not address a common concern about assessing student writing without recourse to a professor's culturally specific standards and/or stylistic preferences. You may be wondering whether students leave first-year writing prepared for their next courses. Will they know how to use MLA or APA format? Will their future instructors in History or Biology find their writing up to par? Are we failing in our responsibility to our students if we do not grade them based on the quality of their essays? We would argue that the most important take-away from first-year writing is rhetorical awareness and critical consciousness around language. Will students practice using citation styles in a contract grading classroom? Of course, if that is part of the curriculum. And they will do so with formative feedback that encourages audience awareness so that they think not so much about the minutiae of a citation, but about the disciplinary norms that govern how different fields understand evidence and ethos. In our experience, students that engage deeply with writing, reflection, and revision will be much more prepared for their future writing contexts than those who learn to meet the expectations of their first-year writing instructor, only to find that all other writing contexts demand different genres and styles. We are making the familiar argument that writing is rhetorical and that a contract grading system prioritizes conceptual knowledge and process awareness over notions of correctness.

This approach is a fundamental shift from the teacher as primary, or sole, arbitrator in the summative assessment of student learning. Many approaches to classroom-level assessment and feedback focus on the distinction between formative and summative assessments. These approaches have often emphasized the value of formative feedback over summative. That is, they advocate for providing more formative feedback, more formative assessment, and more commentary earlier in the process for students. This approach is valuable, and it has moved many faculty members' pedagogical practices away from detailed responses to justify a grade and toward detailed responses that would encourage students to revise. Students learn through revision; classroom response and grading practices that foster revision through an emphasis on formative rather than summative feedback have been widely encouraged.

However, many approaches that encourage teachers to provide formative feedback over summative feedback remain focused on the instructor. In *Writing without Teachers*, Elbow (1998) sketched out methods of response to break away from an instructor-focused approach. Part of Elbow's system is a devaluing of grades. In fact, he has written fondly of Evergreen College and UC–Santa Cruz where undergraduates used to receive course credit, but no grades. And while Elbow's work has been widely read in Composition Studies and is often enthusiastically discussed in graduate seminars on the teaching of writing, operationalizing a system that does not rely on grades has proved more difficult and is less widely accepted and practiced.

Contract grading differs from approaches that emphasize formative assessment over summative assessment and from Elbow's (1998) idealistic "grade-free zone"/"writing without teachers" approach. Contract grading runs into the mechanisms of schooling. That is, it uses the economy of grades and grading to foster student learning. Rather than hoping that students will not worry about grades and focus on a teacher's responses to revise, contract grading embraces the culture and economy of schooling that students know. In contract grading the teacher fundamentally says, "You will receive a grade for your work. Your grade will be an A, B, C, D, or F. You will determine it." Unlike more traditional systems, where the "you will determine it" means that the student will determine it in a limited fashion (i.e., through the work they do as evaluated by the instructor), in a contract grading system, students are genuinely empowered to determine their grades.

Making the Case for Contract Grading in Your Institutional Context

The simplified contract grading system we are advocating is not an anything goes approach. Students must produce the work that they have contracted to complete. They must write a certain number of words, and they must reflect on their composing processes, their revision work, and the qualities—both strengths and weaknesses—of their final essays. When utilized in the California Community College System, we have seen how this approach changes the way students relate to their instructors. In general, contract grading promotes anti-racist praxis and equity because it includes students in conversations about how their writing is assessed. It also gives them ownership and responsibility for their learning in terms that they understand (grades) and that are meaningful to them not only in their writing course but also within the larger ecologies and economies of schooling.

Of course, not every implementation of contract grading has the same level of success. Resistance to contract grading can come from within a writing program or an English department. It can come from students. Or it can come from colleagues across campus. In fact, we have experience with efforts with one community college English department that tried to implement and support contract grading in a program-wide change. In that instance, other departments on campus raised concerns through the Faculty Senate related to the perception and response to contract grading from other departments on campus. Responses ranged from horrified and resistant to puzzled, to expressions of interest and support. Fears were expressed about "allowing the English department to lower academic standards" with contract grading. Contract grading opens up possibilities for anti-racist praxis, but these opportunities are not without risk or tension.

There are many complexities around basic writing and first-year composition in community and junior colleges. Foremost among those may be writing assessment and the relationships among departments at community colleges and the relationships between community colleges and their neighboring four-year institutions. As contract grading is considered by a wider array of writing programs and writing faculty, it is likely that more opportunities to put into practice contract grading systems will emerge in community colleges. The simplified contract grading system we present in this chapter was developed by drawing on the work of Kohn (2011), Blackstock and Exton (2014), and Davidson (2011). Their work on contract grading in open access institutions helped us consider how liberatory practices from within composition studies (i.e., Shor's (1992) work on learning contracts and Elbow's (1998) grade-free writing without teachers) might be adapted for community college students. Given the work within the last five years, across the CCCs to increase equitable outcomes, the ability to develop and employ contract grading assessment systems in writing courses seems vital.

Acknowledgments

We would like to acknowledge Sarah Tinker Perrault's contribution to the idea of a simplified contract structure. The grading contract presented here was adapted by Sarah Klotz for First Year Writing at Butte College in Northern California. We would also like to thank Amy

Clarke, Sarah Faye, and Dan Melzer for providing feedback on an earlier version of this chapter. While we know we have not addressed all of the questions they raised, the chapter is better situated within the context of California and within the emerging literature on contract grading because of their comments.

REFERENCES

Atkinson, W. (2011). From sociological fictions to social fictions: some Bourdieusian reflections on the concepts of 'institutional habitus' and 'family habitus.' *British Journal of Sociology of Education, 32*(3), 331–347. doi: 10.1080/01425692.2011.559337

Blackstock, A., & Exton, V. N. (2014). Space to grow: Grading contracts for basic writers. *Teaching English in the Two-Year College, 41*(3), 278–293.

Bourdieu, P. (1974). The school as a conservative force: Scholastic and cultural inequalities. In J. Eggleston (Ed.), *Contemporary research in the sociology of education* (pp. 32–46). London: Methuen.

Bourdieu, P. (1977). *Outline of a theory of practice* (R. Nice, Trans.). Cambridge, England: Cambridge University Press.

Bourdieu, P. (1984). *Distinction: A social critique of the judgement of taste.* Cambridge, MA: Harvard University Press.

Bulinski, M., Dominguez, A., Inoue, A., Jamali, M., McKnight, M., Seidel, S., & Stott, J. (2009, March). "Shit-plus," "AWK," "frag," and "huh?": An empirical look at a writing program's commenting practices. Paper presented at the Conference on College Composition and Communication, San Francisco, CA.

Campaign for College Opportunity. (2018). Left out: How exclusion in California's colleges and universities hurts our values, our students, and our economy. Retrieved from https://collegecampaign.org/portfolio/left-out-report/

Chen, X. (2016). Remedial coursetaking at U.S. public 2- and 4-year institutions: Scope, experiences, and outcomes. Retrieved from https://nces.ed.gov/pubs2016/2016405.pdf

CCCC. (1975). Committee on Language Statement. Students' right to their own language. *College English, 36*(6), 709–726.

Davidson, C. (2011). *Now you see it: How technology and brain science will transform schools and business for the 21st Century.* New York: Penguin.

Dowd, A., & Bensimon, E. (2015). *Engaging the race question: Accountability and equity in higher education.* New York: Teachers College Press.

Elbow, P. (1996). Writing assessment in the twenty-first century: A utopian view. In L. Bloom, D. Daiker, & E. White (Eds.), *Composition in the 21st century: Crisis and change* (pp. 83–100). Carbondale: Southern Illinois University Press.

Elbow, P. (1998). *Writing without teachers* (25th Anniv. ed.). Oxford, England: Oxford University Press.

Elbow, P. (2011). Good enough evaluation: When is it feasible and when is evaluation not worth having? In N. Elliot & L. Perelman (Eds.), *Writing assessment in the 21st century: Essays in honor of Edward M. White* (pp. 303–325). New York: Hampton Press.

Inoue, A. (2015). *Antiracist writing assessment ecologies.* Anderson, SC: Parlor Press.

Inoue, A. (2019). *Labor-based grading contracts: Building equity and inclusion in the compassionate writing classroom.* Fort Collins: The WAC Clearinghouse and University Press of Colorado.

Kanno, Y. (2018). High-performing English learners' limited access to four-year college. *Teachers College Record, 120*(4), 1–46.

Kohn, A. (2011). The case against grades. *Educational Leadership, 69*(3), 28–33.

Lederman, J., & Warwick, N. (2018). The violence of assessment: Writing assessment, social (in)justice, and the role of validation. In M. Poe, A. Inoue, & N. Elliot (Eds.), *Writing assessment, social justice, and the advancement of opportunity* (pp. 229–255). Fort Collins: The WAC Clearinghouse and University Press of Colorado.

Poe, M. (2016). Re-framing race in teaching writing across the curriculum. In V. Young & F. Condon (Eds.), *Performing anti-racist pedagogy in rhetoric, writing, and communication* (pp. 87–105). Fort Collins: University Press of Colorado.

Poe, M., & Cogan, J. (2016). Civil rights and writing assessment: Using the disparate impact approach as a fairness methodology to determine social impact.

Journal of Writing Assessment, 9(1). Retrieved from http://journalofwriting assessment.org

Poe, M., Inoue, A., & Elliot, N. (Eds.). (2018). *Writing assessment, social justice, and the advancement of opportunity.* Fort Collins: The WAC Clearinghouse and University Press of Colorado.

Reay, D. (2004). 'It's all becoming a habitus': Beyond the habitual use of habitus in educational research. *British Journal of Sociology of Education, 25*(4), 431–444. doi: 10.1080/0142569042000236934

Shor, I. (1992). *Empowering education: Critical teaching for social change.* Chicago: University of Chicago Press.

Steele, C. (1997). A threat in the air: How stereotypes shape intellectual identity and performance. *American Psychologist, 52*(6), 613–629.

6

First-Year Composition: Building Relationships to Teach Emerging Writers

Andrew Kranzman and *Chandra Howard*
MODESTO JUNIOR COLLEGE

Student success in community college writing courses is the keystone to academic transfer. According to the Chancellor's Office of the California Community College (CCC) (2019a) system, "With more than 2.1 million students at 115 colleges, the California Community Colleges is the largest system of higher education in the country." Of this 2.1 million, as the Chancellor's Office observes, 80,000 transfer to the University of California system (e.g., UC Berkeley or UCLA) or the California State University system (e.g., San Francisco State or San Diego State) (California Community Colleges Chancellor's Office, 2019b). Given the diversity of its student body in terms of academic preparedness, those who teach first-year composition (FYC) in the CCC system can attest to the task of preparing incoming students for transfer. This chapter demonstrates how FYC at the community college can prepare students for their post-transfer experiences by (1) building relationships between faculty and students as well as among peers and (2) focusing on innovative ways to teach writing concepts that formerly seemed inaccessible to students who carry previous negative experiences with writing classes into the college setting.

Attending to the affective domain must precede (or at best, fold into) FYC andragogy—that is, methods of teaching adult learners—and curriculum. Therefore, the chapter describes ways to establish positive, trusting relationships with students, focusing on ways to address students' prior poor relationships to educational institutions and to acculturate first-generation college students to the expectations of higher learning. A series of easy-to-emulate activities are presented to build relationships that attend to the affective domain and increase engagement and retention. Also presented are the ways that attending to the affective domain engages students and promotes high-level learning. Specifically, the focus is on concrete activities that expose students to the writing and reading skills needed to succeed in FYC and beyond. These activities include foundational skills, such as writing topic sentences and analyzing paragraphs to demonstrate purpose in writing situations. Other activities include reading comprehension skills, like locating keywords, to show how writers sustain an argument. Activities also develop more advanced skills like synthesizing sources, which fosters the awareness that academic writing never operates in isolation but is always in conversation with other texts.

Theoretical Rationale

Prior research on the importance of affective development and collaborative learning underlie the following learning activities. Lev Vygotsky's (1978) research on peer-to-peer learning emphasizes the importance of social interaction and cognitive development (i.e., the "interpsychological" and the "intrapsychological") (p. 57). He contends that "all higher [cognitive] functions originate as actual relations between individuals" that continually evolve with repeated exposure to learning in a social context (p. 57). Sid Barhoum's (2017) research on the centrality of the "relational domain" in developmental writing programs equally applies to many underprepared students in FYC. Finally, the advocacy of Katie Hern and Myra Snell (2011) of the California Acceleration Project (CAP) highlights the "psychological and emotional" aspects of learning. They emphasize the need to "establish and maintain positive relationships" and to "provide class time for students to process content and practice skills" (p. 2), two design principles of these FYC activities. Considered together, the research of these scholars provides a rationale for creating activities that capitalize on the social dimensions of apprenticing students who are unfamiliar with discipline-specific language and skills, such as purpose, organization, and synthesis.

Addressing the Affective Domain

Building community has a dual benefit for FYC students: It creates a comfortable and flexible learning environment (rather than an exacting one) and illustrates how writing is a site of identity formation and collegiality. Many students entering community college have had negative experiences in English classes, and even students with positive experiences carry anxiety into the FYC classroom. In our experience, one thing remains nearly universal among students: They do not think they are good writers. Adverse experiences have bred not only resentment of English courses, instructors, and general education (GE) requirements, but also low self-esteem as writers in academic settings, which students internalize as personal deficiency. This specific brand of rejection, coupled with fears well outlined in Rebecca D. Cox's *The College Fear Factor* (2009), compound to make incoming students feel like imposters. They do not see themselves as college material. They are often first-generation college students facing very high stakes as they step into FYC classrooms. Therefore, building positive relationships must occur before apprenticing in the practices of FYC.

Activity 1: Apprenticing through *Learning to Read* by Malcolm X

The choice of this book excerpt and accompanying activity intentionally recognize the shifting uses of language while reprioritizing which types of writers typically dominate course reading lists. This exercise introduces aspects of Reading Apprenticeship (WestEd, 2020) andragogy that undergird sound writing practices, illustrates the concept of audience in writing and speaking, and addresses underrepresented voices in the curriculum. This show-and-tell strategy builds self-esteem from the outset and allows the class to establish a concept employed throughout the course when working on academic register.

Set Up

On the first day of class, teachers should discuss the concept of registers. They should explain that different vocabularies are used in different situations and that one is not necessarily more valuable than another. They can confirm that, in an academic setting, other voices are not typically valued; for example, conversational vernacular or "kitchen table" knowledge are not considered scholarly. Then teachers can open discussion to the class about different vernaculars they use in different situations.

Directions

Students take turns reading "Learning to Read," an excerpt from *The Autobiography of Malcolm X* (1965), aloud, paragraph by paragraph, during the class session. The instructor should stop at each paragraph, summarizing Malcolm X's act of recognizing that he only spoke one register and wanted to learn different ways of communicating so that he would feel comfortable in a variety of settings. Ask students to annotate the text to define different settings and the language that was valued. Then discuss the role of context: Who are these people he is describing? How can context clues be used to situate this decontextualized excerpt? What are students learning about Malcolm X and who relates to him? These comprehension questions, reading strategies, and discussion points allow students to:

1. see the arc of an incarcerated youth to esteemed speaker.

2. understand the impetus for his transformation: the desire to speak and write in different registers.

3. identify the value of learning multiple "languages."

<u>Teacher's Note:</u> Focus on the presence of different registers and the recognition of audience and purpose. Dispel linguistic hierarchies by focusing on the idea that every register presents a specialization.

Activity 2: Sharing Journeys: The Educational Letter

The intention of this assignment is threefold in terms of affective domain principles: (1) build a relationship with students by showing trials and successes of your own educational journey; (2) invite students to respond to your letter and share personal stories of their own; and (3) assess their writing with a low-stakes assignment (they are not graded on this personal letter project, and this should not be used as a diagnostic exam).

Set Up

As a homework assignment, ask students to read an educational journey letter written by an instructor. (It may or may not be the one in the class.) Instructors should include successes and failures in school, struggles, and strategies. The letter should offer insight as to how the instructor got to where they are today.

Student Response to Professor's Educational Letter

Instructors can request that students respond with a question or comment after having read the instructor's letter. This often generates conversation, particularly if done over email. In our experience, students often connect with and respond to particular parts. For example, when responding to instructor education letters, students often express camaraderie and empathize with the similar challenges faced by the instructor during their college experience, particularly when balancing finances. In response, for example, to an instructor mentioning a semester-long subsistence on quesadillas, one student mentioned having a "Cup-of-Noodles year" herself.

Assignment Prompt

Similar to my letter to you, please write a 2- to 3-page typed letter (double-spaced) to me in which you introduce yourself and provide some information about you as a student. This will help me get to know you better.

Please consider the following questions in this letter. (Answer in paragraph form—some questions can be answered in the same paragraph. Try combining similar topics.)

You do not have to answer all the questions. They are here to help you generate ideas.

- *What was your high school experience like?*
- *What has your experience in English classes been like?*
- *What is your attitude about reading and writing?*
  - *What did you read for school?*
  - *What do you read for pleasure?*
  - *What kind of writing do you do in your free time?*
- *What is your native language?*
  - *Additional language(s)?*
- *Why have you come to Modesto Junior College?*
- *What are your academic interests and goals?*
- *What are your career goals?*
- *Describe your study skills/academic work habits.*
  - *What kinds of class activities and learning strategies have you found helpful in the past?*
  - *What are your strengths as a student?*
  - *How could you improve as a student?*
- *What do you hope to learn in this class?*
- *What other classes are you taking this semester?*
- *What do you enjoy doing in your free time?*
- *What else should I know about you that would help me teach you more effectively?*

Excerpt from Example Student Educational Letter

Another aspect of this assignment is that students naturally tend to share stories of resilience. We often comment in the margins, encouraging them to remember their comebacks and focus on the things that got them through. This student letter, reproduced with the student's original language and punctuation, is typical of the level of reflection we have grown accustomed to in the project:

> My high school experience was a great one, but it was also difficult. The first three years of high school was great. I was on the soccer team and also was a cheerleader. I was dating the 'popular guy' and I had a whole bunch of friends. But towards the end of my Jr. Year everything started to go downhill my relationship started to become really toxic and my mother became sick. So in a result of bad things happening my grades started to slip, I got kicked off the cheerleading team and was no longer able to play soccer. I became really lazy and let everything that was going on get the best of me. My boyfriend at the time damaged me emotionally and physically and my mother being sick also hurt me. So, my grades were all F's for that whole semester. So, the start of my senior year I had to go to a different school to make up all the credits I lost, also that summer I had to do summer school. The reason why I said my high school experience was great is because that one bad event didn't define the outcome of my future. I was able to work really hard and earn all my credits back. I was even able to go to prom. That one event taught me that when things get bad you just can't give up and let it get the best of you. You have to keep pushing forward. And also, never let your past define your future.

Teacher's Note: Treat this assignment like a letter exchange. Do not correct or grade; anything written on student letters should be supportive commentary on the content.

Teaching Central FYC Concepts

Activities in this section address fundamental practices in reading and writing for FYC students at community college. They are examples of the "low-stakes, collaborative practice" that Hern and Snell (2011, p. 4) see as critical to the affective domain and are useful points of entry for teaching what they view as central FYC concepts. While these activities are designed to be completed during class, they could be given as out-of-class assignments, although the social context and component would be eliminated, and therefore, their efficacy undermined.

Activity 1: Keywords, Quotations, and Paraphrases

This activity introduces foundational skills: organization, quotation, and paraphrase. It can also illustrate how to use keywords to sustain a thesis statement and to introduce summary. Students complete this in class with two to three peers. The activity takes approximately 20–30 minutes if all three skills are taught (this includes a brief set up). Taking time to teach these skills (identifying important keywords, quoting, and paraphrasing) creates ample opportunities to practice foundational college-level reading and writing skills that students need to succeed in coursework throughout the general education sequence and when they transfer. In our experience, students often have difficulty choosing central quotations from a text or tracking a central idea throughout an academic text; instead, they gravitate toward quotes peripheral to the text's thesis. Showing students how to identify keywords helps them choose meaningful quotes in their writing and research and expand their reading comprehension simultaneously. Likewise, students often struggle with paraphrase. They typically forget to signal the quotation or include a parenthetical citation and repeat words from the original text without the use of quotation marks. Teaching quotation and paraphrase at the same time (and repeatedly across the semester as a refresher) often allays any confusion and helps them understand how to avoid plagiarism.

Set Up for Keywords

Teachers should use a class reading to introduce strategies to locate high-impact and high-frequency keywords. Here *keyword* refers to a term or set of terms central to understanding an author's thesis as well as a term or set of terms an author uses to illustrate their thesis. *High-impact keywords* are those that occupy important positions in a reading (e.g., title, subtitles, thesis, italicized or boldfaced words, graphs, bibliography, etc.). *High-frequency keywords* are consistently recurring words in a specific reading.

Directions

Working with peers, ask students to take five minutes and list the high-impact keywords and high-frequency keywords in Carol Dweck's "Brainology" (2008) and to note the page number for each keyword.

> Student Examples: *fixed mindset* (p. 1), *growth mindset* (p. 1), *intelligence* (p. 1), *failures* (p. 2), *motivation* (p. 2), *setbacks* (p. 2), *praise* (p. 3), *stereotypes* (p. 4)

Teacher's Note: *Fixed mindset* (p. 1), *growth mindset* (p. 1), *setbacks* (p. 2), and *motivation* (p. 2) constitute high-impact keywords since they occur in important places in Dweck's article such as the title, subtitles, italicized words, and pulled quotes. *Intelligence* (p. 1), *failures* (p. 2), *praise* (p. 3), and *stereotypes* (p. 4) constitute high-frequency keywords since they occur repeatedly throughout Dweck's article. Ask students how they determined these keywords. Reviewing the generated list of words is useful. Ask groups to respond to these two questions: Which keywords occur in the article title, section subtitles, pulled quotes, descriptions of figures or graphics, topic sentences? Which keywords occur repeatedly throughout Dweck's article?

Directions for Paraphrase

Choose the 3–4 most important keywords from your list and find a direct sentence from the reading that illustrates it. Cite the page number. Restate each direct sentence in your own words, using a signal phrase, reporting verb, and parenthetical citation.

Student Quotation Example: "Many students believe that intelligence is fixed, that each person has a certain amount and that's that" (1).

Teacher's Note: This quotation represents typical student work at the second week of the semester when students are often struggling to identify relevant quotes and passages from a reading.

Student Paraphrase Example: "According to Dweck, students often think they have a set amount of intelligence that cannot be changed" (1).

Teacher's Note: Debrief by asking students how they selected their quotations and how a sentence illustrates a keyword. Be sure to also discuss how they restated the quotation in their own words. What approaches did they use? What difficulties did they encounter?

The keyword activity can also be used to introduce summary (thesis, keywords, and supporting detail) and to help students locate the author's thesis or "big picture idea." This is a good time to talk about how authors often use keywords in their thesis statements as a roadmap to help readers follow the development of their argument.

Activity 2: Research Paper Keystone: Source Synthesis

The multisource research essay is a central assignment in FYC and, as most faculty can attest, it is a struggle for students. This activity uses a Venn diagram to illustrate synthesis. Not only is it a good activity for students to complete at the beginning of the research process, but it also proves useful in discussions of academic writing as a conversation to which multiple parties contribute. This discussion would generally occur toward the start of the semester. Students complete this poster activity with two to three peers. This activity takes approximately 30 to 40 minutes.

Set Up

This activity provides students with a brief overview of synthesis and model use of Venn diagram. Consider starting with something like:

> *Synthesis is a form of analysis that connects multiple sources and/or pieces of evidence. It draws together traits, themes, or relationships from multiple sources and organizes them to show how they overlap. In other words, synthesis creates a dialogue between or among sources.*

Directions

With peers, ask students to create a Venn diagram of Mark Salzman's *True Notebooks* (2003) and Jennifer Siebel Newsom's film *The Mask You Live In* (2015). Students should then paraphrase or quote instances where both readings overlap and cite the page number. They will put this information in the center of the diagram where the circles overlap. Next students paraphrase or quote instances where readings discuss different ideas or topics. They should cite the page number and put this information toward the outside of each circle where no overlap occurs. They should find as many overlaps as possible.

One student's diagram is shown in Figure 6.1.

Teacher's Note: Debrief by asking students how they determined which ideas overlapped and which ideas did not. What criteria did they use? Why did they determine these criteria to be the most representative of shared ideas?

Gallery Walk

Ask students to walk around the room and review the Venn diagrams created by their peers. Or students could write observations or put questions on sticky notes on each diagram. For instance, they may note what they noticed when reviewing peers' diagrams. What were some common

FIGURE 6.1. Student Example: Connecting Sources, Connecting Ideas

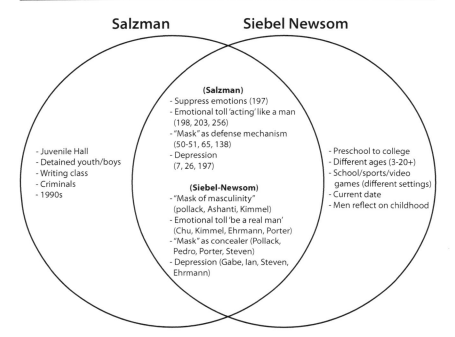

Salzman   Siebel Newsom

(Salzman)
- Suppress emotions (197)
- Emotional toll 'acting' like a man
  (198, 203, 256)
- "Mask" as defense mechanism
  (50-51, 65, 138)
- Depression
  (7, 26, 197)

(Siebel-Newsom)
- "Mask of masculinity"
  (pollack, Ashanti, Kimmel)
- Emotional toll 'be a real man'
  (Chu, Kimmel, Ehrmann, Porter)
- "Mask" as concealer (Pollack,
  Pedro, Porter, Steven)
- Depression (Gabe, Ian, Steven,
  Ehrmann)

- Juvenile Hall
- Detained youth/boys
- Writing class
- Criminals
- 1990s

- Preschool to college
- Different ages (3-20+)
- School/sports/video
  games (different settings)
- Current date
- Men reflect on childhood

themes that diagrams identified as overlapping? What were some themes that each reading discussed separately? If you include this step, be sure to allow additional time for the original group to review the sticky notes and to report out to the class their peers' comments and responses.

Teacher's Note: Debrief by asking students to share their observations. Finally, ask them to reflect on how this exercise demonstrates a conversation between the two authors.

Synthesis Paragraph

Ask students to review a peer example of a synthesis paragraph for the next class. At the start of the next class meeting, briefly discuss the various "moves" made by the peer author (e.g., repetition of keywords, transition words, emphatic order, etc.), including what makes it an effective paragraph. Groups of two to three students should draft a synthesis paragraph using their previous session's Venn diagram and observations from the Gallery Walk.

Note that this student example is reproduced using the student's original punctuation and MLA style citation, which is the preferred style in the class.

> Jimmy Wu is a quiet young man who is much different from the other boys. He doesn't talk about having to wear a "mask," however, he talks about how they're not allowed to show emotions in "juvenile hall." Wu says: [w]e can't even talk about it in here. It's not allowed" (197). The boys are not allowed to talk about the emotions they go through during their trial and sentencing. At this point Jimmy Wu had just got his sentence for robbery. He was really upset and hurt at how much time he had gotten and couldn't let anyone see he was hurting. William Pollack claims that boys are taught "to hide natural vulnerable…feelings behind the mask of masculinity" (qtd. in Newsom). Boys are trained at a young age to conceal their genuine emotions and are forced to hide behind a "mask." Two of the most common things that boys hide behind their "mask" is pain and anger (Newsom). Jimmy Wu hides his anger behind the "mask of masculinity."

Commentary on Student Writing

This sample represents a typical first attempt at synthesis in our FYC. Here, we have asked students to discuss similar themes on masculinity in a full-length book (Salzman, 2003) and a documentary (Siebel Newsom, 2015). We appreciate how the student hones in on the theme of *masking* in both texts, even though, as the student notes, the term is not used explicitly in Salzman's discussion of Jimmy. In a future iteration of this paragraph, we would ask the student to add more detail to their discussion of the conversation between both texts because it is a little vague. However, this is an excellent first attempt at synthesis, and we would draw the writer's attention to how they focus on the explicit and implicit use of masking (a sophisticated move, in our opinion) and how they quote and paraphrase from the original sources.

In conclusion, it is not uncommon to have in the same FYC classroom students who range from marginally proficient in college-level reading and writing to clearly prepared for college course rigors. Moving from basics like keyword identification and summary to paraphrase proficiency and research synthesis in one semester requires instructional sequencing and skill-building. A major challenge at this introductory transfer-level course (often the first of two or three required English courses for the GE sequence, depending on students' majors) is to create a learning environment in which students thrive regardless of their disparate preparedness and past educational experiences. Moreover, the activities presented illustrate community-building in the classroom. These activities illustrate J.E. Roueche's claim that, in the writing classroom, "affective development informs cognitive development" (quoted in Barhoum, 2017, p. 11). While these activities typically take place in an FYC course, they can be applied to an array of learning contexts (like future courses that require research synthesis or register/audience/purpose discernment) and for a variety of student demographics. Indeed, these activities have been used in developmental composition courses, co-requisite composition courses, advanced composition courses, and literature courses. Their collaborative nature makes them suitable for all students—those who are first generation, returning, have poor educational experiences, and have learning differences.

REFERENCES

Barhoum, S. (2017). Community college developmental writing programs most promising practices: What the research tells educators. *Community College Journal of Research and Practice, 41*(12), 791–808.

California Community Colleges Chancellor's Office. (2019a). Key facts. Retrieved from https://www.cccco.edu/About-Us/Key-Facts

California Community Colleges Chancellor's Office. (2019b). Transfer. Retrieved from https://www.cccco.edu/Students/Transfer

Cox, R. D. (2009). *The college fear factor: How students and professors misunderstand one another.* Cambridge, MA: Harvard University Press.

Dweck, C. S. (2008). Brainology: Transforming students' motivation to learn. *National Association of Independent Schools.* Retrieved from https://www.nais. org/magazine/independent-school/winter-2008/brainology/

Hern, K., & Snell, M. (2011). Attending to the affective domain. California Acceleration Project. Retrieved from http://cap.3csn.org/files/2012/02/Attending-to-the-Affective-Domain-outline-v21.pdf

Malcolm X. (1965). *The autobiography of Malcolm X.* New York: Ballantine Books.

Salzman, M. (2003). *True notebooks: A writer's year at juvenile hall.* New York: Vintage Books.

Siebel Newsom, J. (Producer). (2015). *The mask you live in* [Motion picture]. New York: Virgil Films.

Vygotsky, L. (1978). *Mind in society: The development of higher psychological processes.* M. Cole, V. J. Steiner, S. Scribner, & E. Souberman (Trans.). Cambridge, MA: Harvard University Press.

WestEd. (2020). *Reading apprenticeship at WestEd.* Retrieved from https://readingapprenticeship.org/

7

Supporting English Learners with Disabilities in College Composition Courses

Caroline Torres
KAPʻIOLANI COMMUNITY COLLEGE

The number of English learners (ELs) in college has been steadily increasing and is reflective of the nearly 25 percent of community college students who speak a language other than English at home (Community College Consortium for Immigrant Education, 2015). These increases have resulted in a "new mainstream" (Enright, 2011) of much more diverse classrooms. ELs themselves are "superdiverse," coming from different backgrounds, with different schooling experiences, linguistic backgrounds, and many other distinct characteristics (Park, Zong, & Batalova, 2018). Another aspect of diversity is disability, with nearly 13 percent of ELs in U.S. public schools identified as having a disability (U.S. Department of Education, 2014). There is limited information, however, on how many ELs with disabilities enroll in college because colleges are not required to collect and report data on EL enrollment. In addition, few ELs with disabilities have access to college preparation classes (Office of English Language Education, 2017). These barriers result in lower enrollment and success rates for ELs and ELs with disabilities.

Commonly Occurring Disabilities among ELs

Once in college, many ELs struggle to be successful due to the strong emphasis that universities place on language skills (Kanel, 2004), and this is compounded for ELs with the additional challenge of a disability. The Americans with Disabilities Act (ADA), which offers support for and prohibits discrimination against all individuals with disabilities, including college students, defines disability as "a physical or mental impairment that substantially limits one or more major life activities of such individual" (ADA, 2008). In addition, the Individuals with Disabilities in Education Act (IDEA), which ensures free and appropriate public education and protects the rights for students with disabilities in U.S. public education, identifies 13 categories of disabilities (IDEA, 2004). Approximately half of ELs with disabilities have been identified with a specific learning disability and more than 20 percent have a speech or language impairment. Autism, intellectual disability, and other health impairments, which includes Attention Deficit Disorder (ADD) and Attention Deficit Hyperactivity Disorder (ADHD), are the next three most common disabilities (OELA, 2017) (see Table 7.1). This superdiversity of ELs challenges teachers with recognizing students' varied needs and understanding how to support them.

Some of the characteristics of these disabilities—such as atypical communication patterns, lack of focus and organization, and difficulty completing assignments—may be misinterpreted as intentional bad behavior or a lack of motivation. In addition, because of these and other negative misperceptions, students with disabilities are often not given the extra time and care that is required to provide appropriate accommodations. It is essential that teachers be open to alternative root causes for the students' poor performance or atypical behavior. This awareness is the first critical step to providing needed support.

TABLE 7.1. Common Disabilities among ELs, Characteristics, and Possible Supports

Disability	Key Features	Selected Writing Accommodations
Specific Learning Disability	• Disorder that impacts cognitive processing related to understanding/using written or spoken language "which may manifest itself in an imperfect ability to listen, think, speak, read, write, spell, or to do mathematical calculations" (IDEA, 2004), • Individuals with average/above average intelligence • Challenges can also be metacognition, memory, organization, task completion, and persistence. • **Citations:** Harris, Graham, Brindle, & Sandmel, 2009; Pullen, Lane, Ashworth, & Lovelace, 2011	• Explicit strategy instruction • Chunked assignments and organizational support • Instruction on expectations and focused feedback • Models and repeated practice • Support for student's specific challenges (reading, writing, spelling, organization, other) • Support for self-regulation
Speech and Language Impairments	• Challenges with oral language, including limited vocabulary, inaccurate use of grammar • Can include reading & writing challenges (language processing is linked to reading) • **Citations:** Dockrell, Lindsay, & Connely, 2009	• Explicit vocabulary development • Explicit grammar instruction • Reading comprehension support (linked to writing) • Focused feedback on structure
Autism Spectrum Disorder	• Neurodevelopmental disorder: impacts individuals with a range of challenges and severity • Challenges typically include communicating, appropriately responding, understanding non-verbal cues, relationship-building, and processing large amounts of information at once. • Challenges often include managing change, unpredictability, ambiguity, and transitions. • **Citations:** American Psychiatric Association, 2013; Marks, Shaw-Hegwer, Schrader, Longaker, Peters, Powers, & Levine, 2003	• Clear expectations for learning and processes • Clear modeling and examples • Reduced ambiguity • Visual presentation of information: organizers/outlines • Clear structure and support for group work/alternate options • Cues leading up to transitions
Other Health Impairment	• Health impairments that impact academics • Impairments can be asthma, Attention Deficit Hyperactivity Disorder (ADHD), Attention Deficit Disorder (ADD), and many others. • Individuals with ADD/ADHD face challenges focusing, controlling impulses, and executive functions (i.e., task initiation/completion, organization, time management, short-term memory). • **Citations:** IDEA, 2004, Sec. 300.8 (c) (9); Rooney, 2011	• Clear guidelines and guidance • Support, such as outlines for writing, to support focus • Engaging instruction • Support for organization • Step-by-step instructions and chunking assignments (supports task initiation and completion)
Intellectual Disability	• Individuals with IQ of less than 70-75: results in intellectual, functional, and practical behavioral challenges. • **Citations:** Polloway, Patton, & Nelson, 2011	• Clear guidelines provided in small chunks with extensive modeling and guidance

Identification of and Support for Students with Disabilities

U.S. Public schools are required by law to provide testing for students suspected of having a disability and to create and implement an Individualized Education Plan (IEP), outlining supports to help students diagnosed with a disability to succeed academically. High school IEPs include transition planning for attending college. When students who have had these supports transition to college, they have often been advised to provide documentation to continue to receive supports for their disability. Institutions of higher education that receive federal funding are required to provide accommodations for students with documented disabilities. However, approximately 60 percent of college students with disabilities choose not to disclose their disability status (Newman, 2005) and, as a result, do not receive accommodations. Yet, even when students do provide documentation and request services, teachers are only notified of what official accommodations the students are eligible to receive (e.g., extended time and/or a distraction-free area for tests and quizzes). The students' disabilities remain confidential unless they choose to disclose to their teachers themselves.

International students, on the other hand, may be from countries that do not have the same level of support for students with disabilities built into their educational systems, so they often do not have diagnoses for their disabilities, which makes them ineligible for support services in college. Some international students seek out testing, but it can be prohibitively expensive and is often not supported due to culturally different beliefs surrounding disability. This leaves college teachers of ELs to determine the students' strengths and challenges without knowing whether they have a disability.

In addition, in public education, ELs are required to be identified, tested, and provided with language supports. However, unlike for students with disabilities, colleges are not required to provide supports to ELs and, outside of specially designed ESL classes, ELs may not get any accommodations for language development. Many colleges have ESL classes, but teachers in other classes, including FYC, are not required to provide any additional accommodations.

Concerned teachers should not ask students if they have disabilities or what their disabilities are and should not try to "armchair diagnose" their students; however, they can ask if a student has always struggled with writing or school in general in their first language to begin to determine if the challenges that they are noticing are due to language or potential learning difficulties. If a student exhibits similar challenges in their first language, there may be a disability. Understanding learner diversity and characteristics of disabilities helps teachers identify challenges, especially those that may manifest in ways that can be misinterpreted as a lack of caring or motivation. Teachers can implement supports that draw on students' strengths to ameliorate challenges. This type of instructional design benefits all students.

Challenges in Writing for ELs with Disabilities

First-year composition courses can be a hurdle for ELs and for students with disabilities, so it is even more so for ELs with disabilities. In addition to language development needs, many ELs with disabilities struggle in particular to generate and organize their ideas and to understand what is expected in terms of academic writing. In addition, ELs typically make fewer and less beneficial revisions and tend to favor surface-level revisions over those related to meaning. In fact, the writing of struggling writers, including those with disabilities, often does not improve with revision (Berg, 1999). Many of these skills are expected to have been developed prior to college, so teachers may not explicitly address them in composition classes. ELs with disabilities at the postsecondary level benefit greatly from a clear, structured approach with explicit instruction on how to write and revise. These strategies also support native speakers with disabilities and ELs without disabilities who are not proficient in writing.

Rationale

There is very limited empirical research on what works to support ELs with disabilities when it comes to writing, and even less for supporting ELs with disabilities in college writing. Few empirical studies analyze the success of direct instruction and strategy instruction (Viel-Ruma et al., 2010; Wong et al., 2008), which aligns with the suggestion that strategy instruction may have the most positive impact on writing (Graham & Perin, 2007). In addition, Self-Regulated Strategy Development (SRSD) for writing, which provides a foundation for the framework outlined in this chapter, has been identified as an evidence-based practice for students with specific learning disabilities (Baker et al., 2009) and shows promise with students with ADD and ADHD (Jacobson & Reid, 2010) and Autism Spectrum Disorder (Asaro-Saddler & Saddler, 2010), which are three of the five most common disabilities among ELs.

There is a common argument that explicit genre and language instruction leads to students writing only the infamous five-paragraph essay, which stifles quality writing and eliminates critical thinking (Hillocks, 2002), but explicit instruction should not limit students' creativity. As the explicit models and text deconstruction demonstrate different varieties of writing in the genre, students learn what varied styles look like and choose what they apply. To be sure, it is a balance between providing explicit instruction and supporting students to maintain their voice, but without the explicit instruction on genre, strategy, and language, many ELs with disabilities would not be able to produce clear enough writing to showcase their voice and meet college-level demands. Through increased understanding and confidence, they can express their identities and ideas in writing.

Pedagogy

I teach community college composition for ELs (ESL 100), which has the equivalent competencies and credits as the FYC (ENG 100) required of all students seeking a degree, as well as an advanced writing course for non-native speakers of English, which is one level below the ESL 100 class. For both of these classes, I use SRSD, which includes specific genre instruction: using models, writing strategy instruction, and self-regulation to help students self-assess and monitor their writing process and progress (Harris et al., 2008). This approach, adapted to meet the requirements of college-level writing, combined with explicit language instruction and culturally responsive content and teaching provides an effective framework for supporting ELs with disabilities.

Explicit Genre Instruction

The majority of college-level writing assignments are persuasive and informative genres. To support students' success with these genres, teachers should provide explicit instruction on the expectations for each, including required elements: for example, the expectations for a persuasive or informative essay and what types of information and style of language should be included. SRSD includes mnemonics to help students remember the required elements for each genre. I have adapted these to align with college-level writing (see Figure 7.1), and they can be used with students, particularly those with disabilities, who often struggle to remember how to organize and what to include to develop their writing. For example, in persuasive writing, students are expected to take a side and state a claim. Then, they need to support their claim with reasons from sources and often are expected to include and refute a counterclaim to strengthen their argument. To remember this, students can be taught the mnemonic TREE, which stands for Topic, Reasons, Explain and expand, and Ending. Even when they understand the expectations, students are often still confused as to how to apply it in their own writing. Contextualizing and providing a concrete real-life example also helps students understand the expectations. One such example could be a student wanting to ask her boss for a day off. If she simply asks, she knows that the boss may say no; however, if she anticipates why the boss may say no and provides an alternative to the refusal, then the boss may be more likely to agree and grant her the day off. Because many EL college students have jobs, providing this type of example may help them better understand how refuting a counterclaim supports an argument.

Contextualization like this, along with culturally relevant content and teaching approaches, should also be embedded throughout to support students. Finding ways to help students use their background

FIGURE 7.1. Informative: TIDE Mnemonic & Persuasive/ Argument: TREE Mnemonics, adapted from SRSD

TIDE

Informative Writing

T **Topic/ Thesis**
- Introduce the topic with a clear thesis statement.
- Engage the reader.

I **Important Evidence**
- Support thesis statement with *important evidence*.
- Begin a paragraph for each new idea.
  - Introduce the new ideas in each paragraph.

D **Details *to support evidence***
- Provide <u>details to support each piece of evidence</u>
  - Details can be explanations, additional information, facts, and examples.
- Use transitional and cohesive devices to show relationships between evidence and details.

E **Ending**
- End each paragraph with a concluding idea or transition to connect to next important evidence.
- End the essay with a final message and connection to the introduction.

TREE

Argumentative and Persuasive Writing

T **Thesis Statement**
- Introduce the topic by stating a claim.
- Engage the reader.

R **Reasons**
- Support claim with <u>strong reasons</u>.
- Begin a paragraph for each new idea.
  - Introduce the new ideas in each paragraph.

E **Explain/ Expand**
- Provide explanations and examples for each reason.
- Use transitional and cohesive devices to show relationships between reasons and support.

E **Ending**
- End each paragraph with a concluding idea and transition to next reason.
- End essay with a conclusion that provides a final message and connects to introduction.

knowledge and their skills to be successful can provide an assets-based perspective that students may begin to internalize, supporting their persistence in writing.

Text Deconstruction with Models

Beginning writing instruction with text deconstruction of a model essay helps students to understand what different genre elements look like. Teachers can ask students to complete a "reverse outline" based on the model. The students think about the required elements and identify what they look like in a model essay and then practice creating an outline from the essay. When students begin writing their own essays, they better understand how to organize their own ideas into an outline after practicing with the proficient model. They can begin to see how the author connected ideas to support the topic.

Another typical college requirement is to elaborate and develop ideas well. This is often challenging for language learners because in addition to limited vocabulary, they may not understand what it means to develop their ideas, resulting in the same few ideas being repeated in different ways, making longer, but not better, essays. Through genre instruction and text deconstruction, students can be taught explicitly how to elaborate and develop ideas. For instance, TREE can help students remember what to include to develop their ideas well. As students identify these elements and what these types of sentences look like in varied models, they learn to support their reasons with sentences that explain, give examples of, and add other information to support their reasons. Exposing students to different models in each genre also allows them to see variety and not learn or reinforce the myth that essays must have a certain number of paragraphs or a certain number of sentences in each paragraph.

Writing Process

Many ELs with disabilities start writing without planning, focusing, or organizing their thoughts, making it difficult to stay on topic. Thus, teaching students a process for how to prepare to write and organize their ideas can result in higher quality writing and increased confidence. They can be taught to remember this process by using the mnemonic PO²WER (Plan, Organize, Outline, Write, Edit, Revise), which is adapted from SRSD's POW (Pull apart the prompt, Organize my notes, Write and say more). When students take the first step and **Plan** what they will write about, they should be taught to analyze the criteria or prompt. One simple way to do that is to teach them to number each part that they need to write about. This helps students identify and remember to address all aspects of an assignment. In addition, after drafting, they can review their writing by checking that they have written about each numbered part. After planning, students should be taught how to generate and **Organize** their ideas in relation to the different parts of the topic. Graphic organizers can help students organize and focus their ideas on the topic.

After generating their ideas, students should learn how to **Outline**, which includes explicit instruction on how to use keywords instead of complete sentences and how to group ideas into paragraphs, as well as determining how many paragraphs to include. If students write complete sentences on their outlines, they may lose focus or lack persistence when they then **Rewrite** their notes into essay form. Creating quick outlines with just keywords and notes helps students write more quickly and efficiently, which helps them maintain or regain focus and persist in this endeavor. The outlines students create vary depending on the requirements of the assignment, but students can be given the format for an outline initially (see Figure 7.2) so that they can understand, visualize, and remember how to develop their ideas and how to organize. The amount of detail (i.e., prompting) included in the outline will depend on the needs of the students (see Figure 7.3). It is also important that, as soon as students are ready, they begin to create their own outlines without a template and determine how many ideas will make up their different paragraphs and how many paragraphs they will include. This will help them begin to move to independence and, for those who are ready, beyond a prescribed format. To this end, provide outlines with some variation so that students can see how different assignment criteria may require varied lengths and organizational patterns in writing.

Students should then be encouraged to use their outlines to **Write** and help them get back on track if they become distracted. Using the

FIGURE 7.2. Highly Scaffolded Informative (TIDE) Outline

Outline

Make notes about what you will include in your essay –
don't write complete sentences yet!

T: TOPIC & THESIS

- Hook: _____
- Thesis Statement: _____

I: IMPORTANT Evidence: _____

D: _DETAILS_ *to support evidence: (explanation, examples)*

- _____
- _____
- _____

E: _Ending_ *of paragraph/ Transition*

- _____

I: IMPORTANT Evidence: _____

D: _DETAILS_ *to support evidence: (explanation, examples)*

- _____
- _____
- _____

E: _Ending_ *of paragraph/ Transition*

- _____

E: ENDING of Essay/ Conclusion

- Connection to the introduction/ thesis: _____
- Final message: _____

Now Write Your Essay
Don't forget to add transitions!

FIGURE 7.3. Reduced Scaffolding Argumentative/ Persuasive (TREE) Outline

Outline

T

1. Introduction

- Hook:
- Thesis Statement (**Claim**):

2. Development

Organize your ideas into paragraphs. Each paragraph should focus on one reason. Then, explain, expand, and give examples, using persuasive devices and a counterclaim to support your reasons. Make sure to include an ending statement and/ or transition between ideas and paragraphs.

R
E
E
E

R
E
E
E

3. Ending/ Conclusion

E

- Connection to the introduction/ thesis:
- Final message:

outline reduces the cognitive demands while writing, so students have more capacity to focus on language. To internalize and support generalization of these strategies, teachers should gradually wean students off pre-made organizers and outlines. After writing, specific language instruction helps students learn to **Edit** their own writing and to **Revise** after receiving feedback.

Language Instruction

For ELs with disabilities, equally critical as organization is explicit language instruction. Mini-lessons and text deconstruction can be used for explicit language instruction immediately before or after students write, either to prepare them to write or to support them to edit and revise. Often, composition classes do not include explicit grammar instruction or correction; however, ELs and ELs with disabilities typically cannot successfully develop their language and writing without this.

Mini-lessons are recommended for language instruction because they are efficient and narrowly focused to help students to deeply understand and practice one language form or grammar issue in context so that they can learn to apply it in their writing (Ferris & Hedgcock, 2014). An "input analysis" process can be used as a framework in which teachers provide input (e.g., course readings, videos) to raise students' awareness of a relevant language form, highlighting it in the content and having students analyze and practice the pattern (Ford, 2004, as cited in Noji & Yuen, 2012). Pulling language and language forms from content that students are already interacting with creates a context and more relevance for language instruction than stand-alone grammar exercises and quizzes. This text deconstruction and practice should also be paired with explicit language instruction and repeated opportunities for practice. The explicit instruction is essential because many ELs with disabilities will not be able to successfully "discover" a grammar rule through analysis only. These mini-lessons should be integrated throughout to address different aspects of grammar, genre-specific language, or vocabulary. Targeted feedback on what was taught, in conjunction with mini-lessons helps students deepen their understanding, which leads to increased language development and supports them to learn to edit and revise their writing. Too much feedback not directly related to instruction can confuse and overwhelm students and can lead to students rotely fixing errors without learning.

Examples and Evidence of Success

Students' success is shown in their self-efficacy and confidence that they can be proficient writers with the tools and knowledge to continue developing their language and their writing. Success is also shown when students' writing demonstrates that they have written about all parts of the topic through a well-organized piece of writing that includes all of the required genre elements. The structured approach to writing instruction outlined has shown promise with culturally and linguistically diverse college students (Torres & Black, 2018) and high school students transitioning to college in improved overall fluency (as measured by number of words written), quality, organization, and development (as measured by the inclusion of genre elements) in their writing. When assessed by a college English teacher, the students' essays also all improved by one or two letter grades, with the students initially scoring the lowest making the biggest improvement (Torres & Black, 2018). In addition, the students reported starting to plan and understanding how to organize their ideas. Also notable was that several students had reported that they often became distracted when writing and struggled to get started again, but after being taught how to plan and outline through the structured approach, they were able to use those strategies to get back on track (Torres & Black, 2018). Another student who reported always writing "off the top of his head" and who struggled with organization and cohesion, after less than two weeks of instruction, created an outline prior to writing, which he said helped him reduce the "chaos" that he had previously felt with his unorganized writing (Torres, 2016).

Another example of the improved development and organization can be seen with a student with significant challenges with focus and organization. Prior to instruction, this student's writing consisted of very long unfocused sentences, and he often became distracted and struggled to get back on topic. After instruction, he demonstrated an understanding of how to organize and develop his ideas by creating and using an outline. The essay shows that he was able to use the outline to regain focus after becoming distracted. The student did not include a conclusion in the outline, but he used the TREE mnemonic and remembered to include one in the essay. The student's outline and essay are shown in Figure 7.4 with the original spelling and punctuation.

In addition, the focused and explicit language instruction and text deconstruction (or input analysis) seems to help students understand and apply cohesion in their writing. For example, after instruction, one student who struggled this way was able to relate all of his ideas in an essay and to connect them. One technique studied through the text deconstruction was using pronouns, reference words (e.g., *this, those*), and repetition to create cohesion. He was able to apply this in sentences such as "*With this knowledge, my mind will continue to grow. This growth will aide me in my work…*" [emphasis added] (Torres, 2016, p. 74).

Ultimately, students reported increased self-efficacy and self-confidence through their understanding of the expectations of academic college-level writing and how to meet those expectations. These strategies may be unnecessary for students with well-developed study skills, focus, and a strong command of the language; however, for ELs with disabilities, clear modeling with explicit instruction is key to supporting their language development, academic writing, and self-confidence, all of which are instrumental for academic success.

FIGURE 7.4. Excerpt of Student Outline (Argumentative/ Persuasive Writing, Using TREE) and Essay

	Introduction:
Hook:	*Going to college for me was a big challenge. At a young age…*
Thesis:	*Through hard work and dedication…*
R1	*There were many obsticles…*
Exp.	*First person in family to go to college…*
	overcome adversity…
	not a triditional student
R2	*Armed with AA and 3 certificates*
Exp.	*I always had an astute interest in plants…*
	fasinated with endangered species…
	took every botany class that the school ofered…
	volenteer to control invasives…
R3	*Acquireing this degree…*
	Will help find a job/ career

I've always had a dream of going to college but, for me going to college was a big challenge. As a young child I got shuffeled around from school to school, then finally labled with a learning disorder. I was able to overcome any adversity and managed to graduate from high school, but college proved to be very discouraging. Through hard work, dedication, and persiverence, I am know able to be successful in college.

There were many obsticles and challenges for me to get by to become successful. First I had to overcome social anxiety by learning coping skills. Sencond, I am the first person in my family to go to college. furthermore I'm not a traditional student, so working ful time, and going to school ful time forced me to utilize my time efficiently.

Now armed with an AA degree and 3 certificates, I plan to goto UH Manoa and acquire a degree in plant and environmental protection sciences. I always had an astute interest in plants, and endangered species. Sometimes I volunteer to help control invasive species with certain organizations.

If Awarded with this scholarship, It would offset my financial struggles and help me to achieve my academic goals.

References

American Psychiatric Association. (2013). *Autism spectrum disorder*. DSM-5 Fact Sheet. Retrieved from https://www.psychiatry.org/psychiatrists/practice/dsm/educational-resources/dsm-5-fact-sheets

Americans with Disabilities Act (ADA). (2008). Amendment Act, Pub. L. No. P.L. 110-325. 42 U.S.C. § 1201.

Asaro-Saddler, K., & Saddler, B. (2010). Planning instruction and self-regulation training: Effects on writers with autism spectrum disorders. *Exceptional Children*, *77*(1), 107–124.

Baker, S., Chard, D., Ketterlin-Geller, L., Apichatabutra, C., & Doabler, C. (2009). Teaching writing to at-risk students: the quality of evidence for self-regulated strategy development. *Exceptional Children*, *75*(3), 303–318.

Berg, E.C. (1999). The effects of trained peer response on ESL students' revision types and writing quality. *Journal of Second Language Writing, 8*(3), 215–241.

Community College Consortium for Immigrant Education. (2015). *Fast facts: The U.S. immigrant population: Demographics, education, labor force, and the economy*. Retrieved from https://www.cccie.org/resources/fast-facts/

Dockrell, J. E., Lindsay, G., & Connelly, V. (2009). The impact of specific language impairment on adolescents' written text. *Exceptional Children*, *75*(4), 427–446.

Enright, K. A. (2011). Language and literacy for a new mainstream. *American Educational Research Journal*, *48*(1), 80–118.

Ferris, D. R., & Hedgcock, J. (2014). *Teaching ESL composition: Purpose, process, and practice* (3rd ed.) New York: Routledge.

Graham, S., & Perin, D. (2007). A meta-analysis of writing instruction for adolescent students. *Journal of Educational Psychology*, *99*(3), 445.

Harris, K. R., Graham, S., Brindle, M., & Sandmel, K. (2009). Metacognition and children's writing. In D.J. Hacker, J. Dunlosky, & A. Graesser (Eds.), *Handbook of Metacognition in Education* (pp. 131–153). New York: Routledge.

Harris, K. R., Graham, S., Mason, L., & Friedlander, B. (2008). *Powerful writing strategies for all students*. Baltimore: Paul H. Brookes.

Hillocks, G. (2002). *The testing trap: How state writing assessments control learning*. New York: Teachers College Press.

Individuals with Disabilities in Education Act (IDEA) of 2004, Sec. 300.8.

Jacobson, L. T., & Reid, R. (2010). Improving the persuasive essay writing of high school students with ADHD. *Exceptional Children, 76*(2), 157–174.

Kanel, K. L. (2004). Accommodating ESL students in the university. *Thought & Action, 19*(2), 61–68.

Marks, S. U., Shaw-Hegwer, J., Schrader, C., Longaker, T., Peters, I., Powers, F., & Levine, M. (2003). Instructional management tips for teachers of students with autism spectrum disorder (ASD). *Teaching Exceptional Children, 35*(4), 50–54.

Newman, L. (2005). Postsecondary education participation of youth with disabilities. In M. Wagner, L. Newman, R. Cameto, N. Garza, & P. Levine (Eds.), *After high school: A first look at the postschool experiences of youth with disabilities. A report from the national longitudinal transition study-2 (NLTS2)* (pp. 4.1-4.17). Menlo Park, CA: SRI International. Retrieved from www.nlts2.org/reports/2005_04/nlts2_report_2005_04_complete.pdf

Noji, F., & Yuen, S. K. (2012). Developing content based curriculum: Aimed toward superior level of proficiency. *The Korean Language in America, 17*, 93–108.

Office of English Language Education (OELA). (2017). *Fast facts: Students with disabilities who are English language learners.* Retrieved from https://ncela.ed.gov/fast-facts

Park, M., Zong, J., & Batalova, J. (2018). *Growing superdiversity among young US dual language learners and its implications.* Washington, DC: Migration Policy Institute.

Polloway, E., Patton, J., & Nelson, M. (2011). Intellectual and Developmental Disabilities. In J.M. Kauffman & D.P. Hallahan (Eds.), *Handbook of special education* (pp. 175–186). New York: Routledge.

Pullen, P., Lane, H., Ashworth, K., & Lovelace, S. (2011). Learning disabilities. In J.M. Kauffman & D.P. Hallahan (Eds.), *Handbook of special education* (pp. 187–197). New York: Routledge.

Rooney, K. (2011). Attention-deficit/ hyperactivity disorder. In J.M. Kauffman & D.P. Hallahan (Eds.), *Handbook of special education* (pp. 198–208). New York: Routledge.

Torres, C. (2016). Culturally responsive self-regulated strategy development in writing for college students with disabilities. Unpublished PhD diss. University of Hawai'i at Mānoa.

Torres, C., & Black, R. (2018). Culturally responsive self-regulated strategy development in writing for college students with disabilities. *Multiple Voices, 18*(1), 1–18.

U.S. Department of Education. (2014). *2013-14 English language instruction program enrollment estimations.* Washington, DC: Office of Civil Rights. Retrieved from http://ocrdata.ed.gov

Viel-Ruma, K., Houchins, D. E., Jolivette, K., Fredrick, L. D., & Gama, R. (2010). Direct instruction in written expression: The effects on English speakers and English language learners with Disabilities. *Learning Disabilities Research & Practice, 25*(2), 97–108.

Wong, B. Y., Hoskyn, M., Jai, D., Ellis, P., & Watson, K. (2008). The comparative efficacy of two approaches to teaching sixth graders opinion essay writing. *Contemporary Educational Psychology, 33*(4), 757–784.

Part 3

Considering Programmatic Change

8

Teaching Writing in a STEM Learning Community: The Heart and Science of Communication

Gonzalo Arrizon
CAÑADA COLLEGE

> "The community here is super helpful which is a welcome change from my high school experience."
> —*Cañada College STEM Student*

This student's comments speak to what we hope all students find in our college's STEM Center—academic support and a sense of community. Historically, many students interested in STEM majors (Science, Technology, Engineering, and Math) have to prepare academically and psychologically for four-year university contexts, which has been described as "a culture of highly competitive classrooms that [often] do not promote active participation" (National Academies of Sciences, Engineering, and Medicine, 2016, p. 63). Given the rigorous STEM pathways and barriers to transfer for community college students in general, and underrepresented students in particular, Cañada College has continued to build on the learning community models that have proven successful in the past (Bunch & Kibler, 2015).

My work at the STEM Center is funded by a U.S. Department of Education grant named GANAS, an acronym that not only stands for Generating Access to Navigate and Achieve in STEM, but also roughly translates to *grit* in Spanish. GANAS is designed to improve the participation, retention, and success of Hispanic and other underrepresented minority students in STEM (Cañada College News & Events, 2016). As one of the Retention Specialists, I am responsible for coordinating programs for first-year students, including STEM Explorers, a summer bridge program, as well as course-based interventions, such as a one-unit study skills course offered in the fall semester. I also consult with STEM faculty, counselors, and peer tutors and mentors, especially when students experience academic difficulty. In Fall 2018, we piloted STEM Academy, modeled after other learning communities that encourage students to move as a cohort through common classes, and we offer additional support such as a designated counselor. Students are eligible for this program if they are recent high school graduates, qualify for a precalculus math course, and have declared a STEM major with a goal to transfer to a university. In addition to the math course and the study skills course, STEM Academy also includes English 100, a three-unit transfer-level composition course that I teach in my part-time position as an adjunct instructor. My work in the STEM Center inspired me to assign texts and create lesson plans that address how the scientific method and the stories that scientists tell illuminate critical thinking and creativity.

This chapter demonstrates how a writing course can be a valuable resource to STEM students' transition to college. My pedagogical approach and choice of texts and topics seeks to increase student perceptions of relevance, utility, and sense of belonging in STEM through writing, while helping students build key critical-thinking and composition skills. Ultimately, the goal of STEM Academy English is to support students in defining their journeys in the sciences.

Context for Pedagogy

My English 100 course description offers an invitation for all students to consider math and science as viable topics for a composition course:

> This is a writing class that may appeal to budding scientists. This is also a class that will further expose "non-scientists" to the benefits of scientific thinking. In practicing how to construct arguable thesis statements and how to make clear claims backed by solid evidence, we *all* can learn from the "process of science."

At Cañada, the English Department offers about 20 sections of English 100 every fall semester, with a maximum of 26 students per section. Although there are a wide range of course themes across sections, English 100 instructors share common student learning outcomes:

> Upon successful completion of English 100, students learn: (1) How to draft a well-supported, argumentative, text-based essay; (2) how to compose an essay that conforms to the MLA format; and (3) how to construct a compelling thesis statement that controls the argument of the essay. (internal document, Cañada College English Department, 2017 SLOs)

I have been teaching English 100 since Fall 2015, and looking at the past three semesters, my average success rate is 77 percent ("success" meaning students who passed the course with a grade of C or better). This success rate is comparable to the average success rate for all other faculty teaching English 100 in face-to-face sections (67.5 percent) (Cañada College, 2019). Cañada College has a total enrollment of nearly 10,000 students and is also a designated Hispanic-Serving Institution (HSI) where 44 percent of students enrolled are Hispanic (California Community Colleges Chancellors Office, n.d.). Given these demographics, I have a responsibility to design pedagogy that is culturally responsive, student-centered, and inclusive. I hold weekly office hours in our Learning Center because it houses many other student services, and I encourage my students to connect with peer writing tutors there. I emphasize multiple strategies for reading, and I encourage them to embrace writing as a process.

In the Fall 2018 semester, 27 students who had recently graduated high school enrolled in my course; 15 of the 27 were part of our STEM Academy cohort and enrolled in all three target courses. There were 14 women and 13 men in English 100. Sixteen of the students were considered MESA-eligible (Math, Engineering, and Science Achievement Program), meaning that they were low-income, first-generation college students and qualified for additional support services (Cañada College STEM Center, n.d.). Also, 14 of the students identified as Hispanic.

Finally, this cohort of students was interested in a wide range of STEM majors: biology (7 students), engineering (6 students), computer science (6 students), math (3 students), and physics (2 students). One student was a declared business administration major but was open to exploring STEM. A handful of students were also interested in emerging and interdisciplinary STEM fields like biotechnology, computer engineering, and environmental sciences.

Description of Pedagogy

In the classroom, I design my lesson plans according to what Winkelmes (2015) refers to as communicating the "purpose, task and criteria" for activities and assignments to students. In other words, the *why* (purpose), the *what* (task), and the *how* (criteria) of a writing assignment. This level of transparency allows more students to "enter the conversation" of academic discourse (Graff & Birkenstein, 2018) and creates a more equitable learning environment. To that end, I will highlight three activities that are centered on key English 100 texts, describing the purpose, tasks, and criteria for each, followed by a sample of student writing.

Activity 1: Teaching the Thesis: Reaching the Eureka! Moment

Purpose

A core learning outcome is to help students construct compelling and arguable thesis statements. The first text I assign is *Eureka!: Discovering your Inner Scientist* (2014) by physicist Chad Orzel. Through stories of famous scientists and in his own personal and professional experiences, Orzel affirms how we all already practice the scientific process in our everyday lives. In our discussions, students are asked to consider the argument about how, for example, playing video games involves the process steps of "looking, thinking, testing, and telling." My goal is for students to write thesis statements that incorporate Orzel's framework in their analysis.

Task

The prompt is:

> *"For Essay #1, please write a critical analysis of an activity that you enjoy. It can be a game, a sport, cooking, collecting, watching a favorite TV show, or perhaps your experiences with social media. Utilizing Orzel's scientific framework, do a close reading of your activity. How does your chosen activity illustrate the scientific process and why does that matter?"*

Students are given two weeks to complete this essay. One week prior to the due date, I organize a structured peer review session in which each student provides written and oral feedback for one or two peers' first drafts. Two days prior to the due date, I guide students to practice drafting thesis statements based on the rhetorical templates from Graff and Birkenstein's *They Say/I Say* (2018). I ask volunteers to write their thesis statements on the board. Students are exposed to not only different topics but also different approaches to composing thesis statements.

Criteria

During class discussions of the Orzel text, I present a handout on thesis statements to show how a thesis statement is composed of (1) an observation, (2) an interpretation, and (3) a level of significance. One student applied Orzel's framework to her experience as a youth swim instructor: "Orzel describes scientific models as '[providing] a story explaining not just what happened . . . but *why* it happened' (87). Just as scientists create models for their hypotheses, I compare the strokes my students practice to the good form of a professional swimmer, which is beneficial as a professional's stroke is refined to maximize their efficiency."

Another student describes her writing process and how the assignment allowed her to see her passion for anime in a new light: "He gave us enough time to do this essay. I did my essay, I tried to incorporate my interests into this essay, like I'm interested in anime and I know the essay is about the scientific process so that got me thinking that watching anime *is* a part of the scientific process and then I just built something from that" (quoted in Morin & Angelova, 2018).

Activity 2: Teaching By Example: Scientific Role Models

Purpose

Following Orzel's text and his insistence that we all have an "inner scientist," I then assign a memoir *Becoming Dr. Q* (Quiñones-Hinojosa & Rivas, 2011). Dr. Quiñones-Hinojosa describes his journey from working as an undocumented farmworker to becoming a highly respected neurosurgeon. My goal in this unit is for students to be exposed to an alternative pathway to scientific careers. In the process, I guide them to be aware of how the protagonist encounters obstacles, develops useful skills, and learns from his mentors. Given Dr. Q's legal status, I am curious to survey students' experiences and opinions about immigration.

Task

Essay #2: I provide students with a choice of three different prompts. One question is based on analyzing how Dr. Q displays scientific thinking early in his childhood. Another question asks them to consider Dr. Q's mentors. Finally, the third question addresses his views about opportunity, luck, and the persistence toward the "American Dream."

The first activity for this unit is called "Immigration Gallery." On large sticky notes, I transcribe quotes, facts, statistics, and images related to immigration. For example, I post a passage from the 1848 Treaty of Guadalupe-Hidalgo from the Library of Congress, the estimated number of foreign-born workers in Silicon Valley, and artwork that insists that "No Human Being is Illegal." I then ask students if they have ever visited a museum and, if not, I describe how to get the most of that experience.

They then silently walk around, and on small sticky notes, they write comments, reactions, and questions about themes and topics related to immigration. Then they add their notes on to the relevant display. I encourage them to also feel free to respond in languages other than English. Finally, after each student has posted all their comments, they are instructed to walk around and read their peers' comments. I then direct them to write a final reflection of this activity before we debrief orally as a class.

Criteria

Early in the semester, we come up with a list of "community agreements" in which we decide how to have productive and respectful conversations. I tell students that the outcome for this gallery walk activity is for them to process their opinions and express feelings about immigration prior to discussing the *Dr. Q* text. As they proceed to read the book, I want them to be aware of how the protagonist negotiates pursuing a career in science while grappling with the challenges of his legal status. As one student wrote in her concluding paragraph: "Having stricter border security nowadays is just an extra burden that people who try to come to the U.S. have, but it does not limit their ability to reach their goals. . . . This achievement is an exception in history because it changes people's perspectives about who can be a scientist."

Activity 3: Writing My Relationship with Math: The Math Autobiography

Purpose

This activity is both an initial and a culminating assignment across all STEM Academy courses. Inspired by Barbara Oakley's book *A Mind for Numbers: How to Excel at Math and Science (Even If You Flunked Algebra)* (2014), we strive to encourage a "learning how to learn" ethos for students. Students are prompted to reflect on their history with math courses in their middle school and high school years, with the goal of raising their metacognitive awareness about how and why they experience math courses the ways they do.

Task

First, the Math 225 instructor assigns students to read Chapter 1 of the Oakley text, in which the author describes in often painful but ultimately transformative detail her experiences with math and other classes, as well as with uninspired teaching. Based on this example, students then write a reflection of their own experiences with math, both positive and negative. This assignment allows the math instructor to assess the students' mindset about math and level of motivation.

For students enrolled in our STEM study skills class, we first facilitate a Four Corner Exercise, where we read statements that reflect beliefs about math (i.e., "I consider myself a math person") and then we ask students to move to a corner of the room with signs that read Agree, Disagree, Somewhat Agree, and Somewhat Disagree. We then debrief as a group to discuss multiple viewpoints and experiences with math.

Next, they are instructed to write a brief Math Autobiography: "Write about your background in math, beginning as far back as you can remember. Describe successes, failures, pleasant experiences, frustrations, and your confidence with math in the past and present. Discuss your strengths and weaknesses, and how they were developed. Also, describe what kind of math you see yourself doing in the future."

At the end of the semester, my English 100 students revisit this essay and write a longer, more detailed comparison between their experiences and Oakley's narrative. I am able to assess how their self-efficacy with math has shifted, as they practice writing a compare/contrast essay.

Criteria

We provide students with a rubric that details what strong, fair, and poor essays look like. In addition to providing examples for "reflectiveness," "strengths in math," "weaknesses in math," and "organization of ideas," students are also learning how to manage their time to successfully complete the assignment. We make it very explicit that time management is a necessary skill to develop as it promotes approaching learning as a process, a key expectation for college success. On the final exam, one student reflected on her first semester experience with math: "Although I have always wanted to pursue a field of science as a career,

Dr. Oakley and I have both struggled with math from childhood experiences, but have since overcome our shortcomings and view math with fresh eyes of appreciation."

Rationale for STEM Academy English

Thus far with STEM Academy, and similar to the findings of Bunch and Kibler (2015), we have already observed positive student engagement and the value of building support services for students, such as access to a STEM counselor and designated peer tutors and mentors. Linked courses and cohorting play to students' strengths. For example, Yosso (2005) argues that students, especially first-generation students of color, bring to college a set of skills and experiences—what she calls "Community Cultural Wealth"—that we need to build on and enhance. More recently, Huerta and Bray (2013) surveyed more than 1,300 first-year students in a learning community program at Texas A&M University and reported that this program had a positive impact on first semester student GPA. Moreover, collaborative learning activities were especially helpful for Latino students. Given the non-residential culture of community college, learning communities are crucial in giving students the "tools they need to decode academia" (Millward, Starkey, & Starkey, 2007, p. 486) in a communal setting. Also, increasingly in STEM courses, instructors such as Camfield and Land (2017) are integrating "writing as thinking" exercises into their biology curriculum, for example. In my choice of texts, I agree with Hern (2017) that students need to find relevance in what they read for their personal lives and professional futures. Most important, a writing class can offer first-year students the space and opportunities to express what community means to them and solidify a sense of belonging in college (Adams et al., 2017).

Examples and Evidence of Success

As of this writing, I have achieved mixed results with student performance in my course. While some students are thriving, others are struggling with the workload and/or experiencing financial, health, and familial challenges in their transitions to college. Luckily, we have skilled counselors and financial aid staff to address these needs. As faculty, I not only support and care for students' academic success but their personal well-being as well (Berrett, 2015). We see our model of support, skill-building, and personal self-reflection influencing how students themselves view their academic success. We tell students that in community colleges they can practice honing soft skills and help-seeking behaviors that can lead to academic success. As one student who hopes to become a medical doctor writes, "The 'American Dream' is easier to achieve when your family and mentors support you." Another student illustrates growth mindset with a powerful analogy: "Math is like a sport, if you practice, you will get better."

Students continuing in STEM is one measure of success. In Spring 2019 semester, some of our STEM students enrolled in Calculus 1 and an honors counseling course to help them formulate a plan for transfer. A handful of these students enrolled in my advanced composition course (English 165) where we grapple with environmental issues and research. At the end of their first year, the STEM team will view their GPAs and gather and analyze survey results to measure the impact of STEM Academy. Given the rigors of STEM pathways, learning to "think like a scientist" will demand that students grow accustomed to trial and error, refine their initial assumptions about STEM and their abilities, and, ultimately, persist in the face of adversity.

ℛEFERENCES

Adams, P., Gearheart, S., Miller, R., & Roberts, A. (2017). The accelerated learning program: throwing open the gates. In P. Sullivan & C. Toth (Eds.), *Teaching composition at the two-year college: Background readings* (pp. 401–418). Boston: Bedford/St. Martin's.

Berrett, D. (2015, September 21). The unwritten rules of college. *The Chronicle of Higher Education.* Retrieved from: https://www.chronicle.com/article/The-Unwritten-Rules-of/23324

Bunch, G., & Kibler, A. (2015). Integrating language, literacy, and academic development: alternatives to traditional English as a second language and remedial English for language minority students in community colleges. *Community College Journal of Research and Practice, 39*(1), 20–33. doi: 10.1080/10668926.2012.755483

California Community Colleges Chancellor's Office. (n.d.). 2018 student success scorecard. Retrieved from https://scorecard.cccco.edu/scorecardrates.aspx?CollegeID=371

Camfield, E., & Land, K. (2017). The evolution of student engagement: Writing improves teaching in introductory biology courses. *Bioscene, 43*(1). Retrieved from https://files.eric.ed.gov/fulltext/EJ1156693.pdf

Cañada College. (2019). 2019–2020 program review. Retrieved from https://canadacollege.edu/programreview/1920/1920_IPR_English.pdf

Cañada College News & Events (2016, October 18). Cañada College awarded $4.3 million federal STEM grant to support hispanic students. Retrieved from https://canadacollege.edu/news/index.php?postID=7922814204835200789&id=5670366946617807975

Cañada College STEM Center. (n.d.). MESA. Retrieved from https://www.canadacollege.edu/stemcenter/MESA.php

Graff, G., & Birkenstein, C. (2018). *They say/I say: The moves that matter in academic writing* (4th ed.). New York: W.W. Norton & Company.

Hern, K. (2017). Thoughts on selecting readings. In P. Sullivan & C. Toth (Eds.), *Teaching composition at the two-year college: Background readings* (pp. 294–297). Boston: Bedford/St. Martin's.

Huerta, J. C., & Bray, J. J. (2013). How do learning communities affect first-year latino students? *Learning Communities Research and Practice, 1*(1), Article 5. Retrieved from https://washingtoncenter.evergreen.edu/lcrpjournal/vol1/iss1/5

Millward, J., Starkey, S., & Starkey, D. (2017). Teaching English in a California two-year Hispanic-serving institution: Complexities, challenges, programs, and practices. In P. Sullivan & C. Toth (Eds.), *Teaching composition at the two-year college: Background readings* (pp. 482–504). Boston: Bedford/St. Martin's.

Morin, G., & Angelova, M. (2018). STEM Academy student interviews. Unpublished data.

National Academies of Sciences, Engineering, and Medicine. (2016). *Barriers and STEM degrees: Systemic change to support students' diverse pathways.* Washington, DC: The National Academies Press. doi.org/10.17226/21739.

Oakley, B. (2014). *A mind for numbers: How to excel at math and science (even if you flunked algebra).* New York: TarcherPerigee.

Orzel, C. (2014). *Eureka!: Discovering your inner scientist.* New York: Basic Books.

Quiñones-Hinojosa, A., & Rivas, M. (2011). *Becoming Dr. Q: My journey from migrant farm worker to brain surgeon.* Berkeley: University of California Press.

Winkelmes, M. A. (2015). Equity of access and equity of experience in higher education. *The National Teaching & Learning Forum, 24*(2), 1–4.

Yosso, T. (2005). Whose culture has capital? A critical race theory discussion of community cultural wealth. *Race Ethnicity and Education, 8*(1), 69–91.

9

Motivating Students from Afar: Teaching English in a Live Broadcast Concurrent Enrollment Program

Kellyanne Ure, Kade Parry, and David A. Allred
SNOW COLLEGE

In 2011 Howard Tinberg and Jean-Paul Nadeau asked NCTE and CCCC to ensure that high school students receive the best instruction possible in concurrent enrollment (CE) courses. (CE or concurrent enrollment is also called *dual credit* or *dual enrollment*. We use it to mean high school students taking a college class for both high school and college credit.) In their study, they identified core attributes of college-level writing that should be emphasized in CE courses to ensure college-level rigor, including that the subject matter be writing (rather than literature or another subject) and that there be a focus on the writing process and audience awareness. In other words, CE courses should reflect comparable college-level writing courses taught on campus to college students. The CE programs at Snow College—a small, two-year, residential college located in rural Utah—seek to embrace these attributes in response to outside pressures to expand and develop more CE English courses.

Many years ago, Alan Blackstock and Virginia Norris Exton (2005) evaluated similar CE efforts in Utah, particularly at Utah State University. They concluded that the delivery of CE writing and literature

128

courses through live interactive broadcasting can be an effective way to expand CE programs given specific conditions. For various reasons (primarily by state legislative mandate), the development of such programs has since shifted for many parts of the state to Snow College. Our programs respond to these pressures in ways specific to the needs of the area through broadcasting live writing courses to multiple high school sites from the college and managing two other CE programs taught by high school teachers. This chapter, in part, updates the work begun years ago at other schools in the state, with a particular focus on the broadcast courses that make our program unique among CE programs.

The development of technology has been a critical part of making our Interactive Video Conferencing (IVC) CE program more robust and rigorous, as we seek to answer the call of Tinberg and Nadeau (2011) while dealing with the challenges that come with the program. IVC courses use the internet to allow live, interactive class sessions where students at various sites (usually high schools) can participate in the class while it is being taught on Snow's campus. Although IVC uses the internet, it is a closed system that only connects sites based on the location of the students enrolled in the course. As many as 20 sites have been included in an individual class in other departments, but composition classes generally have five to ten sites per class.

As shown in Figure 9.1, current technologies allow for students at different sites to easily interact with the class; they are able to ask questions and make comments that are seen and heard simultaneously by the participants at every other site. Utilizing high-speed audio and high-definition cameras, there is only a 0.3 second delay in the transmission of audio and video to all the sites. In addition to live audio and video, the instructor's location is equipped to allow presentations such as PowerPoint or recorded videos to be broadcast to all the sites during a lecture. IVC classes have recently become more common for teaching concurrent enrollment.

Blackstock and Exton (2005) discussed four categories of challenges professors faced when teaching via broadcast. The first is management issues, including faxing, mailing, and emailing assignments to and from students. These issues have largely been resolved because of Canvas, our

FIGURE 9.1. Representative Screen Layout of What Instructors See during Class

Each room indicates a high school site, with the instructor and PowerPoint broadcast to students on the top. Note the variety of physical situations students may be in. Sites may have one to twenty students. When a student turns on a mic at a high school, their camera view is shown to the other sites, allowing the entire class to see the speaker. Electronic video recordings of each class session can be accessed for students to view, which is especially useful when schools have different schedules for spring break and other holidays.

learning management system (LMS), which provides the resource for instant (or almost instant) communication and management of assignments. The second is lack of personal interaction with students. Admittedly, this is still an issue with the present program. However, as will be discussed, technological developments aid in greater personal interaction with students. The third is tight turnaround time of assignments. This, of course, refers to the additional time mailing assignments takes, and Canvas has largely solved this issue. Finally, the fourth challenge is the vagaries of technology. This includes such things as varying levels of technology quality and technologies available at different high school sites. Although technological developments and generous monetary support from the state government create greater consistency with technology, we still encounter issues. For example, not all high school sites have high-definition quality video and audio, and at times video and audio does not work with 100 percent efficiency.

While many of these challenges are unavoidable, we are dedicated to maintaining a program that will benefit our students through their college years. This chapter covers the unique attributes of Snow's CE programs and explores how we ensure college-level rigor, establish relationships with students from a distance, and deal with challenges associated with managing these programs.

Administering Concurrent Enrollment Composition Classes

Much of what ensures that IVC classes are rigorous and engaging happens on the course level with the teacher-student interactions. However, students and teachers are also influenced by class sizes, curriculum guidelines, course outcomes, and even classroom space. Each of these are largely dependent on department and campus administration as well as government stakeholders on the state level. These administrative entities have had an influence on what happens with concurrent enrollment writing classes at Snow College.

Utah's Concurrent Enrollment Environment

Snow College operates within a higher education system that has strong legislative support for CE. This support has led to the college needing to administer three different, legislatively mandated programs (see Table 9.1). The first is a traditional concurrent enrollment program with high school teachers teaching a year-long, college-level first-year composition class. These classes are held at the high schools. The year-long

TABLE 9.1. Comparison of Three Different CE Programs at Snow College

Program	Face-to-Face CE	Technology Intensive CE	Interactive Video CE
Description	• Year-long course taught by high school faculty at high school.	• Semester-long, college-dictated curriculum taught face-to-face at high schools with K–12 faculty.	• Semester-long college course taught by Snow faculty and broadcast live to high school sites.
Scope	• Nine sites in 150-mile radius with about 300 students per year.	• One site with fewer than 75 students per year.	• Around ten sections of composition classes per year with about 250 students per year.
Strengths	• Popular with parents and high schools.	• College control of content. • Closer supervision because of LMS.	• College faculty. • Clear supervision and assessment.
Challenges	• Providing sufficient oversight of curriculum and pedagogy. • High school environment.	• High school environment. • Less popular with high school faculty.	• Conducting site visits. • Mastering the interactive video teaching environment. • Higher cost to the college.

format allows high school teachers to fulfill Language Arts outcomes (including literature) as well as college-level composition outcomes; in other words, the class fulfills requirements for high school and college English. Because of the rural location of Snow College, these high schools may be 100 miles away, meaning that regular visits from college faculty are difficult.

The second program, technology-intensive concurrent enrollment (TICE), received legislative funding in recent years to develop courses that would be offered through learning management systems and without textbooks. Like the CE program, high school teachers are instructors of record, but TICE classes are taught in a semester and use only curriculum designed by the college and housed in the LMS. Because the curriculum is more tightly controlled, the literature content that is found in a year-long course is excised because of time restraints.

Finally, while Snow has taught classes via broadcast technologies for years, in 2014 the state legislature provided an ongoing appropriation at the request of superintendents in rural school districts for Snow to offer CE courses delivered by interactive video conferencing. The goal was to offer enough classes that high school students could complete any general education requirement. For the English Department at Snow College, this meant hiring two tenure-track faculty to expand the department's IVC offerings (the authors Ure and Parry were those two hires). This also created more institutional resources for CE such as dedicated academic advisors and financial support for Snow faculty to visit remote sites.

English Department Efforts for Rigor

Ensuring educational structures that support high-quality concurrent enrollment classes and rigor is an ongoing task, and Snow College's staff and the English Department have achieved several key successes in these efforts.

Some IVC classes at other Utah institutions have 50–100 students even though disciplinary standards recommended much lower enrollment caps. Indeed, it is relatively simple to add more students when they do not all need a desk in the classroom. However, such high enrollment caps can compromise the rigor of composition courses, which require intensive feedback on written drafts. Beginning in 2014, Snow's English Department was able to establish that the same enrollment caps as in on-campus composition courses would apply to IVC courses, which means that no IVC class will have more than 25 students. This gives instructors the ability to engage students and to offer meaningful feedback.

One danger of CE is that students may not have access to college-level academic advising and therefore may be less than intentional when choosing classes, which may result in duplicate classes in general education areas and the lengthening of the progress to a college degree. The addition of academic advisors has made student schedules more efficient in addition to adding another college contact point for high school students. This has helped with placement in concurrent enrollment composition classes.

The same state funding that supports advising also enables differential pay so that IVC instructors have a small financial incentive for teaching in the challenging IVC mode. Instructors also receive a small stipend for visiting remote sites to visit with students, providing valuable moments of face-to-face teaching in a distance education class. Finally, the department also instituted a summer training for CE teachers in all of the programs, offering support for assessment projects, curriculum sharing, and dialogue. These details are less significant than the classroom-based activities described, but they have helped create an environment where quality teaching can take place, specifically in IVC classes.

College-Level Rigor and IVC Concurrent Enrollment

Our pedagogical efforts happen both at the system level and within the classroom, where learning and rigor become most important. One of the concerns with the CE classroom is that it does not always have the level of rigor normally associated with a college-level classroom. Our IVC CE courses are carefully designed to address this issue and are taught by college faculty, rather than high school teachers.

Our approach as faculty is to make the IVC courses as much like college courses as possible, though there are obvious challenges. We teach the same as we do in our on-campus college courses. In addition to having the same curriculum, including content and assignments, we have the same grading standards. We have the same level of expectations for behavior and quality of work as we do with our on-campus college first-year students. We require the same level of participation of all students in class discussions. In fact, most of our IVC classes have on-campus college students in them as well. However, these expectations pose some unique challenges in a broadcast setting because the courses cannot be the same; by definition, they are not. What are those challenges, or barriers to ensuring an equal experience to a college-level writing class? They fall into two broad categories—students and technology.

Benefits of the High School Students

We teach students who are in a variety of situations. Some students are at small high schools, with no more than a couple of dozen students at the entire school. Other students are in large metropolitan areas and attend state charter schools or private schools, and we occasionally have several primarily home-schooled students who attend virtual high schools and participate in our classes individually from their homes. Our primary service area tends to be the small rural school, but we do teach to a variety of situations.

Whatever the general location or situation of the school, the students are usually among the top 5–10 percent academically of their high schools. They are required to have a B or higher average in courses, have an English ACT score of at least 17, and, for our composition courses, they must be seniors. In general, we recruit and target students who are academically prepared for college and who know how to be successful students.

They tend to be inquisitive and love to learn. They tend to look for challenges, so many take multiple college courses, averaging two or three college courses during their last two years of high school. Some of them are working toward an associate's degree (which leads to a scholarship offered by the state if they complete the degree by the time they graduate from high school). They are often very excited about learning and attending college, and they are generally ambitious and anxious to please and do well.

Alhough there is always a moment of rough transition, our students pick up quickly how college classes differ from high school in content and intellectual rigor. One of the purposes and great benefits of our program is that we can expose them to college and teach them what college is like. We try to help them to be more prepared for college, so that they will be more successful when they go to college full time.

Our students also bring in fresh perspectives on life because of diverse experiences. For instance, in a single semester we have had a student at a military base high school who grew up mostly in Germany and another student who moved to rural Utah from San Diego. We have had the children of farmers and ranchers, of immigrants and some who are immigrants themselves (documented and not); we have had students in an urban area attending a charter high school for filmmakers and students from upper middle-class, white collar families. This diversity adds to class discussions and enriches the course with different viewpoints on life. Overall, the students are rewarding to teach and get to know. They are, for the most part, hard-working students who are eager to learn and be successful.

Challenges with Students

In addition to offering rewarding teaching opportunities, the students in our program also come with added challenges. They are often motivated by grades, and they are at a disadvantage in that their grade in the class affects both high school and college. A B in a college composition class is not a bad grade, but it does lower their high school GPA, which may have repercussions for scholarships and financial aid and other accomplishments, such as being a valedictorian. This is a particular problem with students who do poorly in the class; their eligibility for high school graduation or to participate in extracurricular opportunities, like sports, may be impacted if they fail.

Students also have a harder time shifting from a high school to a college behavioral mentality, so they think behaviors appropriate in high school are acceptable for college. For instance, we have seen such things as students throwing paper airplanes or balls around the class at each other. Although this high school mentality can be typical of all first-year college students, the learning curve is harsher for the high school students, especially since the high school perspective is still most prominent, at least part of the time. They are still sitting in their physical high schools, so they do not have the added advantage of moving to a different location, which would imply different expectations. This leads to class discipline issues that we normally do not see with college students.

Our courses include facilitators, who are meant to help with some of the challenges of teaching IVC courses. Facilitators are individuals at both the originating site (Snow College campus) and high school sites who manage the technology so that professors can focus on teaching and students can focus on learning. Facilitators at the college are college students hired by the college to manage the technology during a live broadcast. Facilitators at high schools are trained to deal with technology issues and to act as an extension of the professors in helping maintain order in the classroom. They are hired by the high school and are often teachers or parents of students.

However, high school facilitators do not always properly represent faculty. Blackstock and Exton (2005) advised that "the role of the facilitator is crucial" (p. 385). Evidently, this has always been an issue with broadcast courses. We have found that the best on-site facilitators respect and maintain our course policies, such as helping students stay on task during class time, reminding students of assignment deadlines, and collecting in-class assignments or journals and submitting them to us in a timely manner (usually through regular mail). Ideally, facilitators fill in when there may be less-than-ideal situations; for instance, facilitators have even done the required reading with the class so that students alone at their sites may have someone to discuss questions with during group discussions. Facilitators are trained to be extensions of the professor; however, occasionally, facilitators will not meet these expectations.

The additional adults that are required for the program to work can cause other challenges, including the involvement of parents. Parents are required to sign a release form indicating that their underage child is mature enough for college-level work. However, we hear much about "helicopter parents," parents who oversee much if not most of their children's activities and become too involved at times. This usually ends when students reach college, but because our students are still minors in high school, we deal with more parents than we typically do on campus. Generally, this does not cause major issues, in part because of the Family Educational Rights and Privacy Act of 1974 (FERPA). However, issues of privacy associated with FERPA can become muddled because of the additional role of facilitators and high school counselors. These adults, including parents, are important to students' success in our programs, but roles are often complicated and can hinder the educational experience of students.

When we first started teaching CE courses, we saw many underprepared or overwhelmed students, students who were pushed into taking a college class by parents, teachers, or counselors despite already having a heavy high school load, or students who just barely met the high requirements of our program. This puts students at a great disadvantage, and they are more likely to fail. In more recent semesters, this issue has become less common mostly because of improved recruitment of our Snow College academic advisors and better understanding of course rigor by high school teachers and counselors. We still see occasional students who are not truly prepared for college-level work or (more often) who are overwhelmed with teenage and high school life, and they do struggle more in our classes. For instance, because students are usually at small high schools, they tend to have multiple roles. One student may be a student body officer, on the cheer squad, an Honor Society officer, and a track-and-field participant. Because of the great distances these students must travel for various functions, they are on the road often. They miss class and have difficulties submitting assignments.

Those of us who teach IVC courses look at these challenges as opportunities: How can we develop strategies that creatively address these issues to give these students the best educational opportunity possible? This is the question of our teaching practice, and we are always looking for innovative ways to answer it.

The Benefits of Technology

Part of the answer comes from the benefits of technology. In their early report on the program, Blackstock and Exton (2005) recommend using technology in the classroom, noting it is difficult to teach broadcast classes without it. We use technology to enhance our students' learning; some beneficial technologies come from such things as Smart podiums, apps that turn devices like tablets and phones into clickers, real-time editing ability in various word processing programs, and Canvas. These technologies allow us to replicate some of the live in-class activities used in our regular on-campus classes.

As has been mentioned, the greatest benefit of the entire program and the technology that allows for our IVC classes to function is our ability to reach students all over the state of Utah. These students would not have the opportunity to take advanced classes (or college classes) without the technological infrastructure that the State of Utah invested in years ago. This enhances the educational opportunities of people who live in some of the most distant areas of Utah. Technology will only get better, and we are looking forward to additional technological developments that will make our classes even more effective and easier to teach.

Challenges of Technology

As wonderful as technology is, it also poses some unique and obvious problems. It is the intermediary between instructor and student, which compounds challenges that might exist in an on-campus classroom yet creates others. We notice the biggest challenge with expectations for class participation. Because we teach composition through workshopping, peer reviewing, and discussion, it can be difficult using a technology system that is designed for lecture-based courses. Getting students out of the mindset of passively listening to their professor on a TV screen can be challenging.

Students forget that the course is live and that they can be seen at all times. Students already have difficulty shifting from a high school to a college mentality, and the limitations of the technology compounds this issue. For instance, mics must be kept muted, unless students are speaking, to avoid electronic feedback. Because students cannot be heard, they will openly chat with their site-mates when they should be listening to classmates at other sites or the instructor. It is also harder to monitor and deal with such class disruptions, since we usually have several sites. Because of other duties onsite facilitators might have (including facilitating multiple classes at one time), we have found that they are not always available to help remind students.

Since technology is the intermediary, it is also more difficult to establish rapport and to "read" students and how they are feeling or learning. Short delays in the broadcast to the sites mean student reactions are not as instantaneous as they are in an on-campus classroom. Students are also more reluctant to ask questions and make comments through the technology. This can lead to miscommunication. Developing relationships with students is more difficult from a distance and through technology.

Technology is not completely reliable, and we know that if something can go wrong, it will go wrong. Though problems do not happen every class, we must be prepared for technologies not to work and for variable technologies at the high school sites. For instance, because the servers are housed in Salt Lake City, if there are power or server issues there, our classes will not broadcast. Electricity service is at times unreliable in some remote parts of Utah, and this often means individual sites will not connect. If students do not have reliable internet during class, some interactive class activities can be a problem. Some high schools also block student internet access or filter internet sites, and students are not always able to access resources online that they might need, such as library databases.

As with any technological issue, we must have a backup plan almost every class period (though we especially are prepared during the winter months when the weather has the biggest impact on technology and power). The key, we have found, is not getting flustered but simply and calmly dealing with issues and planning extra class periods into the schedule in case of a problem; we must also constantly remind students that problems will arise and be dealt with appropriately so that they remain calm as well. Still, these technological challenges are becoming less of a problem as technologies improve and as we learn to use technology in pedagogically intelligent ways that ensure college-level rigor.

Best Practices

To best address some of the unique challenges of teaching IVC courses, we recognize the importance of keeping composition courses as similar to on-campus classes as possible; our IVC teaching experiences have revealed several helpful practices to keep IVC class discussions engaging, conduct effective teacher-student writing conferences, and provide useful interactive feedback.

Class Participation

To be successful, IVC classes must be at least as engaging as on-campus classes. To avoid lecture-heavy teaching, we seek to engage students through daily class discussions that help students build communication skills and enhance critical-thinking abilities. To meet this challenge, we set high expectations for students to regularly participate in class discussions. Because IVC students are expected to comment frequently, we have developed policies that we include in the syllabus. An example is: "At the end of the semester, I will assign you a participation score which I record daily throughout the semester. Students who attend regularly, elevate the classroom discussions with critical comments and questions, and participate in group activities will do well." Although we each have different philosophies and use different practices when grading in-class participation, we all recognize the importance of making it clear to students early in the semester that IVC composition courses are highly collaborative and require students to share their thoughts with their peers in class.

There are several tactics we use to help make class discussions as effective as possible. Unlike in an on-campus course, we find it essential to take several minutes during the first IVC class session to train students on how to use the IVC microphones (mics). Although mic devices will vary at different high school sites, students must be trained on the functions of using the mics to be comfortable participating in the class discussions. We give students commenting instructions on the first day of class and then spend some time practicing, such as going from site to site and asking each student to share their name and favorite book. Before commenting or asking a question in class, we ask students to begin their comments by stating their name (at least early in the semester) and to be sure they turn the mic off when they finish commenting (to avoid everyone hearing noises at their site like high school bells ringing). We also consider how to manage class comments: Is it best to ask students to raise their hands and wait to be called on (which requires instructors to constantly be monitoring the screen) or should students simply turn on the mic and start talking (which can result in multiple students commenting at the same time and require the instructor to assign one to speak first)?

Perhaps the most effective way to motivate students to participate in class is to record the number of quality comments they make throughout the semester and base part of their participation grade on the total number of comments. This can be done by simply putting tally marks on a class roll for each comment the student gives; there are also apps that allow instructors to easily keep track of participation electronically. Although it might seem tedious, having this record assists us when grading students as well as providing useful data to update students on their participation in comparison with class peers. Additionally, students usually find added motivation to participate when they know they are being actively evaluated and their comments are being recorded. We generally tell students they should aim to comment at least once during each class session. Even on days when we are in peer workshop or doing group work in class, we usually take several minutes to ask students to share the highlights of their discussions with the rest of the class. By using these practices—along with frequently observing colleagues' IVC classes to share specific discussion tactics—we have significantly enhanced the quality of class lessons and ensured students are engaged in regular discussions as active participants in the course.

Student Conferences

In *A Writer Teaches Writing* (2004), Donald Murray suggest that "conference teaching is the most effective—and the most practical—method of teaching composition" (p. 147). Murray explains his conference methods and argues that conference teaching is practical and efficient, despite many views to the contrary. However, conferencing in an IVC setting is significantly less practical and efficient; because of the geographical distance between instructors and students (which can sometimes be hundreds of miles), it is difficult—though not impossible—to conference together one-on-one with students. Despite the challenges distance sites create, we have found several effective ways to implement teacher-student conferencing into our IVC courses.

The most effective method, yet also the most challenging and time-consuming, is to travel to the various high schools once or twice a semester to meet with the students in person. These conferences provide an opportunity for us to work with students on their individual writing needs, to review grades and performance in class, to address questions or concerns the student might have about the course, and to discuss topics unlikely to be addressed in email conversations. Additionally, because site visits also allow us to meet with students in person (something that is often taken for granted in on-campus classrooms), they help to show students that we genuinely care about their success in class and help to establish a working relationship of respect and gratitude. Students frequently mention the value and impact of site visits in their end-of-semester course evaluations. As previously noted, our college incentivizes these visits with a small stipend to help make the travel possible.

If visiting students in person at their high schools is not a possibility (and even when it is), there are other means of communication that are also effective. We also use less time-consuming methods like conferencing online with Voice Over Internet (VOI) software like Skype, Google Hangouts, or Zoom. Similarly, our Canvas site provides a web conferencing system called BigBlueButton that, like other tools, allows students to connect with their instructor and upload essay documents to review and discuss. Even setting up phone conferences or instant message conversations have proven to be effective ways to communicate with students one-on-one.

Interactive Feedback

In addition to teacher-student conferences, providing interactive feedback can create a virtual conversation with students and produce similar benefits for students and instructors. Requiring students to respond to instructor feedback (perhaps with questions and plans for revision) leads to a useful conversation that shows that students understand the feedback and are prepared to revise effectively. Even using different forms of feedback can help to substitute for in-person conferencing. For instance, using audio feedback (a.k.a. recorded feedback or digital commentary) is the method of a teacher verbally recording writing feedback to students. Audio feedback has actually been used for decades in composition courses, dating back to recording with tapes in the 1960s, but technological advances have made this easier and more efficient. Audio feedback offers many of the advantages of face-to-face conferencing with students. For instance, audio comments allow us to give more detailed feedback because we can communicate more quickly when talking than typing. Kelly Gallagher (2006) reminds us that "you can achieve more in a two-minute conference than you can by spending five to seven minutes writing comments on a paper" (p. 167). However, when conferencing one-on-one with every student is not possible, audio feedback serves as a suitable substitute that is both effective and efficient.

Instructors interested in using audio feedback can consider a variety of different software programs. For those looking for a program to record and send audio-only remarks, there are programs like Audacity or WavePad Audio Editor that essentially provide an electronic version of a tape recorder. Embedded audio is an alternative form of audio feedback where certain programs allow instructors to "insert" short audio comments directly into electronic versions of a student's work. Finally, our strongest recommendation, screen capture, is an application that allows instructors to record audio feedback with a visual image of the computer screen as well (usually showing the student's paper or a webcam). Internet websites such as Screencast-O-Matic, Loom, or Jing provide this service for free. These applications record all audio and screen activity so that teachers can have an electronic document of the student's writing open on the screen while using the mouse pointer to draw attention to certain passages or sentences and simultaneously talk about the paper and provide in-depth feedback. Teachers can easily send students access to these videos electronically where they can view them and listen to the feedback the teacher gave.

Using a combination of these methods can help instructors develop a working relationship with students that can help strengthen their writing, motivate them to succeed, and assist them in becoming more prepared for the challenges of college.

In conclusion, colleges and universities across the country find themselves working within a unique constellation of pedagogical, geographic, demographic, and economic pressures and must find productive ways forward. This chapter has outlined the steps Snow College has taken with addressing these in our concurrent enrollment composition classes, particularly in our IVC courses. These efforts will continue, as further technological advances, economic booms or busts, and trends in composition studies affect the way the college navigates higher education for high school students.

Acknowledgments

We would like to thank Landon Peterson, Mike Daniels, and Doug Johnson for their assistance in preparing this essay.

REFERENCES

Blackstock, A., & Exton, V. N. (2005). "Drive-by English": Teaching college English to high school students via interactive TV. *Teaching English in the Two-Year College, 32*(4), 379–389.

Gallagher, K. (2006). *Teaching adolescent writers.* Portland, ME: Stenhouse Publishers.

Murray, D. M. (2004). *A writer teaches writing* (2nd ed.). Boston: Heinle Cengage Learning.

Tinberg, H., & Nadeau, J. P. (2011). Contesting the space between high school and college in the era of dual-enrollment. *College Composition and Communication, 62*(4), 704–725.

10

Contextualized FYC Courses for Career Technical Education

Erin B. Jensen
BELMONT ABBEY COLLEGE

Jennifer Stieger & Whitney Zulim
GREAT BASIN COLLEGE

Great Basin College (GBC) is a community college located in the rural Northern Nevada town of Elko. GBC offers 30 associate's degrees and 20 certificate programs and has recently added 13 bachelor's degrees. GBC has almost 4,000 students, and the most popular degrees are in Career and Technical Education (CTE) and nursing. GBC campuses are mainly surrounded by gold and silver mines, and our CTE programs have strong connections to those mining companies.

The CTE program offers five technical programs: Diesel Technology, Electrical Systems Technology, Industrial Millwright Technology, Instrumentation Technology, and Welding Technology. Students have the opportunity to earn a Certificate of Achievement or an Associate of Applied Science degree in a 36-week period. Through collaboration efforts between CTE and the local mines, there are multiple scholarships offered including the Maintenance Training Cooperative (MTC) Scholarship. MTC scholarship recipients earn monetary value toward their tuition along with a paid internship to the specific company who awarded them the scholarship. The MTC scholarship allows students to simultaneously attend school and be employed through a paid internship. This gives them the opportunity to apply their classroom knowledge and writing skills to the workplace. About half of all CTE students are recipients of the MTC Scholarship.

CTE students at GBC have the unique opportunity to take English 107: Technical Communications I and English 108: Technical Communications II instead of the traditional first-year composition courses (FYC). These two courses are equivalent to the two FYC courses that students in other majors take but are specifically focused on the workplace writing needs of CTE students. When students are admitted to the college, they take a test to determine their first course; while the majority of students are placed in English 107, some students place into English 108. The few transfer students who have already taken a first-year writing course at another institution are placed into English 108.

This chapter focuses on the pedagogy of creating these two English courses (English 107 and 108) that focus on the types of writing CTE students need. It provides an overview of why these courses were created, describes our experiences teaching these courses, and includes examples of successful student writing within the courses. While the assignment and workplace writing are more specific to GBC and the mining industry, these same assignments and curriculum could be implemented in other community college CTE programs.

Description of the Courses

As CTE students learn information at an accelerated pace, face-to-face classes offer advantages toward our teaching goals. The one-on-one connection with students allows us to effectively reach and engage with students. GBC offers CTE programs at its main campus in Elko and also at several other rurally based satellite campuses. The students at the other campuses are also able to attend live classes through Interactive Video (IAV) systems. We structured our assignments and in-class learning around common workplace communications students will experience upon program completion. In addition to workplace writing assignments, we also included some essay assignments more typically found in many FYC courses and used these essays as a platform for students to develop stronger writing skills. Students also learned about research and using sources to support their arguments in their essays.

During their CTE courses, students learn in a classroom environment and spend time applying that knowledge in the diesel, millwright, welding shop, or electrical lab. Since students are familiar with active and hands-on learning in their respective CTE courses, we include as much hands-on teaching as we can creatively incorporate. Students become more receptive to and engaged in a learning environment that keeps them actively involved. We provide in-class activities and teaching strategies that translate effectively to the workplace. The various techniques used range from problem-solving for real-life scenarios, open discussions on relevant workplace topics, individual and group presentations regarding key points of the textbook, examples of documents that need improvement, peer editing of student writings, and use of the computer lab.

English 107 and 108 are taught during the same semester as half-semester courses. This schedule was created to accommodate the CTE accelerated associate's degrees and certificates. ENG 107 is taught during the first half of the semester, and ENG 108 is taught during the second half of the semester. Each is a three-credit course and meets twice a week for 150 minutes each day to fit with other CTE courses. Currently, the instructors for English 107 and 108 have a background in technical writing and are instructors who have an interest in CTE. We believe the interest and background of our faculty make the course successful. The current syllabi and assignments are designed to engage students and connect directly to workplace-based writing. For these classes, the three CTE-English instructors use the same textbook, syllabi, and assignments.

ENG 107 was designed to teach students to write documents such as reports, proposals, resumes, and business letters. The focus skills are identifying and incorporating quality research; coherence of information with introduction, body, and conclusion; informing, persuading, and describing information to a specific audience; and document formatting. It is necessary for students to apply these skills as they advance directly to ENG 108.

The transition from English 107 to English 108 is seamless, as the purpose for technical writing assignments is still to either inform, instruct, or persuade, but the emphasis is now on document design. The purpose of English 108 is for students to create clear, concise business documents that are not only well-written and well-researched, but are visually appealing as well. Student outcomes for English 108 state that students understand the audience and purpose of a document. By employing appropriate research methodologies, students also learn how to think and write critically. Table 10.1 includes the main assignments for English 107 and 108.

Rationale

In designing these courses, we focused on creating assignments that best meet the needs of CTE students. To help us in re-designing these courses, we used a social constructivist approach (Vygotsky, 1978). We thought about how to incorporate scaffolding into the courses so each assignment built on the previous assignment and then English 107 led into English 108 assignments. We also thought to connect students' previous knowledge with what students would be learning in the course. We emphasized group learning through partner discussions, small group work, and large class discussions. Students also participated in peer-review writing workshops and gave each other feedback on all major writing assignments.

We were also heavily influenced by Howard Gardner (1993) and his research on multiple intelligences and how to incorporate differ-

TABLE 10.1. Overview of Main Assignments

English 107	English 107
Informational essay	Cover letter and resume
Instructional essay	Product and process instructions
Persuasive essay (final essay)	Informal and formal report
Oral presentation	Formal proposal

ent types of learning into the courses. Following Gardner's suggestions, we incorporated visual, kinesthetic, and logic learning activities in the course activities and assignments.

Engagement Activities and Assignments

The focus of English 107 and 108 is to actively engage students in learning workplace writing skills and academic writing skills through both in-class activities and writing assignments.

In English 107, students used Lego® bricks as they learned about creating a Task Analysis Document. Legos of various shapes and colors were arranged on a main table. In groups of three to four, students assembled five Legos into a team design. They were required to include a task analysis with appropriate main tasks and subtasks. They had to critically think of what information their audience needed when performing assembly instructions. They placed their Legos back on the main table and exchanged their instructions with a different group (readers). That group had to find the correct Legos and assemble them into the correct design. The readers were required to provide feedback by answering questions to assess the instructions for usability (Gurak & Lannon, 2016). Students appreciated being able to manipulate and build with Legos, which appealed to their visual and kinesthetic learning styles. Similar activities were built into the course activities for English 108 as well.

During English 108, students were preparing to write product descriptions. One in-class assignment instructed small groups of students to write a product description for a rudimentary, mundane office item (Gurak & Lannon, 2016). The instructor brought three products to the classroom—a stapler, a staple remover, and a three-hole punch. After placing the students into groups of three or four, they were instructed to write a detailed description of their product as if they were manufacturing it for a sales company. To make the exercise even more challenging, the students were told that their audience was made up of customers who had never before used this product. Students were instructed to include spatial, functional, or chronological sequencing to explain how the product looks, operates, or fits together. After the group completed their written descriptions, they assigned a team member to present the description—and their product—to the class.

The purpose of this assignment was for students to use detailed and specific language to explain how their product functions. By providing the students with tangible, 3D items they could touch and feel, they were able to successfully communicate how their product operates. Imagine the laughter in class that day as students explained the inner workings of a staple remover! Students were engaged in this assignment, laughed through the process, and were prepared to then write an individual and more complex product description.

In English 107, students wrote an informational essay about something related to their technical degree. We wanted students to understand audience and purpose of various writings, so they were writing this assignment to an audience (their English instructor). We were specifically looking for coherent flow of the whole document (introduction, body, conclusion); paragraph cohesiveness (topic sentences, supporting sentences, and concluding sentences); incorporating and citing quality research; and using correct spelling, grammar, and punctuation.

An example from the introduction of an informational essay by an MTC student in the Electrical Systems Technology program is shown as it was written. His topic was the importance of electricity in mining. The student provides research including in-text citations to support his information.

> Mining plays a major role in our economy. Mining in the United States produces metals, industrial minerals, coal, and uranium. Our society cannot function without minerals the products that are made from what mining produces. What most people do not understand, though, is how important electrical systems is for a mine to keep running. As Duddu (2011) explains, "New technologies [such as] wireless radios, connecting machines, flowmeters, automatic switches, sensore, and other technologies" make mining more productive. Electrical systems are critical for mines to be run smoothly and be productive.

In English 108, students wrote an informal proposal formatted as a memo. The purpose of the document was to persuade the instructor to approve the topic for their formal report, which was the final assignment for the course. Students needed to include specific design elements such as headings, bullet points, white space, appropriate font size and style, and effective visual aids. Consider one student's use of headings, bold-face, line spacing, justification, and numbered lists shown in Figure 10.1.

The writer, an electrical student, chose to write about a topic related to his field of study. While we specifically assign writing topics relevant to students' educational interests, assignments such as the proposal and report also have a strong research component. For primary sources, students conduct interviews with experts in their field, most often an instructor, employer, or even a family member. Students are required to delve deeper for secondary sources, scouring academic journals and

FIGURE 10.1. Student Informal Proposal in Memo Format

Proposed Study

To answer your request on April 16th for a research paper due by the end of our English course in May, I propose to study electrical safety in residential, industrial and DIY applications.

Statement of Problem

In my multiple years working with electrical systems for jobs and personal projects, I have experienced a lot of problems with the safety of electricity. I have not only witnessed the various problems that come along with electrical safety first-hand, but have also seen many seminars and videos that show the struggle of electrical safety. This is a hard topic to accomplish in many workplaces because there is so much unknown to electricity and also cost for proper safe circuits is very high. To try to find a viable solution to the problem I will research the topic and interview experienced professionals from the field to offer potential solutions to the problem.

Scope of Proposed Study

I will explore and explain the following issues with electrical safety:

1. A lay out of the various types of electrical hazards along with some examples.
2. The proper personal protective equipment and training.
3. Implementation of safety devices.
4. Effective methods of properly working on electrical circuits.
5. How properly used safety can save lives, equipment and time.
6. The pros and cons of using or not using electrical safety correctly.
7. Preventative maintenance for electrical system.

articles. The research in English 108 challenges students to question preconceived assumptions, laying the foundation for critical and analytical thinking.

The formal report assignment in English 108 asked students to write on a topic of their choice about the field they were studying. Students wrote an abstract and included a report with graphics to illustrate their main points. Figure 10.2 shows how the student used headings, justifi-

FIGURE 10.2. Student Example of Formal Report for English 108

ABSTRACT

The purpose of this report is to explain the many benefits tied to autonomous mining equipment, and its subsidiaries. Many companies in the national mining industry have made the change to autonomous mining equipment. Autonomous mining has resulted in an increase in profits, lowered operating costs, and increased safety for people. Some mining companies are resistant to going autonomous, but the future of mining is very much focused on autonomous mining. The high startup cost can be a factor, but the research proves that autonomous mining will not only pay for itself but will increase the company's profit.

TECHNOLOGY

When someone thinks about autonomous, they often think of highly complex machinery such as, robots or artificial intelligence. Autonomous equipment can include complex machinery, but does not have to. Some autonomous equipment needs a human to run it. Surface mines that use autonomous equipment generally use a GPS-based positioning system to navigate (See Figure 1). An IT operator will input GPS coordinates that correspond to the mining plan and monitor the trucks systems without being anywhere near the equipment. Autonomous equipment progress through several stages of communication. First, it starts with a remote that can control all the degrees of freedom on the vehicle. The next step is called "tele-remote operation" and this is where the operator can't see the vehicle, so they are dependent on video feed. The next level is called, "fully autonomous," which is also referred to as (blind), where GPS and mapping software give the machine the ability to execute a sequence of paths and actions commanded by the user. Fully autonomous is the typically used system; however, it can be the most reckless, because the operator cannot see the truck. The truck must rely on a countless number of sensors to avoid possible road hazards. These hazards are then computed by the onboard computer system and the operator is alerted. Then the system will plan out the best action to avoid the hazard. With this type of control system, equipment would travel at the right speed all the time, and do its directed job with consistency.

[Figure 1 is an image of Autonomous Mining Control taken from a copyrighted source so it is not reprinted here.]
Student writing appears here as it was written.

cation, line spacing, a visual of the process, and white space to create a crisp, clean document.

In conclusion, English 107 and 108 were created with specific goals in mind—to create two English classes that were specifically designed for CTE students to learn workplace related writing skills. Writing assignments such as reports, proposals, memos, business letters, and research projects prepare students for writing skills needed in the workplace. The completion of English 107 and 108 provides students with strong written communication skills that allow them to be successful as a working professional. While these courses were created to be specific to the needs of CTE students at GBC, these courses and assignments can easily be adapted to other CTE college programs.

ℛEFERENCES

Gardner, H. (1993). *Frames of mind: The theory of multiple intelligences*. New York: Basic Books.

Gurak, L.J., & Lannon, J. M. (2016). *Strategies for technical communication* (3rd ed.). New York: Pearson.

Vygotsky, L. S. (1978). *Mind in society: The development of higher psychological processes*. Cambridge, MA: Harvard University Press.

Part 4

Considering Curriculum: Research and Policy

11

Heterogeneity among Community College English Learners: Who Are Our ELs in FYC and How Do They Compare?

*R*ebecca *M.* *C*allahan
UNIVERSITY OF TEXAS–AUSTIN

*C*atherine *E.* *H*artman
UNIVERSITY OF SOUTH CAROLINA

*H*ongwei *Y*u
TEXAS STATE UNIVERSITY–SAN MARCOS

In 1980, 23.1 million U.S. Census respondents reported speaking a language other than English in the home (Ryan, 2013); by 2016 that number reached 65.5 million, a 184 percent increase when the total population grew by only 42 percent (U.S. Census Bureau, 2016). Distributed across the *life course*, the nonnative–English speaking population is rapidly expanding among youth aged 5–24, 23 percent of whom speak a language other than English (U.S. Census Bureau, 2016). In response, K–12 schools systematically identify multilingual youth who both speak a language in addition to English *and* who are identified as needing linguistic support services as English learners (ELs). In 2015, 4.6 million (10 percent) K–12 students were EL-identified, an increase from 3 million (7 percent) in 2000 (U.S. Census Bureau, 2016). As a result, considerable K–12 research, policy, and practice have focused on this growing population. In turn, postsecondary systems struggle to consistently identify EL students and meet their diverse academic and linguistic needs (Núñez et al., 2016). While K–12 EL identification is relatively consistent and universally understood (Linquanti & Cook, 2013), higher education has neither a common EL identification process nor a clear understanding of EL status and student needs.

Prior research suggests that the postsecondary equivalent to the K–12 EL population may be more heterogeneous, at minimum consisting of three distinct groups. First, postsecondary systems enroll former K–12 EL-identified students, some of whom were exited from EL status prior to leaving high school, some of whom were not (Bunch, 2008; Bunch et al., 2011; Núñez et al., 2016). Second, many two- and four-year colleges offer adult ESL programs for recent immigrants who hope to learn English to better navigate the workplace (Teranishi, Suárez-Orozco, & Suárez-Orozco, 2011) but who do not attend the community college otherwise. Third, ESL programs in higher education also serve international students who come to the U.S. primarily for educational purposes, including obtaining a bachelor's degree (Kanno & Varghese, 2010). While federal legislation such as No Child Left Behind (NCLB, 2001) and the Every Student Succeeds Act (ESSA, 2015) requires that K–12 systems provide linguistic support services for ELs in the primary and secondary levels (Abedi, 2004; Mitchell, 2017), no such policies exist to govern postsecondary offerings. Instead, community colleges and other postsecondary institutions generally assess multilingual students' English proficiency upon enrollment to determine whether they might require ESL services or other language supports (Hodara, 2015). For the purpose of the present study, we refer to those multilingual students identified as needing linguistic support services as community college ELs (CCELs), though no such formal, legislatively mandated designation exists otherwise. Frequently, CCELs must complete the college's ESL sequence and/or Developmental English in reading and/or writing prior to enrolling first-year composition (FYC) and other credit-bearing coursework; none are credit-bearing (Hodara, 2015; Hodara & Xu, 2018).

Unlike the highly prescribed EL support and programming in K–12 education, linguistic support services at the community college level often depend largely on the training and impetus of the ESL faculty (Núñez et al., 2016). Few federal, district, or institutional policies or requirements exist to regulate the provision of linguistic support services in higher education (Núñez et al., 2016). The lack of institutional oversight regarding their instruction and access may limit the likelihood that CCELs will transfer to a four-year institution compared to their non-EL peers (Kanno & Cromley, 2013). To date, no comprehensive work has identified who, exactly, comprises the CCEL population, much less how they compare to their K–12 counterparts.

The Educational Aspirations of CCELs

Community colleges occupy a unique niche in the postsecondary realm, serving as a crucial bridge between secondary educational attainment and entrance to a four-year college or university. Prior research suggests that multilingual students hold equal, if not more ambitious, educational goals compared to their monolingual peers (Santibañez & Zarate, 2014). Data from the Beginning Postsecondary Students Longitudinal Study (BPS) of 2004 reveal that out of a sample of approximately 16,500 students from about 7,400 two-year schools nationwide, multilingual students reported expecting to pursue a bachelor's degree or greater at rates higher than monolinguals: 84 percent and 79 percent. Multilingual students in BPS also reported expecting to transfer to four-year schools at a higher rate than monolinguals: 70 percent versus 63 percent (Núñez & Sparks, 2012). However, whether and how these differences are meaningful is less well understood, as multilinguals often differ significantly from their monolingual counterparts on a wide array of factors (Callahan & Gándara, 2014).

Since the emergence of Astin's (1993a, 1993b) seminal work framing the relationship between postsecondary engagement and student success, scholars have worked to better understand how engagement as a broad construct shapes students' academic and social integration and persistence and how it varies across groups. Student engagement comprises the energy and effort that students put toward activities and services, as well as the support(s) institutions provide students (Greene, Marti, & McClenney, 2008; Kuh, 2001). Since 2000, two national datasets have emerged to explore student engagement: the National Survey of Student Engagement (NSSE, 2000, 2003) and the Community College Survey of Student Engagement (CCSSE, 2018). In this chapter, we use CCSSE data to better understand not only the characteristics of the large and growing CCEL population but also how CCELs experience engagement as it is associated with college achievement and attainment.

First we review the extant literature on community college student engagement and consider what this might mean for CCELs' experiences in FYC and other courses. Then we present data comparing CCELs nationally to their non-EL counterparts on a wide range of individual and school characteristics. Finally, we consider how CCELs experience engagement relative to their peers, both native English speakers and multilinguals not placed in ESL or developmental English. These analyses also take into account a number of factors associated with both engagement and CCELs' multilingual status.

Student Engagement in Community Colleges

Students who are more connected to their campuses by engaging with staff, peers, and support services and who actively put forth effort in their coursework are more likely to persist and to meet their educational goals than those who do not (Braxton, Hirschy, & McClendon, 2004). In turn, research has shown a relationship between student engagement and transfer, as well as persistence toward a four-year degree (Bahr, 2008; Karp, Hughes, & O'Gara, 2010). Student engagement consists of, but is not limited to, these constructs: student and faculty interactions (Pascarella & Terenzini, 2005); peer relationships (Astin, 1993a; Pascarella & Terenzini, 2005); active and collaborative instructional experiences (Astin 1993a, 1993b); and institutional, familial, and social supports (Pascarella & Terenzini, 2005). These findings have motivated postsecondary leaders and educators to prioritize programs and practices that foster student engagement on their campuses with the end goal of improved achievement (Zepke & Leach, 2010). However, student engagement research has yet to focus specifically on ELs in community colleges (Reyes et al., 2012), as it has on their K–12 counterparts.

Prior research finds that linguistically diverse students often participate less in class, are less comfortable in their coursework, and may perceive themselves as less academically capable than native speakers and speakers of standard varieties of English—all the markers of overall college engagement. The authors of these studies attributed these disparities to peers' and instructors' linguistic biases (Dunstan & Jaeger, 2015). Likewise, research focusing on racial and ethnic minorities finds that neither African-American nor Hispanic youth experience the same gains in achievement that high levels of engagement bring for their White peers (Greene, Marti, & McClenney, 2008).

Discursive Engagement: Academic and Social

Prior research suggests that discursive engagement, both *academic*—talking with peers and instructors about classwork, ideas, and theories—and *social*—developing ongoing rapport with peers and instructors—is associated with more positive college outcomes (Astin, 1993b; Kuh, Pace, & Vesper, 1997). Social discursive engagement, in the form of peer relationships and rapport, has been found to shape students' personal and academic growth and development (Chang, Denson, Sáenz, & Misa, 2006), while academic discursive engagement may be particularly salient for students from nondominant groups, including ELs. For example, Swigart and Murrell (2001) found African-American students experience greater returns for their academic efforts than White students. Early on, some researchers questioned the ability of two-year colleges to foster such engagement; however, Karp, Hughes, and O'Gara (2010) found community college students to be as likely to engage in social and academic discourse as four-year students, with its benefits evidenced in students' second-year persistence. ELs in particular, as relatively new users of English, may be uniquely positioned to benefit from rich discursive engagement, both academic and social.

Pedagogical Engagement

At the core of any learning context, instructors' pedagogical practices often determine whether or not a student finds reason to learn, much less stay in school (Pascarella et al., 1996; Schwitzer et al., 1999). Not only does pedagogy need to be engaging and thought-provoking, but research has found that diverse learners are more likely to engage when material is presented in a culturally relevant manner (Greene, Marti, & McClenney, 2008). ELs in particular may benefit from culturally and linguistically engaging pedagogies that promote critical-thinking skills. At least some of the racial and socioeconomic disparity in academic attainment and success can be attributed to a lack of cultural awareness in pedagogy and programing (Hudson, 2003; Jacobson et al., 2001; Szelenyi, 2001). Considerable K–12 research recommends that teachers incorporate strategies to promote critical-thinking skills to improve multilingual and EL student achievement (Calderon & Slakk, 2018). In an ethnographic study, Harklau (2000) documented how CCELs who had attended U.S. high schools chafed not only at instructors' stereotyping of all ESL students as new to the country and unfamiliar with U.S. culture, but also at the overall lack of academic challenge provided.

Support: Elements and Networks

The role of institutional agents and programs available are particularly important for student engagement because "engagement is about two elements: what the student does and what the institution does" (Wolf-Wendel, Ward, & Kinzie, 2009, p. 413). Importantly, encouragement from staff, faculty, and peers can lead to an increase in rates of student transfer to four-year institutions (Cejda & Kaylor, 2001). At the same time, however, minority students may also lack or experience poor-quality relationships with faculty and staff (Astin, 1993a; Pascarella & Terenzini, 2005); evidence to this point has been found regarding ELs in the K–12 system (Ream, 2003; Lewis et al., 2012). Mentoring as a form of engagement is particularly salient as minority community college students appear to benefit uniquely from positive interpersonal relationships with instructors and peers (Szelenyi, 2001). Advisor and other mentor relationships in particular have proven critical to the success of underprepared students (Bahr, 2008), a category likely to include former K–12 ELs once in college (Callahan & Humphries, 2016). Bunch and colleagues (2011) highlight the importance of funding and counseling to support multilingual community college students. However, despite the relatively rich literature regarding the relationship between institutional and interpersonal supports, to date no comprehensive studies have examined how EL students engage with community college instructors, administrators, and peers relative to their peers.

Challenges

Ultimately, we find it important to consider the challenges to community college success. Students who have external influences and commitments that limit their time on campus may not develop a sense of connection to faculty and others at their schools (Nora, 2003; Schudde, 2019). Importantly, K–12 ELs tend to experience greater exposure to academic (and other) risk factors relative to their peers (Kieffer, 2008). Specifically, we hypothesize that CCELs may internalize dominant ideologies that equate English proficiency with intelligence (Dunstan & Jaeger, 2015; Kanno, 2018) and, as a result, may face additional barriers to course and degree completion. We include an indicator of such challenges as a key, substantive control in our models.

Methods

CCSSE Dataset

For the purposes of this study, we draw from the Community College Survey of Student Engagement (CCSSE) 2014–2016 survey dataset, which consists of 434,288 students nested in a random sample of 701 community colleges across the U.S. The CCSSE survey (http://www.ccsse.org/aboutccsse/aboutccsse.cfm) administered to community college students, asks questions that assess institutional practices and student behaviors correlated with both achievement and retention. Notably, the survey asks community college students about various college experiences, including what activities they spend their time doing; what activities they have completed both inside and outside of class; their interactions with students, faculty, and staff; and what sort of academic support services they utilize on their campuses, among other items (CCSSE, 2018). Designed to provide input into how colleges can improve students' experiences while monitoring institutional trends and effectiveness, the CCSSE is a paper survey containing multiple choice items about student engagement and background (CCSSE, 2018). Two-year colleges pay fees for CCSSE administration, after which it is randomly distributed among courses at member schools each spring academic term, with sample sizes ranging from 600 to 1,200 students per site, depending on student enrollment (CCSSE, 2018).

Variables of Interest

Community College English Learners (CCELs)

Our foremost variable of interest is an indicator designed to identify the equivalent of K–12 ELs among the community college student population (CCELs). To construct this variable, we first identified multilingual students, those who report speaking a language other than English (N=355,822). As the CCSSE data lack any measure that might approximate English proficiency placement test results among the multilingual population, we then identified those students who have taken, or who are currently taking, ESL or developmental reading or writing coursework (N=33,399). Among CCELs, three-quarters took ESL and some iteration of either developmental reading or writing. Specifically, 30.4 percent took only ESL (N=9832), and an additional 43.9 percent (N=14,210) took ESL plus developmental reading and/or writing. In addition, one-quarter only had developmental English coursework, either reading alone (2.8%, N=891), writing alone (6.6%, N=2147), or both (16.4%, N=5316). The decision to include this latter group in our analytic sample owes to prior research that finds a conflation of ESL and developmental English placement for multilingual youth (Bunch, 2008; Harklau, 2000; Razfar & Simon, 2011). Specifically, Hodara (2015) finds evidence of the misplacement of multilingual students into ESL and developmental reading and writing courses. In preliminary analyses not shown here, Hartman (2019) documents how community college administrators describe systematically placing multilingual students who did not graduate from a U.S. high school in the ESL sequence and those who did graduate from U.S. high schools in developmental reading and writing coursework in lieu of ESL.

Engagement into and with Community Colleges

In an attempt to identify several factors associated with different aspects of student engagement in the community college system, we ran a series of exploratory factor analyses (EFA) on select empirically motivated items in the CCSSE dataset. In the process, we developed nine independent variables of interest in the framing and shaping of community college student engagement. The three engagement constructs are described: Discursive Engagement, Pedagogical Engagement, and Supports: Institutional and Interpersonal.

- *Discursive Engagement.* From a series of items related to academic experiences during the school year, with responses regarding frequency ranging from 1=Never, 2=Sometimes, 3=Often, to 4=Very often, we extracted two distinct factors. The first relates to **academic discourse** and draws from five items (*degree to which students discuss grades, ideas, or career plans with an instructor; emailed an instructor; worked outside of class with classmates; worked harder than expected; worked to integrate ideas from multiple sources*) with a factor loading ≥ 0.50 (Mean=2.43, SD=0.58). A second factor emerged representing **social discourse** and draws from two items (*had serious conversations with students (1) of different race/ethnicity than your own, or (2) who differ from you in* *terms of religious or political beliefs and opinions*) with a factor loading $\geq$ 0.77 (Mean=2.41, SD=0.99). (Here, and throughout this chapter, the Mean represents the average of all student responses to the item. In this case, it represents the average frequency, in between sometimes and often, with which students report engaging with academic issues and ideas. The Standard Deviation (SD) describes the spread of values out from the average (mean); a low SD indicates that the distribution is close to the mean, and a high SD is widely spread out.)

- **Pedagogical Engagement.** In response to the literature examining pedagogical quality and student achievement, we captured two additional factors with responses gauging emphasis and intensity ranging from 1=Very little, 2=Some, 3=Quite a bit, to 4=Very much. The first factor approximates **critical thinking** skills and consists of five items (*synthesizing, organizing ideas; applying theories; analyzing basic elements and theories; making judgments; application of information to new skill*), with a factor loading $\geq$ 0.66 (Mean=2.80, SD=0.72). The second factor draws from a single item, **memorization** of facts, ideas, and methods for recall (Mean=2.88, SD=0.89).

- **Logistical Support.** From a series of items attempting to address the multiple supports that students might experience with responses gauging emphasis and intensity ranging from 1=Very little, 2=Some, 3=Quite a bit, to 4=Very much, an additional three factors emerged. The first is **institutional** support, both affective and logistical (*help necessary to thrive socially, to succeed at this college, to cope with non-academic responsibilities, to encourage contact across diverse peer groups, as well as providing financial support*), with a factor loading $\geq$ 0.66 (Mean=2.52, SD=0.75). Second is **interpersonal skill development** (10 items: *developing a personal value code; effective speaking; self-understanding; working effectively with others; critical/ analytic thought; career goal development; understanding across racial/ethnic groups; clear, effective writing, independent learning, contributing to the larger community*) with a factor loading $\geq$ 0.67 (Mean=2.70, SD=0.74). Finally, **workforce**

skill development (five items: *career information; computing, IT use; educational preparation; work/ job related skills; numerical problem solving*) has a factor loading ≥ 0.58 (Mean=2.76, SD=0.71).

- *Support Networks.* Finally, we identified three types of support networks associated with student success. The first factor to emerge measures the strength and resiliency of a student's **school-based support network** of instructors, administrative personnel, and other students, with availability ranging from 1=unhelpful, inconsiderate, rigid, to 7=helpful, considerate, and flexible, with a factor loading ≥ 0.60 (Mean=5.41, SD=1.14). In addition, we include two indicators of a student's **family support network** (Mean=3.51, SD=0.80) and **friend support network** (Mean=3.24, SD=0.89) with responses measuring intensity from 1=Not very, 2=Somewhat, 3=Quite a bit, to 4=Extremely.

Background Control Variables

To understand how the CCEL population fares in FYC and other classes, it is important to first consider how they compare on any number of indicators associated with both success at the community college level and overall engagement. Social background is critical to consider, as K–12 ELs tend to be more economically disadvantaged and attend lower quality schools (Gándara et al., 2003) than native English speakers and more English-proficient multilinguals. **Individual demographic** controls include age, gender, multilingualism, full-time enrollment, concurrent enrollment, international (foreign) student, marital status, whether respondent has children, full-time work, intent to transfer, grades, race/ethnicity, credit hours completed, respondent's highest prior education, respondents' mother's and father's education level, and sources of school funding. In addition, evidence of frequent challenges and risk factors (e.g., greater likelihood of working full-time, limited economic supports) is noted in the EL education literature (see, for example, Gándara et al., 2003), so we include a measure of challenges as well. **School-level** controls include school size and urbanicity (rural, suburban, or urban).

Findings

Demographics

Not only how the CCEL population compares to non-EL students but to the K–12 EL population is discussed. Table 11.1 displays differences in background characteristics of the CCEL sample of CCSSE respondents relative to their non-EL peers.

Relative to K–12 ELs

It is notable to consider that Latinos comprise nearly half of CCELs in the CCSSE dataset, compared to 77 percent of K–12 ELs nationally (McFarland et al., 2018). In contrast, more than one-quarter (26 percent) of CCELs identify as Asian or Asian American, a group that comprises only 10 percent of the national K–12 population. In addition, just over one-third (36 percent) of CCELs are foreign-born, suggesting that a sizeable share graduated from U.S. high schools; unfortunately, CCSSE data do not include this variable. The fact that at least two-thirds of CCELs come from the local K–12 systems suggests both a need and an opportunity for greater collaboration across systems, with FYC and ESL instructors engaging in ongoing dialogue with their local high school English and ESL colleagues to ensure curricular alignment and supports.

Relative to Other Community College Students

Our analyses also show that CCELs are more likely than the non-EL population, including other multilingual students, to be married, parents, first-generation college enrollees, and working more than 30 hours a week. They are also more likely to have enrolled with the intent to transfer to a four-year institution and less likely to be traditional aged (18–24 years old) or to have prior four-year college experience. A greater share of CCELs also report having begun their postsecondary experience at their current institution (80 percent) relative to non-ELs (70 percent). Together, these patterns suggest a certain degree of stability

TABLE 11.1. Demographic Composition of CCSSE Sample by CCEL Status

	Community College	
	ELs	Non-ELs
Variable Name	**(N=33,399)**	**(N=398,758)**
Male	0.39	0.43
Multilingual (Speaks a language in addition to English)	1.00	0.09
Traditional Age (18–24)	0.62	0.67
First-Generation College Student	0.54	0.31
Enrolled Full-Time	0.42	0.41
Began at this Community College	0.80	0.70
Attended a Four-Year Institution after Graduating from High School	0.17	0.20
Foreign-Born	0.36	0.03
Married	0.24	0.16
Has Child(ren)	0.31	0.27
Works More than 30 Hours a Week	0.42	0.41
Goal: Transfer to Four-Year School	0.86	0.75
Degree to Which Experiences External Pressures	2.42(0.87)	2.19(0.89)
Race/ Ethnicity		
White, non-Hispanic	0.11	0.61
Black, non-Hispanic	0.10	0.12
Latinx	0.46	0.16
Asian or Asian American	0.26	0.05
American Indian, Native American, or Native Hawaiian, or Other	0.07	0.07
GPA (4.0 Scale)		
A Average	0.13	0.16
A- to B+ Average	0.35	0.31
B Average	0.22	0.23
B- to C+ Average	0.22	0.20
C Average	0.06	0.07
C- or Lower Average	0.02	0.03
Credits Completed		
No Credits Completed	0.08	0.10
1–29 Credits Completed	0.55	0.54
30–44 Credits Completed	0.15	0.14
45–59 Credits Completed	0.12	0.12
60 or More Credits Completed	0.10	0.09
Paying for College with:		
Own Money	0.68	0.66
Parent, Spouse, Significant Other Pays	0.51	0.47
Employer Sponsored	0.18	0.13
Grants and Fellowships	0.56	0.57
Loans	0.24	0.34
Public Assistance	0.19	0.14

Source: CCSSE (2014–2016). *Share of sample and means (with standard deviations)*. www.ccsse.org/aboutsurvey/aboutsurvey.cfm.

within the CCEL population; however, they may also experience somewhat more severe financial challenges. Consistent with prior literature (Núñez & Sparks, 2012), CCELs are markedly less likely to access student loans (24 percent) to fund their college attendance than non-ELs (34 percent). We encourage institutional efforts that support ESL and FYC instructors to learn about and understand the strengths and needs of the EL student community specific to their campus. Ideally, such efforts would foster development of programs and practices for CCEL students that will improve overall levels of academic achievement. This apparent stability among CCELs has the potential to improve the campus climate overall.

Engagement

In addition, to determine whether CCELs in our sample might differ significantly on any of the important indicators of engagement associated with community college success in general, and successful completion of FYC in particular, we constructed multiple regression models to predict engagement. Specifically, we regressed CCEL status, as well as the multiple demographic controls listed, while also accounting for community college location (urbanicity) and size. In addition, for each facet of engagement (*discursive, pedagogical,* and *supports*), we included factors from the other two constructs as controls. Due to space constraints, full tables are not presented here but rather are available upon request. Table 11.2 displays mean levels of each engagement factor, as well as the as the parameter estimates for CCELs included in the final multiple regression models.

Discursive Engagement

Despite the rigorous background, academic, logistical, and affective controls, we find that CCEL students differ significantly from non-EL students on each engagement construct. Specifically, CCELs alternately report taking part in significantly more academic conversations

TABLE 11.2. Sample Means and Standard Deviations: CCEL Coefficients from Multilevel Regression Models

Engagement Factor	CCELs (N=33,399)		Non-ELs (N=398,758)		CCEL Estimate
	Mean	St.Dev.	Mean	St.Dev.	Coefficient
Discursive: Academic	2.52	0.55	2.42	0.58	0.02****
Discursive: Social	2.21	0.99	2.43	0.98	-0.24****
Pedagogy: Critical Thinking	2.89	0.68	2.80	0.72	-0.01*
Pedagogy: Memorization	2.92	0.87	2.88	0.89	-0.02*
Support: Institutional	2.73	0.75	2.50	0.74	0.15****
Support: Interpersonal Skills	3.00	0.64	2.68	0.74	0.15****
Support: Workforce Skills	2.96	0.66	2.74	0.71	0.12****
Support Network: School-based	5.52	1.10	5.40	1.14	0.09****
Support Network: Family	3.44	0.86	3.51	0.79	-0.02**
Support Network: Friends	3.12	0.91	3.25	0.89	-0.08****

Source: CCSSE (2014–2016); *$p<0.05$; **$p<0.01$; ***$p<0.001$; ****$p<0.0001$. www.ccsse.org/aboutsurvey/aboutsurvey.cfm

and fewer conversations with peers from different backgrounds. For the former, relative to their peers, CCELs are more likely to engage in *academic discourse* with peers or instructors (b=0.02, *p*<.0001). On the other hand, they are also less likely to engage in *social discourse*, and by extension, develop friendships, with peers from different social or political backgrounds (b=-0.24, *p*<.0001). CCELs may be less likely to initiate conversations with peers due to cultural differences or a lack confidence with their English abilities, or they may simply not feel welcome in the classroom space (Dunstan & Jaeger, 2015; Harklau, 2000). CCEL students might not know how to initiate conversations with others, or might be hesitant to do so, both of which could impact their engagement not only in ESL and developmental English courses but also following their transition into FYC and other credit-bearing coursework. Together, these discursive engagement patterns suggest that CCELs have remarkable potential for academically powerful discursive engagement but will need support to engage with and experience the benefits to social discourse.

Pedagogical Engagement

Initial, baseline comparisons indicated that CCELs reported more instructional experiences that engaged their critical-thinking skills, but they also reported experiencing more memorization-driven instruction. However, once the models took into account an array of background characteristics (Hartman, Callahan, & Yu, forthcoming), we found that the opposite, in fact, held true. Not only were CCELs less likely to experience instruction designed to develop critical-thinking skills ($b=-0.01$, $p<0.05$), but they also reported fewer instructional experiences focused on memorization relative to non-EL students ($b=-0.02$, $p<0.05$). The reader will note, however, that these differences might be attributed to statistical artifact due to the large sample size ($N=434,288$) and p values significant only at 0.05 level. These findings should be interpreted with caution.

Given these patterns of pedagogical engagement, FYC instructors and others may find the inclusion of instructional strategies that prioritize critical-thinking skills to improve academic persistence among their EL students; we are less certain about the memorization activities. Alternately, the findings may suggest more broadly that CCELs simply experience less academic focus in their classes, regardless of whether the pedagogy is innovative (critical-thinking skills) or more traditionally oriented (memorization). If that is in fact the case, then educators and community college leaders will want to focus on improving the academic experiences overall in ESL, as well as developmental English classes and any other coursework that targets students relatively new to the language. We venture that pedagogy and curriculum in FYC and other courses can be structured in such a way as to facilitate meaningful connections with all students' lived experiences, regardless of linguistic status (Murie & Fitzpatrick, 2009). In addition, pedagogical approaches that incorporate peer feedback can be especially valuable (Reynolds, Bae, & Wilson, 2009) for CCELs and other multilingual students, with the true benefits emerging later on, via student retention and educational attainment.

Logistical Supports and Support Networks

First, we consider the numerous facets of support that students: receive from the institution, bring with them, and foster once enrolled. Not surprisingly, given the literature on immigrant students and community college outreach (Teranishi et al., 2011), we find that CCELs report accessing higher levels of *institutional support* (b=0.15, p<0.0001), as well as greater access to the support required to develop *interpersonal* (b=0.15, p<0.0001) and *workforce* (b=0.12, p<0.0001) *skills*. In addition, CCELs reported significantly greater access to *school-based support networks* in their colleges (b=0.09, p<0.0001), even though they experience less robust support networks among *family* (b=-0.02, p<0.01) and *friends* (b=-0.08, p<0.0001), suggesting they may be at greater risk of departure from their program (Pascarella & Terenzini, 2005).

Combined, these patterns suggest while CCELs receive constructive institutional supports from the community college context itself, they report receiving suboptimal support from family and friends, which has the potential to hinder their academic progress and academic achievement during their time in the community college. We suggest that FYC and other educators may consider how innovative approaches that promote greater interpersonal engagement in their classes might allow CCELs and others to develop stronger friendships and support networks within the confines of the FYC classroom and beyond. Like their EL counterparts at the secondary level, CCELs report feeling more socially isolated, likely due to linguistic and cultural differences. While the most effective K–12 EL programming (Santos et al., 2018) invites pride and respect toward all cultures, its day to day application and students' social integration may matter most. One need look no further than the innovative student-led *Global Minds* initiative (http://globalminds.world/) developed by and for high school students to more fully incorporate refugee and other EL students, to see the academic and social benefits such integration brings to the campus overall.

Implications

Our findings suggest that not only do CCELs differ greatly from their non-EL peers on any number of characteristics but that they also differ markedly from the K–12 EL population. While a solid share of CCELs appear to come from the U.S. high school system, there are marked differences in nativity, race, outside commitments, and English proficiency that must be taken into account. While there is much to learn from the past trials and tribulations of K–12 EL programming, it is clear that simply replicating these efforts for community colleges remains insufficient. Effective CCEL programming must focus attention on the specific linguistic, social, and academic needs of this linguistically, racially, and culturally diverse population.

Our findings suggest that campus engagement matters, highlighting the importance of efforts by multiple offices to support CCEL success. ESL and developmental English faculty require the support of library and support lab staff, academic advisors, counselors, international advisors, and a whole host of individuals across campus (Braxton et al., 2004; Pascarella & Terenzini, 2005) to ensure degree completion, transfer, and persistence for CCELs. In addition, instruction tailored to the needs of the local CCEL population has the potential to greatly improve the likelihood of educational and career goal attainment among this population. Nationally, Núñez and Sparks (2012) found that 70 percent of multilingual community college students reported an intent to transfer to a four-year institution; in the CCEL group within that larger population, we find that 84 percent reported an intent to transfer.

Our analyses suggest that not only may CCELs be particularly predisposed to want to transfer but also that there are key facets of their engagement experiences while enrolled that can be leveraged to facilitate this transfer. Transfer is a process that, by definition, necessitates a different level of instruction and support than attaining an associate's degree, specific certification, or professional or linguistic improvement. We recommend that FYC instructors incorporate activities that require or encourage students to visit counselors, advisors, the writing center, and/or the skills lab on campus (Hoekje & Stevens, 2018). Additionally, instructors can facilitate writing and conversation groups to foster collaboration inside and outside of class, allowing students to develop social, as well as academic, relationships. Developing cross-cultural friendships has the potential to improve outcomes for all students, not only CCELs, as they promote cross-cultural awareness and empathy, both of which benefit non-EL students.

In addition, we take a moment to expand on the potential of pedagogical engagement. We offer as an example two local community college students who are perfectly matched on all factors, other than ESL enrollment; Lisbet is a CCEL and Elizabeth is not. Lisbet reports markedly less engagement with the instructional practices she is exposed to than Elizabeth. Given the robust relationship between students' pedagogical engagement and college retention (Tinto, 1994), we suggest that focused attention to CCELs' pedagogical experiences in FYC and other courses will result in important returns to the college via their long-term achievement and retention. Prior research sheds light on this; Bunch et al. (2011) found placement in lengthy ESL sequences to constrain students' pedagogical engagement. Long course sequences pose particular challenges for CCELs for a variety of reasons, one of which was that the longer students spend in ESL, the less likely they are to persist to transfer. Using longitudinal data, Patthey-Chavez, Dillon, and Thomas-Spiegel (2005) found that while less than 10 percent of beginning CCELs progressed to and passed a college-level English course, advanced CCELs did not fare much better, with only 29 percent meeting this goal. CCELs trapped in long developmental English or ESL sequences may forgo their educational goals or drop out entirely (Bailey, 2009; Bailey, Jeong, & Cho, 2010). Careful consideration of the length and scope of developmental and ESL course sequences has the potential to vastly improve CCEL persistence and successful transfer.

Like their K–12 counterparts, CCELs appear vulnerable to exit at key junctures marking educational or institutional transitions (e.g., postsecondary application/enrollment, (see Castleman, Page, & Schooley, 2014)); course selection and scheduling/navigation of institutional enrollment, degree, and transfer requirements (Szelenyi & Chang, 2002); and completion of ESL or developmental English sequences (Hodara, 2015). We urge community college faculty and leaders to carefully define success for CCELs specific to their institution, acknowledging the unique strengths and challenges of their particular context, and the characteristics of their local CCEL population. In fact, we argue that the potential for CCEL success rests in those very educational transition points that pose the greatest challenges. Specifically, the point at which CCELs complete ESL or developmental English and enroll in FYC and other credit-bearing coursework is critical for future certification, fulfillment of associate's degree requirements, and/ or transfer. FYC educators can contribute to CCEL success by listening to students' goals and aspirations, connecting students to support services on campus, and identifying meaningful ways for students to connect course content with their goals. In addition, FYC course and campus activities to bolster CCEL engagement will result in returns to their overall academic attainment and retention. Meaningful interactions with staff on campus, mentoring around academic or job planning, and peer collaboration all prove equally important as indicators of community college success.

ℛEFERENCES

Abedi, J. (2004). The No Child Left Behind Act and English language learners: Assessment and accountability issues. *Educational Researcher, 33*(1), 4–14.

Astin, A. (1993a). How are students affected? *Change, 25*(2), 44–50.

Astin, A. (1993b). What matters in college? *Liberal Education, 79*(4), 4–17.

Bahr, P. R. (2008). Cooling out in the community college: What is the effect of academic advising on students' chances of success? *Research in Higher Education, 49*, 704–732.

Bailey, T. (2009). *Rethinking developmental education in community college* (CCRC Brief #40). New York: Community College Research Center, Teachers College, Columbia University.

Bailey, T., Jeong, D. W., & Cho, S. W. (2010). Referral, enrollment, and completion in developmental education sequences in community colleges. *Economics of Education Review, 29*, 255–270.

Braxton, J. M., Hirschy, A. S., & McClendon, S. A. (2004). Understanding and reducing college student departure. *ASHE-ERIC Higher Education Report, 30*(3).

Bunch, G. (2008). Language minority students and California community colleges: Current issues and future directions. *Community College Policy Research, 1*, 1–17.

Bunch, G. C., Endris, A., Panayotova, D., Romero, M., & Llosa, L. (2011). *Mapping the terrain: Language testing and placement for US-educated language minority students in California's community colleges.* Menlo Park, CA: William and Flora Hewlett Foundation.

Calderon, M. E., & Slakk, S. (2018). *Teaching reading to English learners, Grades 6–12: A framework for improving achievement in the content areas.* Thousand Oaks, CA: Sage.

Callahan, R. M., & Gándara, P. C. (Eds.). (2014). *The bilingual advantage: Language, literacy, and the U.S. labor market.* Clevedon, England: Multilingual Matters.

Callahan, R. M., & Humphries, M. H. (2016). Undermatched? School-based linguistic status, college going, and the immigrant advantage. *American Educational Research Journal, 53*(2), 263–295.

Castleman, B. L., Page, L. C., & Schooley, K. (2014). The forgotten summer: Mitigating summer attrition among college-intending, low-income high school graduates. *Journal of Policy Analysis and Management, 33*(2), 320–344.

Cejda, B. D., & Kaylor, A. J. (2001). Early transfer: A case study of traditional-aged community college students. *Community College Journal of Research and Practice, 25*, 621–638.

Chang, M. J., Denson, N., Sáenz, V., & Misa, K. (2006). The educational benefits of sustaining cross-racial interaction among undergraduates. *The Journal of Higher Education, 77*(3), 430–455.

Community College Survey of Student Engagement (CCSSE). (2018). About the community college survey of student engagement. Retrieved from http://www.ccsse.org/aboutccsse/aboutccsse.cfm

Dunstan, S. B., & Jaeger, A. J. (2015). Dialect and influences on the academic experiences of college students. *The Journal of Higher Education, 86*(5), 777–803.

Every Student Succeeds Act (ESSA), Pub.L. 114-95 C.F.R. (2015).

Gándara, P., Rumberger, R., Maxwell-Jolly, J., & Callahan, R. M. (2003). English learners in California schools: Unequal resources, unequal outcomes. *Education Policy Analysis Archives, 11*, 36.

Greene, T. G., Marti, C. M., & McClenney, K. (2008). The effort-outcome gap: Differences for African American and Hispanic community college students in student engagement and academic achievement. *The Journal of Higher Education, 79*(5), 513–539.

Harklau, L. (2000). From the "good kids" to the "worst": Representations of English language learners across educational settings. *TESOL Quarterly, 34*(1), 35–67.

Hartman, C. E. (2019). Understanding student engagement and intentions to transfer among community college English learners. Unpublished PhD diss. University of Texas at Austin.

Hartman, C.E., Callahan, R.M., & Yu, H. (forthcoming). Optimizing their intent to transfer: Community college English learners' engagement. *Research in Higher Education.*

Hodara, M. (2015). The effects of English as a second language courses on language minority community college students. *Educational Evaluation and Policy Analysis, 37*(2), 243–270.

Hodara, M., & Xu, D. (2018). Are two subjects better than one? The effects of developmental English courses on language minority and native English-speaking students' community college outcomes. *Economics of Education Review, 66*, 1–13.

Hoekje, B. J., & Stevens, S. G. (2018). *Creating a culturally inclusive campus: A guide to supporting international students.* New York: Routledge.

Hudson, L. (2003). Racial/ethnic differences in the path to a postsecondary credential. *Education Statistics Quarterly, 5*(2), 129–133.

Jacobson, J., Olsen, C., Rice, J. K., Sweetland, S., & Ralph, J. (2001). *Educational achievement and Black-White inequality* (NCES Publication No. 2001-061). Washington, DC: National Center for Education Statistics.

Kanno, Y. (2018). High-performing English learners' limited access to four-year college. *Teachers College Record, 120*(4), 1–46.

Kanno, Y., & Cromley, J. G. (2013). English language learners' access to and attainment in postsecondary education. *TESOL Quarterly, 47*(1), 89–121.

Kanno, Y., & Varghese, M. M. (2010). Immigrant and refugee ESL students' challenges to accessing four-year college education: From language policy to educational policy. *Journal of Language, Identity, and Education, 9*(5), 310–328.

Karp, M. M., Hughes, K. L., & O'Gara, L. (2010). An exploration of Tinto's integration framework for community college students. *Journal of College Student Retention: Research, Theory and Practice, 12*(1), 69–86.

Kieffer, M. J. (2008). Catching up or falling behind? Initial English proficiency, concentrated poverty, and the reading growth of language minority learners in the United States. *Journal of Educational Psychology, 100*(4), 851.

Kuh, G. D. (2001). *The National Survey of Student Engagement: Conceptual framework and overview of psychometric properties.* Bloomington: Indiana University, Center for Postsecondary Research.

Kuh, G. D., Pace, C. R., & Vesper, N. (1997). The development of process indicators to estimate student gains associated with good practices in undergraduate education. *Research in Higher Education, 38*(4), 435–454.

Lewis, J., Ream, R., Bocian, K., Cardullo, R., Hammond, K., & Fast, L. (2012). Con cariño: Teacher caring, math self-efficacy, and math achievement among Hispanic English learners. *Teachers College Record, 114*(7), n7.

Linquanti, R., & Cook, H. G. (2013). *Toward a "common definition of English learner": A brief defining policy and technical issues and opportunities for state assessment consortia.* Washington DC: Council of Chief State School Officers. Retrieved from https://files.eric.ed.gov/fulltext/ED542705.pdf

McFarland, J., Hussar, B., Wang, X., Zhang, J., Wang, K., Rathbun, A., … Bullock Mann, F. (2018). *The condition of education: English Learners in public schools.* Government Printing Office. Retrieved from https://nces.ed.gov/programs/coe/indicator_cgf.asp

Mitchell, C. (2017, January 4). ESSA's impact unclear for English-learners; advocates are keeping close tabs on states over concerns about resources, staff, and know-how to meet the law's mandates. *Education Week.* Retrieved from https://www.edweek.org/ew/articles/2017/01/04/essas-impact-unclear-for-english-learners.html

Murie, R., & Fitzpatrick, R. (2009). Situating generation 1.5 in the academy: Models for building academic literacy and acculturation. In M. Roberge, M. Siegal, & L. Harklau (Eds.), *Generation 1.5 in College Composition* (pp. 153–170). New York: Routledge.

National Survey of Student Engagement (NSSE). (2000). *National benchmarks of effective educational practice.* Bloomington: Indiana University Center for Postsecondary Research.

National Survey of Student Engagement (NSSE). (2003). *Converting data into action: Expanding the boundaries of institutional improvement.* Bloomington: Indiana University Center for Postsecondary Research.

No Child Left Behind Act (NCLB), Pub. L. No. 107–110, 115 Stat. 1425 (2002).

Nora, A. (2003). Access to higher education for Hispanic students: Real or illusory? In J. Castellanos & L. Jones' (Eds.) *The majority in the minority: Expanding the representation of Latina/o faculty, administrators and students in higher education* (pp. 47–68). Sterling, VA: Stylus.

Núñez, A. M., Rios-Aguilar, C., Kanno, Y., & Flores, S. M. (2016). English learners and their transition to postsecondary education. In M.B. Paulsen (Ed.), *Higher education: Handbook of theory and research* (pp. 41–90). Switzerland: Springer International Publishing.

Núñez, A.-M., & Sparks, P. J. (2012). Who are linguistic minority students in higher education? An analysis of the beginning postsecondary students study 2004. In Y. Kanno & L. Harklau (Eds.), *Linguistic minority students go to college: Preparation, access, and persistence* (pp. 110–129). New York: Routledge.

Pascarella, E. T., Edison, M., Nora, A., Hagedorn, L., & Terenzini, P. T. (1996). Influences on students' openness to diversity and challenge in the first year of college. *Journal of College Student Development, 67,* 174–195.

Pascarella, E. T., & Terenzini, P. T. (2005). *How college affects students: A third decade of research.* San Francisco: Jossey-Bass.

Patthey-Chavez, G., Dillon, P., & Thomas-Spiegel, J. (2005). How far do they get? Tracking students with different academic literacies through community college remediation. *Teaching in the Two-Year College, 32*(3), 261–277.

Razfar, A., & Simon, J. (2011). Course-taking patterns of Latino ESL students: Mobility and mainstreaming in urban community colleges in the United States. *TESOL Quarterly, 45*(4), 595–627.

Ream, R. K. (2003). Counterfeit social capital and Mexican-American underachievement. *Educational Evaluation and Policy Analysis, 25*(3), 237–262.

Reyes, M. R., Brackett, M. A., Rivers, S. E., White, M., & Salovey, P. (2012). Classroom emotional climate, student engagement, and academic achievement. *Journal of Educational Psychology, 104*(3), 700–712.

Reynolds, D. W., Bae, K.-W., & Wilson, J. S. (2009). Individualizing pedagogy: Responding to diverse needs in freshman composition for non-native speakers. In M. Roberge, M. Siegal, & L. Harklau (Eds.), *Generation 1.5 in college composition* (pp. 185–203). New York: Routledge.

Ryan, C. (2013). Language use in the United States: 2011. *American community survey reports, 22,* 1–16.

Santibañez, L., & Zárate, M. E. (2014). Bilinguals in the US and college enrollment. In R. M. Callahan & P. C. Gándara (Eds.), *The bilingual advantage: Language, literacy, and the U.S. labor market* (pp. 211–233). Clevedon, England: Multilingual Matters.

Santos, M., Palacios, M. C., Cheuk, T., Greene, R., Mercado-Garcia, D., Zerkel, L., Hakuta, K., & Skarin, R. (2018). *Preparing English learners for college and career: Lessons from successful high schools.* New York: Teachers College Press.

Schudde, L. (2019). Short- and long-term impacts of engagement experiences with faculty and peers at community colleges. *Review of Higher Education, 42*(4), 385–426.

Schwitzer, A. M., Griffin, O. T., Ancis, J. R., & Thomas, C. (1999). Social adjustment experiences of African American college students. *Journal of Counseling and Development, 77,* 189–197.

Swigart, T. E., & Murrell, P. H. (2001). Factors influencing estimates of gains made among African-American and Caucasian community college students. *Community College Journal of Research and Practice, 25,* 297–312.

Szelenyi, K. (2001). Minority student retention and academic achievement in community colleges. *ERIC Digests, ED451859.*

Szelenyi, K., & Chang, J. C. (2002). Educating immigrants: The community college role. *Community College Review, 30*(2), 55–73.

Teranishi, R. T., Suárez-Orozco, C., & Suárez-Orozco, M. (2011). Immigrants in community colleges. *The Future of Children, 21*(1), 153–169.

Tinto, V. (1994). *Leaving college: Rethinking the causes and cures of student attrition* (2nd ed.). Chicago: The University of Chicago Press.

U.S. Census Bureau. (2016). *Language Spoken at Home: 2016 American Community Survey 1-Year Estimates.* Washington, DC: Author.

Wolf-Wendel, L., Ward, K., & Kinzie, J. (2009). A tangled web of terms: The overlap and unique contribution of involvement, engagement, and integration to understanding college student success. *Journal of College Student Development, 50*(4), 407–428.

Zepke, N., & Leach, L. (2010). Improving student engagement: Ten proposals for action. *Active Learning in Higher Education, 11*(3), 167–177.

12

Avoiding the "Cliffs": Korean International Community College Students and Rhetorical Flexibility

Justin G. Whitney
TENNESSEE STATE UNIVERSITY

College writing education is transforming on a global scale, and U.S. community colleges (CCs) are an important part of that transformation. Whereas international students traditionally have matriculated at four-year universities, increasing populations of international students are now choosing to enter higher education through alternative routes made possible by CCs, and populations overall are predicted to grow (Altbach, Reisberg, & Rumbley, 2009, p. 7).

A community college education has important implications specific to South Koreans. Although English is a required course in Korean public schools, many Korean families pay significant sums of money for their children to attend extracurricular education focusing on English learning or preparation for English proficiency exams, such as the Test of English as a Foreign Language (TOEFL®). Consequently, students from lower-income backgrounds have fewer opportunities to develop English fluency and therefore, fewer opportunities to enter and be successful at U.S. universities, many of which require the TOEFL® for admission.

Today, however, U.S. CCs offer an important alternative for lower-income Korean families. The tradition of open access maintained by CCs allows students from all over the world to begin taking classes regardless of educational background. Furthermore, first-year composition (FYC) course credit from a community college is regularly accepted by top universities in place of a TOEFL® score. FYC in the community college allows Korean international students to gain access to U.S. higher education, which otherwise may not be possible. These students also benefit from the academic preparation and language learning that FYC offers.

Nevertheless, it is important to consider the significance of international student educational trajectories that are increasingly including U.S. CCs. The educational goals of universities can be very different from those of the community college, and these differences influence both writing curriculum and the kinds of learning students gain. Opening educational opportunity for international students from around the world is important, but it is also important to take stock of what it means for students to replace university FYC with community college FYC, including the kinds of academic preparation and language learning opportunities offered there.

This chapter draws on data gathered during a multi-year study of Korean international students at Salt Lake Community College (SLCC), a large urban community college in the U.S. intermountain West. I situate FYC at SLCC as responding to worldwide educational exigence and *obligating* innovative response to the needs of all its students. First some of the exclusionary conditions of the English education industry in South Korea are identified, followed by details about the writing course sequence at SLCC. Aspects of FYC at SLCC that are not shared by universities but that are distinctively beneficial for Korean international and other students will be discussed using the data. The chapter concludes with a discussion of how the educational opportunities offered at SLCC extend far beyond educational attainment or credentialization for Korean international students.

Education in Korea

For many Koreans, admittance into a good university means far more than just a quality education. Educational success is likened to being successful, something that reflects on one's whole family and community. Yeoreum (a pseudonym), a former colleague at the University of Utah from South Korea, said that everyone in Korea is "working toward one pathway," adding that if "somebody goes a different way," they are considered "a failure, a loser." To illustrate her point, she held up her phone, horizontal to the ground so that the screen faced the ceiling, and said there is only "one pathway," pointing to her phone. There are "cliffs on both sides," she continued. As she said the word *sides*, she chopped her hand down along the edges of her phone to show the steep drop off awaiting anyone who strays from the established path.

"We are not allowed to go another way," she told me. While in the United States success is broadly defined, she explained that in Korean society there is a clearly delineated sequence expected of everyone. Koreans are expected to excel as high school students, do well on the national college entrance exam, get into top tier four-year universities, and then move on to a good job at a big company. The "finish line," she says, is a salaried position at a prominent business like Samsung or Hyundai, and that only comes from following the previous steps.

Historically, Yeoreum's "finish line" was once much easier to reach because the education necessary to get there was more equally allocated. In fact, Korea's secondary education system was founded on a philosophy of egalitarianism. Byun and Kim (2010) write that "South Korea's egalitarian approach to education can be best described by its randomized school assignment policy" (p. 162). Under this policy, "Most secondary school students are assigned to schools . . . by a random lottery system" (p. 162). With this policy in place, little variation has emerged in academic performance or school resources and curriculum between public and private education. Such an egalitarian system has historically guided students from diverse backgrounds onto similar educational trajectories with similar chances of reaching a high paying job after graduation.

In the mid-1990s, however, South Korea began shifting away from an egalitarian model and toward a more neo-liberal approach that sees "educational excellence . . . as a key issue regarding national competitiveness in the global market" (Byun & Kim, 2010, p. 162). By 1996, limited school choice was allowed that has slowly proliferated into "independent" schools and "autonomous private" high schools that parents can choose and then pay to have their children attend (pp. 163–164). Perhaps the most significant move away from egalitarianism is the explosion of extra-curricular or "shadow" education that is paid for by parents and commonplace for many Koreans. Further, because part of an educational focus on global competitiveness includes obtaining fluency in English, the quest for English literacy makes up a substantial portion of the shadow education that occurs in Korea (Jahng, 2011). Park (2009) reports that in 2005 alone, the amount of money spent on English education in South Korea reached nearly $15 billion U.S. dollars (p. 51).

Unsurprisingly, education available through personal expenditure significantly impacts families from lower socioeconomic backgrounds. A growing body of research shows that disparities in educational access for Korean students mean differential educational attainment (see, for example, Kim, 2005; Park & Kim, 2014). The effects of socioeconomic status on educational attainment in South Korea are particularly apparent when it comes to English fluency. Wealthier families can pay for their children to attend private schools or for shadow education focusing on English learning or a standardized English proficiency exam such as the TOEFL®. However, as Byun and Kim (2010) write, "Because parents must pay for various types of shadow education for their children" and "because poor parents generally cannot afford the high cost of shadow education," there is a growing gap in educational opportunity and achievement "between children from high- and low-income families" (p. 165). A lifetime of increased access to English education culminates in greater levels of English fluency that play an important role in university admission and job availability. Byun and Kim (2010) maintain that because English fluency plays such an influential role for "gaining admission to selective universities and finding prestigious jobs, the English achievement gap between children from high- and low-SES families will likely lead to persistent inequalities in terms of access to future opportunities" (p. 30; see also Lee, 2005).

Due to a scarcity of research, it is difficult to pinpoint the importance of English language writing education in Korea. Nevertheless, when researchers (such as Ahn, 1995; Kim & Kim, 2005) have addressed writing in English in South Korea, they tended to focus on the problems. Perhaps foremost among the critiques is that English writing teachers focus heavily on grammatical correctness (see, for example, B.E. Cho, 2004; Shim, 2009). Other problems include students not being taught academic writing genres (Kim, 2008) or a lack of "genre specific writing across the curriculum" knowledge (Kim & Kim, 2005, p. 3). These criticisms may hold merit in that not only did Kwon et al. (2004) find that "Koreans scored extremely low on writing tests" in a comparison between Korean, Japanese, and Chinese high school students (p. 3), but Cho (2009) has shown that "writing journal papers in English is a burden to professors and graduate students of science and engineering schools in Korea due to their lack of English proficiency" (p. 230).

A need for college-level English fluency was an important factor for why the students participating in this study chose to enter higher education by coming to the U.S. and enrolling in SLCC. Student participants maintained they wanted to learn more English before entering a university and had little familiarity with writing in English upon arrival at SLCC. Further, apart from minimal study for the TOEFL®, they had almost no familiarity with college writing in the United States.

On a final note, like educational attainment, prestigious employment in South Korea grows increasingly difficult to secure. For example, the percentage of working-aged Koreans (ages 25–64) with bachelor's degrees has seen a 20 percent increase between 2001 to 2015, from 25 percent to 45 percent (National Center for Education Statistics, 2017). Furthermore, while an expanding technology industry created high-paying careers requiring college degrees, less emphasis on other sectors of the Korean economy has diminished high-paying jobs that require no college education. Koreans graduating college today enter a job market with far greater competition and with fewer options than their parents enjoyed. A respectable salaried position at a prominent business such as Samsung or Hyundai is today harder to achieve than ever before.

Through differential access to English education and uncertain job prospects after graduation, Korean students are still expected to follow the cultural pathway Yeoreum identified. Yet, at any point, students can fall off this path and, in doing so, lose critical future job prospects. Students from families who cannot afford the shadow education have a harder time gaining the English fluency necessary to be admitted into top universities that will help them on the job market. For students from lower-income families, there are few alternatives. These students do not get the salaried position at Samsung or Hyundai; they get the cliffs instead. Or, they get something else. Some Koreans who are unable to take up the expected path have found another route to the finish line via U.S. CCs, which offer Korean international students and many others from around the world the opportunity to enroll at a four-year university and obtain the level of education and credentials employers want. Not following the cultural pathway no longer equates to failure. Not only does the tradition of open access offered by CCs provide a route that can lead to a university degree, but CCs offer other opportunities that benefit Korean international students in ways universities cannot.

Methodology

This IRB approved qualitative inquiry draws largely from interview data gathered from eight South Korean international students who were attending or had recently transferred from SLCC. I transcribed all interviews. When representing participants' spoken words in written form, I punctuated minimally to avoid changing their meaning. I have also made only minimal changes to grammar, such as adjusting prepositions, to increase clarity and avoid miscommunication. Data also include interviews with a former colleague as well as faculty and administrators at SLCC. I further draw from classroom observation notes as well as writing samples and institutional texts.

I conducted three sets of interviews, as suggested by Seidman (2013). The first interviews focused on understanding the students' history before coming to SLCC, as well as their plans for the future. The primary function of the second student interview was to learn more about their experiences in learning to write after arrival at SLCC. Final interviews ensured that the conclusions I had made were consistent with the way that participants wanted to be understood. Analysis was thematic and took place holistically after each set of interviews. Analysis of the themes were used to interpret the experiences of Korean international students studying writing at SLCC.

First-Year Composition at SLCC and Rhetorical Flexibility

Salt Lake Community College is a comprehensive institution serving a diverse student population, including a small percentage of international students from South Korea. At the time of this study, SLCC served more than 61,000 students per year (2016–2017). Based on third-week figures from the fall semester of 2016, they were majority (50.4 percent) female and at an average age of 25 (SLCC, 2018). SLCC is majority white (69 percent) with Hispanic students (17.5 percent) as the second largest demographic (SLCC, 2018). Asians are 3.8 percent of the student population. Further, in the spring of 2015, 82 percent of students self-identified as first generation, "meaning that neither parent has achieved a Bachelor's degree" (Rousculp, 2015, p. 23).

SLCC has a robust writing program with a host of writing classes designed for different interests and skill levels. Writing class numbers begin with ENGL 0900 (Integrated Reading and Writing I) followed by ENGL 0990 (Integrated Reading and Writing II), what SLCC terms "basic" and "college preparatory" writing before beginning with their transferrable FYC credits. What I refer to as FYC (first-year composition) includes two main courses, ENGL 1010 and ENGL 2010. ENGL 1010 is required for most Associate-level work, and ENGL 2010 is necessary for a Bachelor's degree. Because most SLCC students are pursuing an Associate's or Bachelor's degree through transfer, ENGL 1010 and 2010 are popular classes. An administrator indicated to me that SLCC offers approximately 116 sections per fall/spring semester of ENGL 2010 with each section capped at 25 students. Placement in ENGL 0900, 0990, 1010 and 2010 are dependent on tests administered either at the community college (ACCUPLACER) or through a third party (for example, LOEP—Levels of English Proficiency Test), both common to community colleges.

The majority of the students participating in this study came to the U.S. with developing English fluency, particularly in writing. Five out of the seven participants took all four writing courses before transferring to a university. Of the remaining two participants, one had not yet taken any writing courses at the time of the interviews, and the other began his course sequence with ENGL 1010 but also indicated he thought he needed "to take it again." Although most participants were required to take a year's worth of coursework before entering classes for which they gained transferable credit, SLCC admitted all participants and accommodated their developing English writing fluency with classes designed for novice writers.

Because SLCC is not a university, neither its students nor its institutional goals equate exactly to those of a university. Not only does a tradition of open access often mean more diverse student populations than at exclusive institutions, but the educational goals of SLCC students include and go beyond those of university academic pursuits. Many students arrive at community college having never considered transferring to a four-year institution, seeking instead a terminal Associate's degree or industry certification before moving on to employment. Further, for various reasons, not everyone who envisions a future leading to a university ends up as a student at a university. As a result, a writing education focusing solely on academic preparation would not provide considerable portions of their student population with the education they want, need, or deserve.

Confronted with this challenge, faculty and administrators at SLCC design their English composition course sequence to exceed traditional academic pursuits. With the purpose of fostering "critical awareness and rhetorical flexibility," students study ways of understanding writing so they can "write effectively across multiple situations" (SLCC, 2016–2017). While full-time faculty are not required to use a standard syllabus, all composition courses focus on the same objectives—Need,

Critical Thought, Conventions, Genre, Audience, and Processes—with the idea that writing in any situation is improved with attention to each. Such a varied approach to writing is designed to help prepare students to be successful writers "in their other classes, at work, and for civic and personal reasons" (SLCC, 2016–2017).

One SLCC faculty member explained that FYC at SLCC is often (though not exclusively) taught using a "genre approach." A genre approach is grounded in research that shows that learning to write a particular genre within a particular context does not necessarily help students be rhetorically effective across other genres and contexts (Beaufort, 2008). Students benefit more from meta theories that help to interpret how to effectively write across variable contexts, according to the faculty member. For example, rhetorical theory is meta because it is equally applicable across contexts; as a result, studying rhetoric improves the ability to communicate effectively across variable contexts. Such a benefit is based on the idea that broad overarching conceptual models "should be made explicitly available to students so they have a framework... to analyze writing tasks and complete them" (Yancey, Robertson, & Taczak, 2014, p. 30; see also: Beaufort, 2008). Teaching "genre awareness," for example, can help students see not only how writing often takes recognizable forms but also that such forms are context dependent. "The idea," Clark and Hernandez (2011) remind us, is that "a metacognitive understanding of genre can help students make connections between the type of writing assigned in the Composition course... and the writing genres they encounter in other disciplines" (p. 65), or across their "academic, professional, civic and personal lives," as specified on the SLCC English Department website.

Educational Possibilities at Community Colleges

Most, if not all, universities require international students to demonstrate college-level English fluency for matriculation, often in the form of a standardized English proficiency exam such as the TOEFL®. Community colleges, however, have a tradition of open access that includes less emphasis on standardized examination for acceptance (Hagedorn & Lee, 2005), and thus regularly accept students at all levels of English fluency. The students participating in this study were able to begin a college career that would have been much more difficult to achieve if access were dependent on passing a difficult language exam, the preparation for which must be paid for out of pocket.

FYC course credit from a community college also helps students gain access to a four-year institution. While the University of Utah requires a TOEFL® score of 80 or higher for incoming international first-year students, international transfer students can use FYC grades in place of the TOEFL®. If students receive a grade of C or higher in their FYC classes at a community college, this credit is recognized as a demonstration of English fluency, and the English proficiency test requirement is waived. Further, the same is true at many highly competitive public research universities across the country.

This tradition of openness regarding admission at CCs allows Korean international students (and others like them) to begin their education and gain credentials with which they can then enter a university. The TOEFL® is, as one participant put it, "hard for international students," but it is even harder for those who cannot afford the kinds of English education necessary for passing the TOEFL®. So, although "open access in admissions" allows students to begin taking college classes, it is the FYC course credit they earn that allows students to bypass the TOEFL® and matriculate at many prestigious universities across the United States. Community colleges support Korean students from lower-income backgrounds into U.S. higher education, but they also support students in their Korean cultural pathway.

And there's more: a writing education that offers preparation for rhetorical success beyond strictly academic contexts goes further than university transfer credit. An education in rhetorical flexibility may better position newly arrived international students (and many others such as immigrant and refugee students) to accomplish the rhetorical goals of their daily lives. Writing to audiences beyond those of U.S. academia, for example, is preparation for interacting effectively with the various audiences with which students will communicate outside their classrooms. One participant spoke in detail about an open letter assignment where she was asked to write a "letter to a specific group of people but it should be understandable to other people who are not the intended audience." She indicated that this assignment emphasized the ways writing for a particular audience can provide direction for the author to "go the right way." She maintains that this and other assignments helped develop a sense for how to avoid letting her "topic get broad," but also that "there should be an audience to [know how to] do the right things." Such a rich interpretation of the role audience plays in writing effectively, coupled with practice writing to non-academic audiences, positions students to communicate effectively across the varied audiences in their day-to-day activities outside of school. While still preparing for academic contexts, students are also preparing to write, for example, to landlords or prospective employers, both situations encountered by my participants.

A writing education preparing students for rhetorical success across contexts means also increased engagement with the world outside U.S. academia, and thus with the broader culture of the United States. The open letter assignment, for example, asks students to consider what kinds of rhetorical choices are best suited for audiences beyond the college. Such a consideration involves asking questions not just about what reading audiences in the United States find compelling but also the culture in which one's writing can be recognized as more or less compelling.

Participants agreed that success at the university level requires not only academic literacy but also literacy in the culture of the United States. Being a college student (in and out of school) in the U.S. is not the same as in South Korea, so students new to the U.S. must learn to accomplish their educational and personal goals in a new cultural context as well. Several student participants remarked that taking classes at SLCC before transferring to a university helped them to learn about U.S. culture and that this learning was helpful both during and after the transfer process. For example, when I asked one participant "Who should go to community college?" he told me that he thought "every Korean needs to study [at community college] first... because Koreans need to understand American culture first... and then... transfer." Not only can a writing education in rhetorical flexibility help prepare students for rhetorical success across the varied audiences they regularly encounter, but students may also gain cultural knowledge with which they are better equipped to accomplish the goals of their daily lives.

Participants overwhelmingly expressed positive experiences with FYC at SLCC. When I asked if FYC helped student participants improve their writing in English, everyone answered affirmatively. One participant, for example, indicated that when he initially arrived at SLCC he was not prepared for the writing asked of him; he said he was "bad at writing." But he also explained that he learned many things in the U.S., such as that he used to "spend lots of time [considering what words] to start [writing]" and now he had "learned how to make [his writing process] fast." In addition, consistent with the writing instructor guide for the English department at SLCC that states that "students will develop an ability and confidence to navigate writing processes," students unanimously indicated they gained confidence in their writing. Given these experiences, it may come with little surprise that all students successfully transferred to a university, and most to the University of Utah.

Avoiding the "Cliffs"

All of the student participants expressed satisfaction with the education they received at SLCC, education that may not have been possible otherwise. Whether it's the institutional access afforded students through community college acceptance, the ability to bypass difficult standardized English proficiency exams necessary for entrance into a university, or the language and cultural learning that FYC offers, students have educational opportunity not otherwise possible, and with it, a chance at the "finish line."

The participants in this study were aware of the Korean cultural pathway that was expected of them. Participants knew that not only did they need a college degree for a higher-level position at Samsung or Hyundai, but they were also in competition with others who had college degrees. The students also knew that they would need to make themselves stand out from others with similar credentials.

For better or for worse, the United States has some of the best institutions of higher education in the world. For South Koreans, however, a university education in the United States has specific social capital different from other countries. For example, in 2011 a professor from Seoul National University published an article in *The Korea Herald* and indicated that "American universities are well known for their rigorous academic training in undergraduate education," but if South Korean people "have no aptitude for study" they should "not enter college in America" but should instead start a "professional career early by finding a job" (S.K. Kim, 2011, para. 1). In fact, a student participant once told me that "having a degree from an American college can be... something special... compared to other students who went to college in Korea."

What I take from this is that the "American college" is not just one part of the culturally established pathway; it's a *good* part, and one with the opportunity to reach that finish line without going off the "cliffs on both sides." I'm not saying that a college degree from a university in the United States or the education that degree entails equates directly to a good job in South Korea, but the value many in Korea interpret for a U.S. university education might be enough for some to get their feet in the door. Moreover, given the learning that participants found at SLCC and beyond at their transfer institutions, a foot in the door might be all that is needed to reach that "finish line." Completing FYC at a community college or transferring to a prestigious university is not the same as a salaried career, but it offers students a route to that level of success from which they may otherwise have been excluded.

Community colleges do not provide all the higher education Korean international students want, but they can keep some students away from those cliffs. For those unable to afford an expensive English language education, for those unable to pass difficult language proficiency exams necessary for entering a university in the U.S., and for those who come to the U.S. with no local peer support group, there is an alternative. Community colleges across the U.S. offer educational opportunities that give South Korean international students a world-class education and a chance at a salaried career. Community colleges do far more than accept and educate students—they take students one step closer to their hopes and dreams.

On a final note, in light of the alternative paths made possible through community colleges, if there is more than one path, then there cannot be cliffs on both sides.

REFERENCES

Ahn, B. K. (1995). The teaching of writing in Korea. *Journal of Asian Pacific Communication, 6*(1), 67–76.

Altbach, P. G., Reisberg, L., & Rumbley, L. E. (2009). *Trends in global higher education: Tracking an academic revolution: A Report prepared for the UNESCO 2009 World Conference on Higher Education.* Paris: United Nations Educational, Scientific and Cultural Organization.

Beaufort, A. (2008). *College writing and beyond: A new framework for university writing instruction.* Boulder: University Press of Colorado.

Byun, S Y., & Kim K.K. (2010). Educational inequality in South Korea: The widening socioeconomic gap in student achievement. In E. Hannum, H. Park, & Y. Butler (Eds.), *Globalization, changing demographics, and educational challenges in East Asia* (pp. 155–182). Bingley, England: Emerald.

Cho, B. E. (2004). Issues concerning Korean learners of English: English education in Korea and some common difficulties of Korean students. *The East Asian Learner, 1*(2), 31–36.

Cho, D. W. (2009). Science journal paper writing in an EFL context: The case of Korea. *English for Specific Purposes, 28*(4), 230–239.

Clark, I. L., & Hernandez, A. (2011). Genre awareness, academic argument, and transferability. *The WAC Journal, 22*, 65–78.

Hagedorn, L., & Lee, M. (2005). *International Community College Students: The Neglected Minority?* ERIC Document Reproduction Service No. ED490516.

Jahng, K. E. (2011). English education for young children in South Korea: not just a collective neurosis of English fever! *Perspectives in Education, 29*(2), 61–69.

Kim, K. K. (2005). Educational gap in Korea and determinant factors. *Korean Journal of Sociology of Education, 15*(3), 1–27.

Kim, S.-K. (2011, 30 August). Korean vs. American universities. *The Korea Herald.* Retrieved from koreaherald.com/view.php?ud=20110830000055

Kim, T. (2008). Korean L2 writers' previous writing experience: L1 literacy development in school. *University of Hawai'i Second Language Studies Papers, 27*(1), 103–154.

Kim, Y., & Kim, J. (2005). Teaching Korean university writing class. *Asian EFL, 7*(2), 1–15.

Kwon, O., Yoshida, K., Negishi, M., & Naganuma, N. (2004). A comparison of English proficiency of Korean, Japanese and Chinese high school students. *English Teaching, 59*(4), 3–21.

Lee, C. J. (2005). Korean education fever and private tutoring. *KEDI Journal of Educational Policy, 2*(1), 99–108.

National Center for Educational Statistics. (2019). International education. Retrieved from https://nces.ed.gov/programs/coe/indicator_cac.asp

Park, H., & Kim, K. K. (Eds.). (2014). *Korean education in changing economic and demographic contexts.* Dordrecht, The Netherlands: Springer.

Park, J. K. (2009). 'English fever' in South Korea: Its history and symptoms. *English Today, 25*(1), 50–57.

Rousculp, T. (2015, March 15). *The state of writing at Salt Lake Community College: Writing inventory and climate assessment.* Retrieved from www.slcc.edu/wac/docs/state-of-writing-at-slcc-inventory-and-climate-assessment.pdf

Seidman, I. (2013). *Interviewing as qualitative research: A guide for researchers in education and the social sciences* (3rd ed.). New York: Teachers College Press.

Shim, E. (2009). An investigation of secondary English teachers' perceptions of writing instruction. 현대영어교육, *10*(1), 114–130.

Salt Lake Community College. (2016–2017). English composition sequence. Retrieved from http://www.slcc.edu/wac/required-composition-sequence.aspx

Salt Lake Community College. (2018). Student demographics. Retrieved from http://performance.slcc.edu/Factbook/2017-18/B_student_demographics/index.html

Yancey, K., Robertson, L., & Taczak, K. (2014). *Writing across contexts: Transfer, composition, and sites of writing.* Boulder: University Press of Colorado.

13

First-Year Composition Faculty in a Changing Community College Policy Landscape: Engagement, Agency, and Leadership in the Midst of Reform

George C. Bunch
UNIVERSITY OF CALIFORNIA, SANTA CRUZ

Ann Endris
CABRILLO COLLEGE

Kylie Alisa Kenner
UNIVERSITY OF CALIFORNIA, SANTA CRUZ

The community college policy landscape is changing—at times dramatically—in ways that have a direct impact on first-year composition (FYC) courses and students' preparation for them. In states across the country, reform efforts are calling for the acceleration of students' progress into and through college-level composition, by changing testing and placement policies, shortening or eliminating developmental English sequences, moving toward concurrent co-requisite supports for underprepared students, and asking students to enroll in "guided pathways" that provide streamlined course-taking options for students from the beginning of their community college studies (Bailey, Jaggars, & Jenkins, 2015; Rodriguez, Cuellar Mejia, & Johnson, 2018).

Some reforms have been initiated by the ranks of composition faculty members themselves (Hern & Snell, 2013; TYCA, 2016). In other cases, the policies have been the result of external pressure from what Adler-Kassner (2017) has called the Educational Industrial Complex: "a collection of NGOs (nongovernmental organizations), granting agencies, businesses, consulting firms, policy institutes, actions, and actors" (p. 320). English faculty have expressed concerns about "legislative imperatives" that exclude faculty from the decision-making, fail to draw on their disciplinary knowledge and "ignore the academic and material realities of two-year college students' lives" (TYCA, 2015, p. 229).

Warnke and Higgins (2018) describe two dominant, and opposing faculty positions in the current community college reform landscape: "*enthusiastic reformer*" and "*reform resister*." Many faculty members feel torn between colleagues on these two ends of the spectrum—that is, between those who "work to design, implement, and scale reform models within the local context, often with little more than cursory knowledge of national trends or disciplinary grounding" and "those who adopt a posture of totalized resistance to protect a legacy of faculty autonomy, academic rigor, institutional knowledge, and humanist endeavor" (pp. 363–364). As a way out, Warnke and Higgins argue for "a position of critical engagement" with reform: "a 'third space' of resistance to both corporatization *and* the instructional status quo" (p. 363, emphasis in original). They argue that this third position allows faculty "to move from an ad hoc, defensive posture to a consistent, offensive position with a reliable framework and value system" (p. 363).

This chapter discusses how, in the context of impending change in policies governing testing, placement, and curriculum, English faculty members at one community college have positioned themselves as agents and leaders in ways that complicate Warnke and Higgins' categories. We describe the context and process under which changes in the college's writing sequence and curriculum have occurred and analyze a range of current faculty perspectives toward programmatic reforms. We acknowledge that reform is always negotiated, constructed, enacted, and resisted at the local level, and that each college has particular institutional histories and contexts that must be taken into account. None-theless, we offer recommendations that we hope will be of some value for faculty in a variety of contexts as they work to improve the quality and impact of their programs in ways that allow them to marshal their professional and disciplinary experience, expertise, and judgment—simultaneously advocating for students' successful progress toward academic and professional goals and the writing outcomes that English faculty desire.

We bring several perspectives to these issues. George, a former high school ESL teacher, is currently a university researcher studying K–12 and community college issues of policy and practice impacting linguistically diverse students. Ann, an adjunct faculty member in a student-success program at the college described here, was hired by the college to coordinate a state grant designed to involve full-time English faculty in preparing for the reforms. Kylie has taught FYC in four-year public universities and is currently a doctoral candidate studying student support initiatives at community colleges. This chapter draws primarily on three sources: Ann's experience working with English faculty preparing for and implementing reforms at the college, responses from an anonymous survey of English faculty at the college, and an interview with the dean overseeing the college's English department.

National and State Context

Rodriguez, Cuellar Mejia, & Johnson (2018) summarized national and state research demonstrating a number of issues with community college testing and placement policies that led to recent reforms. The authors documented problems such as the inadequacy of placement tests to predict students' capacity, the fact that many students placed in developmental education would have been more likely to succeed if placed directly into transfer-level courses, and the "profound effect" that placement decisions have on the probability of students reaching their degree and transfer goals. Student success rates for groups traditionally underrepresented in higher education have been particularly concerning. Our own past research has explored problems with testing and placement at California community colleges for students who grew up speaking languages other than English, including minimal or misleading information provided by many colleges to students about testing and placement policies and their impacts. We also researched the use of tests not designed for language-minority populations, and the fact that "multiple measures," despite being required for placement by state law, were often "unavailable, unsolicited, or underutilized" at most colleges we studied (Bunch et al., 2011, p. ix; see also Bunch & Endris, 2012). In terms of instruction, Grubb (2013) found that the dominant pedagogical approach in developmental English courses in the California community colleges he studied was "remedial pedagogy"—that is, a focus on teaching discrete subskills in the same ways that have failed students in the past.

In California, the changes facing English departments in community colleges are significant. Assembly Bill (AB) 705, a new law intended to widen access to transfer-level English, was passed unanimously and signed into law in October 2017. The law states that for those intending to transfer to four-year institutions, colleges "shall maximize the probability that a student will enter and complete transfer-level coursework in English and mathematics *within a one-year timeframe*" (AB 705, 2017, emphasis added). It also mandates that high school coursework, grades, and/or GPA—instead of placement tests—be used as the primary mechanism for placement into English courses. Colleges may require students to enroll in "concurrent support" while they take a transfer-level English course, "but only if it is determined that the support will increase their likelihood of passing" the transfer-level course.

At the time we conducted our study, the state was moving to fully implement AB 705 by the next academic year. "Default placement rules" issued by the California Community College Chancellor's Office and the Academic Senate for California Community Colleges stated that, without statistical evidence that alternative placements lead to greater student success into and through transfer-level English courses, colleges could not block access to transfer-level courses for *any* student, regardless of GPA, who graduated from high school within the past ten years and who has an identified goal of earning a community college degree or transferring to a four-year institution (Hope & Stankasas, 2018; Rodriguez, Cuellar Mejia & Johnson, 2018). As a rationale for this policy, the Chancellor's implementation guidelines cited completion data demonstrating that even students with the lowest high school GPAs (below 1.9) placed directly in college-level English had a dramatically greater chance of passing FYC in one year (42.6 percent) than did with those with similar GPAs placed in one level below (12 percent).

Colleges could still *offer* a developmental English course to be taken before transfer-level English, but such a course could not be required unless data established that students placed in that course have a greater likelihood of success in transfer-level English than those placed initially into the transfer-level course. Further, the regulations stated that "the placement must not result in the student being required to spend more than two semesters …to complete the transfer-level work," effectively ending the existence of multiple-semester developmental English sequences, previously common at many colleges. (Some requirements were differentiated for speakers of languages other than English. For example, the law provided a three-year window, instead of the one year established for other students, as the timeframe in which colleges must maximize the probability of students' enrollment in transfer-level English.)

As a result of the new legislation, English departments across California's 115 community colleges, like those in other states responding to similar policies, had to decide what to do with their current developmental English courses; how to best support culturally, linguistically, and academically diverse populations; and what curricular and pedagogical approaches to take to FYC itself. This chapter discusses how English faculty at the college studied addressed these issues during a two-year period that began about a year before AB 705 was passed and ended one year before full implementation of the law was required. The period discussed stretched from the faculty's initial exploration of issues and potential solutions to the adoption of new placement procedures and development of a new developmental English sequence. Implementation of the new structures is not addressed.

Reform at One College

The college studied, located on the central coast of California, is a public Hispanic Serving Institution that enrolls roughly 17,000 students. The college has one main suburban campus serving a medium-sized city that is approximately 75 percent white and 20 percent Latino, and a smaller campus in a nearby agricultural town with a Latino population of over 80 percent. The college's demographics have changed dramatically over the years, from an overwhelmingly white student body several decades ago to today's overall enrollment in which 44 percent of students identify as Hispanic and 45 percent identify as White students.

The English Department is one of the largest departments at the college, with 17 full-time faculty members and 27 adjunct faculty. About a decade ago, the faculty approved an acceleration model for a small learning community allowing students placing two levels below transfer-level English to bypass the one-level-below course based on a portfolio reviewed by a committee of English faculty. However, as has been the case with such reforms across the country, only a tiny fraction of the colleges' students were enrolled in that particular program, which targeted "high-risk" students, included an intensive course at the start of the semester, and required students to enroll simultaneously in English, student success courses, and other academic courses specific to the goals of the learning community. At that time, the faculty seriously considered an acceleration model for the entire English department that was being used at a nearby college but ultimately decided against it due to limited data available at that time on its success.

When the opportunity presented itself in 2015 to apply for a grant from the newly established, state-funded Basic Skills Student Outcomes and Transformation (BSSOT) Program, the English faculty agreed, although not enthusiastically. Faculty were interested in the financial resources the grant would bring for professional development and tutoring but generally wary of the impending placement reforms. The BSSOT program provided funding for selected colleges to adopt evidence-based principles and practices for basic skills assessment, placement, instruction, and student support. Similar to the reforms that would later be mandated by AB 705, the program was designed to promote greater access to transfer-level courses, given data showing (1) that more than three-quarters of incoming students in the California community college system were assessed and placed into developmental courses in mathematics, English, or reading; (2) that few of these students successfully complete transfer-level coursework in these subjects and reach their educational goals; and (3) that research showed that many students would have had a higher probability of success by enrolling initially in transfer-level courses ("BSSOT Program", 2018).

The focal college was awarded a three-year BSSOT grant in July 2016. The two primary initiatives of the college's proposal, supported by the local Academic Senate and English and math departments, were (1) incorporating the use of high school GPA and transcripts for placement among the "multiple measures" used in addition to placement test scores and (2) researching "acceleration" models to pilot an "instructional and/or acceleration redesign" of the English course sequence by Spring 2018. In moving toward these goals, the college promised to establish a "redesign team," review relevant research, engage in professional development, and examine "throughput" data, which shifts the focus from individual course success rates to the percentage of students placed in remedial coursework who eventually pass a transfer-level course within a given time frame.

Although few faculty members expressed enthusiasm about the project at its outset, in hindsight the grant provided faculty the opportunity to delve into the research, study acceleration models implemented at other colleges, have difficult but productive conversations with their colleagues, and develop local ownership of reforms that were ultimately mandated statewide.

The department began by forming a small faculty "acceleration team," consisting of the BSSOT grant manager (Ann) and three full-time English faculty members, who agreed to meet twice per month. Based on the grant proposal, the committee was charged in the first year with examining English "pipeline" data with the support of institutional researchers, reviewing acceleration models and relevant national research, creating a proposal for acceleration and/or other instructional redesign to pilot in 2018, and informing and updating the full English department on the team's work. The team was also asked to explore the work of the California Acceleration Project (CAP), which would ultimately become influential in faculty efforts throughout the reform process. CAP is a faculty-led professional development network that supports efforts to provide high-challenge, high-support pedagogy and advocates for student access to transfer-level coursework with co-requisite support (Hern & Snell, 2013).

To provide time and space for research and exploration, the grant manager urged English faculty to refrain from decision making until after the committee's first academic year of work (2016–2017). Over the course of this year, the team conducted a literature review, attended CAP conferences where they participated in workshops presented by faculty from other colleges that had implemented co-requisite designs, and listened to student speakers describe their experiences of direct placement into transfer-level courses with and without co-requisite models of support.

Simultaneously, the faculty group became knowledgeable about findings from the Multiple Measures Assessment Project (MMAP), a statewide project aimed at developing a placement tool that used high school performance for placement into college courses and to assess the predictive validity of such data (Multiple Measures Assessment Project Research Team, 2014). The acceleration team also met with their own college research analysts to review local data regarding placement and throughput rates. Local data showed that, similar to statewide data in California and elsewhere, only a small percentage of basic skills students were successfully completing transfer-level English. These outcomes were particularly alarming to the acceleration committee members when coupled with data showing that placement tests disproportionately placed students of color into remedial courses.

When, during spring of that first year, it came time for the English department as a whole to determine if it would implement MMAP statewide rule sets and use high school GPA for placement, the faculty at large was skeptical of research demonstrating the accuracy of high school GPA data for placement. Some faculty were particularly concerned that the varied preparation students receive at different local high schools and the potential for grade inflation at particular schools would render predictions made by GPA invalid. The acceleration team presented MMAP statewide rule sets and the success rates of students at colleges with varying demographics that had already implemented the use of high school GPA for placement. The team also strategized how best to speak to a group of faculty who were not necessarily convinced by numbers alone, no matter how dramatic the statistics. Ultimately, we believe that it was the combination of compelling data, presentations from the acceleration committee to the full English faculty, and multiple individual conversations that led the department to vote affirmatively toward the end of Spring 2017 to move forward with utilizing high school GPA in addition to placement tests—about six months *before* the passage of AB 705 that would ultimately mandate the use of GPA and the elimination of most placement tests altogether.

At the close of the first academic year, about the time that the English department was voting to implement the MMAP recommendations, the acceleration team discussed eliminating entirely the lowest level remedial English course (two levels below transfer) and implementing a model of co-requisite support for transfer-level courses. The committee recruited five additional full-time English faculty members, and this larger group attended a three-day CAP Summer Institute together. The expanded committee spent the second year of the grant calibrating the team's vision, proposing major reforms to the larger department, galvanizing support from administrators, counselors, and other departments, and conducting two full-day workshops on curriculum and pedagogy for the English faculty at large.

At the start of this second year (Fall 2017), the acceleration team brought a structural reform proposal to the full English department for discussion and a vote. The department voted to dramatically increase access to transfer-level English by eliminating the lowest-level English course and developing the new co-requisite course model. As outlined in Table 13.1, a new assessment process would begin utilizing cumulative high school GPA for placement for Fall 2018. Students with a GPA below 2.3 would receive a placement *recommendation* of English 100 (one level below transfer-level English), although all students, regardless of GPA or assessment test scores, could gain access to English 1A Plus by participating in a learning community. Students could additionally gain access to transfer-level English through placement test scores.

TABLE 13.1. English Course Placement Procedures Before Fall 2018 and During 2018–2019 Academic Year

| Level | Before Fall 2018 | | Fall 2018–Spring 2019 | |
	Placement based on	Course	Placement based on	Course
Transfer level	Placement test	English 1A	Placement test OR GPA: 2.6 or above	English 1A
			Placement test OR GPA: 2.3–2.59	English 1A Plus co-requisite
One level below	Placement test	English 100	Placement test OR GPA: 2.3 or below	English 100
Two levels below	Placement test	English 255		

Note: During 2018–2019 academic year, students who elected to participate in a learning community were all placed into English 1A Plus co-requisite regardless of high school GPA or placement test score.

To further broaden the engagement of the English department, the acceleration team facilitated two six-hour workshops during the Spring 2018 semester that focused on the curriculum and pedagogy for the new co-requisite course to be piloted in Fall 2018. The team built the first workshop around the five CAP principles for accelerated curricula and pedagogy: (1) "backward design" from the transfer-level courses, (2) student relevant, thinking-oriented curriculum, (3) built-in, "just-in-time" remediation, (4) low-stakes, collaborative practice in preparation for individual assessment, and (5) intentional support for students' affective needs (Hern & Snell, 2013). Acceleration team faculty recognized in each other expertise in different parts of these five core areas and designated faculty pairs to develop materials and facilitate experiential activities during the workshop. For the second workshop, the acceleration team designed opportunities for their colleagues to integrate the co-requisite model with other relevant endeavors such as Reading Apprenticeship (Schoenbach, Greenleaf, & Murphy, 2012), OnCourse (Downing, 2017), and Culturally Responsive Teaching (Gay, 2000).

The workshops were attended by about 30 English, ESL, and library faculty as well as interested administrators and staff—a good turnout in the eyes of the team. The workshops not only provided a venue for the acceleration team to further explain the reforms, but they also created a space for cross-departmental conversations and collaborations. For example, the attendance of the library faculty initiated a collaboration to re-design a one-unit library course that continues to be a required co-requisite for transfer-level English.

The reform efforts at the start of this second year were truly faculty-driven. In contrast to the assumption that current reforms are necessarily advanced by administrators against the will of resistant faculty members, it was administrators at this college who initially displayed a tepid response to the acceleration team's proposal to eliminate the course two levels below transfer-level and to establish a co-requisite course. Administrators were initially concerned about the financial implications of eliminating established courses and developing new co-requisites, the ability for students to succeed in the proposed model, and potential negative consequences for enrollments in other departments, such as ESL and Reading. The administration began to embrace the faculty-proposed reforms as it became clear from the statewide context that redesigning basic skills sequences was a critical step for implementing Guided Pathways, another reform gaining notice (and resources) in California and nationally (Bailey, Jaggars, & Jenkins, 2015). Materials provided by the statewide Chancellor's office defined a key principle of Guided Pathways design as broadening access to transfer-level courses through accurate placement via multiple measures and allowing students to enroll in college-level curricula with supports as an alternative to placement into developmental English and math ("Guided Pathways Electronic Toolkit," 2016).

With the passage of AB 705 legislation later that same semester, the reforms spearheaded by the English faculty had prepared the department, at least structurally, for the major implementation requirements being prepared by the Chancellor's Office that would be released the following summer. That is, the structural reforms enacted by the English department had already significantly broadened access to transfer-level English. The college's enrollment data for developmental and transfer-level English courses in Fall 2017 (before departmental reforms) show that 54 percent of students were enrolled in transfer-level English, with that percentage increasing to 88 percent in Fall 2018, when the department piloted the use of high school GPA for placement and the co-requisite support model. To meet AB 705 implementation requirements by Fall 2019, the department had only 12 percent of students remaining for which to provide open access to transfer-level English. The previous structural work allowed the faculty to focus on the even more difficult work of determining how to provide critical support services to students in transfer-level coursework, including the pedagogical and curricular changes needed in the AB 705 context.

Faculty Perspectives

Responses from nine English faculty members to a brief questionnaire sent to all department members reveal a range of perspectives on the reforms, right before the college's piloting of the new placement system broadening access to transfer-level English and the co-requisite support course. Using Google Forms so that respondents could be assured of anonymity, we sent a short qualitative survey to all 17 full-time and 27 adjunct English faculty members. Among other questions, we asked about the promises and challenges they saw associated with the reforms, how their thinking had changed during the process, what kind of support they had received to prepare for the changes, and what additional supports would be helpful. Given the relatively low response rate, we make no claims that the comments are representative of the experiences of the department as a whole. Nonetheless, the range and evolution of faculty members' perspectives are illuminating.

Promises and Challenges

In response to whether they would recommend similar reforms to other states, a question we asked to gauge individual support for the reforms, five of the nine respondents wrote that they strongly recommended the reforms, three indicated they were not yet sure, and one recommended against the reforms. When asked about the reforms' promising aspects, instructors pointed to increasing opportunities for students' success. Several noted advances in equity and social justice and argued that the reforms addressed the problem of students being "mired in remediation" and the "systemic racism" built into higher education generally. One instructor took a more pragmatic approach, explaining that the new system "saves both taxpayers and students money, and it potentially saves students time."

In contrast, one respondent had difficulty envisioning any promise of the reform, suggesting that the reform was a "conscious effort" to hurt—and subsequently push out—students of color and students with disabilities to support "the academically privileged" and to save money. Perhaps not surprisingly, this instructor also offered a vehement critique of the reforms when responding to the question about challenges: "The proposal sets [students] up for failure. They will be unprepared and ill equipped to handle rigorous academic writing."

Respondents who generally indicated support for the reforms also raised concerns. When asked about challenges associated with the reforms, four respondents explained that the largest challenge was changing the perspectives of faculty members committed to the status quo. One described this process as addressing "antiquated ideas" from some faculty, and another (a veteran with 30 years of experience) characterized the largest challenge as confronting "resistance by naysayers." Others had substantive concerns with various aspects of the reforms, including communicating the changes to students, collaborating with advisors and faculty who might be resistant to the changing landscape, and rethinking teaching practices to support a wider range of students. Three respondents spoke specifically about the challenge of communicating the co-requisite course to students due to inconsistent messages from counselors and instructors and because students were reluctant to take an additional course.

When asked about the implications of these changes for students designated as English learners in high school and students with disabilities, instructors also held various views. Some commended a new transfer-level, first-year composition ESL course being developed at the college, and others suggested that AB 705 would pose no additional challenges to second language learners or that it would actually increase equity for these students. In contrast, some felt that the reforms would present challenges for students designated as English learners during their K–12 schooling, and one wondered whether the changes would deter those students from enrolling in community college. Three respondents worried that students with disabilities may not get the support they need, and one of those three explained that the reforms could push students with disabilities out of college. Two faculty members, though, were adamant that the reforms gave students with disabilities a "seat at the table" and opportunities for more equitable education.

Changing Perspectives

Although two of the nine respondents reported that the reforms matched what they had previously believed about teaching and learning, five explained that their views had changed after discussions with colleagues and access to student data. One instructor was "skeptical" at first, but with support and information from colleagues "quickly came to see that the reforms not only needed to be embraced by individual teachers but by our college community as a whole and statewide." On the other hand, two respondents explained that their skepticism remained despite reform preparation and implementation: One was waiting to see how the pilot semester would unfold, and the other continued to firmly believe the reforms would hurt students.

Access to data, professional development experiences, and involvement as members of the acceleration team or other faculty leadership groups all seemed related to instructors' evolving engagement in and support for the reforms. Access to both quantitative and qualitative data about the reforms was an important factor in instructors' developing ideas about the state-mandated changes. One respondent had "conducted research, read widely on the subject, held meetings, formed committees, sub-committees, and then expanded this work to reach out to our department through training, discussion, and again more meetings." Three respondents noted that access to data had gradually helped change their positions from skeptical to positive, and three highlighted the important role that they felt future data collection would play in the continued implementation of the reforms in California and across the country. On the other hand, the faculty member opposed to the reforms who complained of receiving "little to no training" remained unconvinced: "I've been assured there's sound data behind it. I wonder."

Faculty pointed to the importance of leadership opportunities for themselves and their colleagues, reporting that such opportunities allowed them to access data and professional development, to explore how other colleges were navigating the changing landscape, and to advise colleagues. Two individuals who said that they did not have the time or resources to serve on a team saw the leadership roles played by their colleagues as invaluable. Finally, instructors pointed to the importance of professional development to prepare for the new course structures. Four respondents noted the important role of the BSSOT grant and team in guiding their understanding of and preparation for the reforms. More generally, faculty discussed learning directly from professional development opportunities provided by the department, including those described earlier developed by the acceleration team, as well as learning from colleagues who had been studying and beginning to implement the changes. Respondents also discussed the role that "communities of practice" played in their preparation for the legislative change. At the same time, almost all respondents pointed to the need for more professional development than they had currently received. Three emphasized the need to pay instructors, including the large number of adjunct faculty, for engaging in professional development activities.

Comments from the Dean

The dean overseeing the English Department generally shared perspectives expressed by faculty members who were sympathetic to the aims of the reforms, but he also raised sharper concerns than most faculty about the rapid pace of implementation, the potentially deleterious impact on particular students, and the limited resources available for faculty development. Describing himself as having a "love-hate" relationship with AB 705, he found the data on improved student success in acceleration models "compelling." But he also worried about how to effectively implement AB 705, especially for the one-quarter of students who he said the research shows are likely to be unsuccessful in passing college-level English, even at the higher GPA grade bands—"those folks who are going to need a little more help," especially second language learners, students re-entering college from the workforce, and students with disabilities.

The dean said that one of his biggest concerns was that English faculty are not typically prepared to tackle the kinds of challenges that they will face in teaching students from a wider variety of backgrounds in college-level composition courses under the new legislation. Despite the significant increase in the number of students who will now have access to FYC, the dean argued that neither graduate school preparation nor employment qualifications for English faculty have changed to match the new state of affairs. He maintained that, except for those prepared by the few universities with graduate programs in college composition, most full-time community college writing faculty were trained by English departments in either literature or creative writing, without significant preparation in teaching writing. He said faculty typically have had even less preparation in teaching reading, working with students who are learning English as a second language, or accommodating students with disabilities, all areas that they will need to be familiar with in light of the reforms. The dean also noted the limited funding available for professional development on campus and pointed out that there was no designated funding allocated in AB 705 for faculty professional development, making it "one of those unfunded mandates."

The dean emphasized that English faculty members themselves were doing everything possible to prepare to meet students' needs:

> The faculty here have really jumped in with both feet and said, "Okay we're going to do this—let's do this." And I like seeing that excitement. I like seeing the camaraderie of the folks who are working together. I think they've also been understanding of their colleagues who have had qualms about change.

He also pointed out that even the faculty who have not "embraced" the changes are open to learning: "They've said 'look I just need more convincing.' And their colleagues will do that. Or they'll direct them to somebody else. I mean it's not always smooth sailing, but I've seen it a lot worse." But the dean also worried that faculty would expend more effort than was advisable and sustainable "because they want to do the right thing even if they haven't been adequately trained" and "sometimes that's a recipe for burnout for our faculty . . . taking on more than they should. Trying to assure everybody that they can beat the learning curve—while also teaching their classes and trying to catch this moving target."

He said that, moving forward, especially without a large budget for professional development, the college would most likely rely on the "train the trainer" model, with individuals or small groups of faculty members attending conferences and workshops and sharing materials and learnings with their colleagues back at the college.

Conclusions and Implications

Returning to the categories suggested by Warnke and Higgins (2018), one faculty member responding to our survey could fairly be characterized as a "resister," and undoubtedly others who did not complete the survey might also fit that category. Several faculty members began the process as "enthusiastic reformers," and others came to this position over time. However, as indicated by their responses to the survey and our own work with the department over the past several years, most faculty approached the suggested reforms initially with caution or skepticism, neither as resolute resisters or passionate reformers. Through their work over the two years of grant-supported work, digging into data, consulting alternative placement systems, considering curricular reforms, and interacting with their colleagues, first a core small group of English faculty and then others in the department began to take on these issues as agents—and even leaders—of the reforms. Through this process, there was something different going on than what Warnke and Higgins (2018) describe as the "familiar clash" between, on one hand, "corporate-minded forces seeking to address demonstrable gaps in equitable student success" and, on the other, "instructional solidarity" among resisting faculty "who see themselves as doing inherently good work beyond reproach" (pp. 363–365). It could be argued that many of the English faculty members at the college could be placed into the "third space" category that Warnke and Higgins term "critical reformers." But, in contrast to those who "make it their business to engage with the structural *consequences* of reforms" presumably put in motion by others (Warnke & Higgins, p. 364, emphasis added), the faculty members at this college exercised more agency and leadership in identifying and researching the nature of the problems at hand and in developing, piloting, and advocating for potential solutions themselves.

Data released by the college in January 2019 indicated that these faculty efforts might have paid off: Despite broadly widening access, success rates in transfer-level English sections remained the same from Fall 2017 to Fall 2018 (69 percent). But we do not want to present an overly rosy portrait of the reform process at this college. The English department had difficult conversations while grappling with challenging decisions over a two-year period. While the majority of the department ultimately voted to support the proposed reforms, there remained critical concerns, some highlighted in our discussion of faculty responses to our survey, that continue to this day. Throughout the process, faculty also voiced concerns regarding the validity of statewide data to predict success rates at the local level, especially regarding students graduating from different high schools within the district, and whether allowing students to self report their GPA would result in students' inflating their records. They were also concerned about whether the reforms might result in students passing transfer-level English with a weaker set of writing skills that could jeopardize their success in future classes, English or otherwise. With the passage of AB 705, faculty expressed fear that the Chancellor's Office was advocating a "one size fits all model" that would leave some students behind and have other unforeseen consequences.

Nor is it our intention to downplay the power of the "Educational Industrial Complex" (Adler-Kassner, 2017), the problems associated with larger neoliberal influence on higher education, or the serious concerns that many English faculty, across California and the United States, have about impending reforms (TYCA, 2015, 2016). We are not endorsing AB 705 itself nor any other particular version of the reforms we discuss.

It is true that, given problems with students' outcomes in "basic skills courses" and into transfer-level English, we are sympathetic to the need for rethinking community college developmental English and ESL sequences and curriculum, and we have been among those highlighting problems with the status quo and advocating for changes (Bunch & Endris, 2012; Bunch et al., 2011; Kibler, Bunch, & Endris, 2011). On the other hand, we are also mindful of potential problematic consequences of AB 705, especially given the unforgiving timeframe in which the law is being implemented and the lack of resources devoted to faculty professional development. As we write, English faculty members at the college studied are coming face to face with both the promises and challenges of teaching students with a much wider array of needs than those previously enrolling in transfer-level courses. Future inquiry and discussion within and across colleges, as well as continued financial support for professional development, will be necessary to capitalize on the opportunities presented by the new policies and to address the challenges.

But ultimately, we want to complicate the narrative that community college reform can easily be characterized as corporate Goliaths against English faculty Davids, with the only possible positions being embracing, resisting, or adopting a critical defensive posture against policies put in motion by others. In the spirit of this volume's focus on agency and empowerment for community college FYC faculty, we conclude by offering several recommendations for faculty at other colleges based on what we have learned from listening to and working with faculty in this setting. The challenges and possibilities associated with each recommendation will obviously vary according to a number of contextual factors at different colleges, but we are confident that faculty at every college will be able to engage in some version of each of them.

Some Recommendations

- **Engage as early as possible.** It takes time to study the underlying issues leading to the call for reforms, to deliberate and plan solutions, to seek intellectual and material resources, to negotiate with college administrators, to evaluate pilot efforts, and to reach out to colleagues who have concerns. At the college discussed in this chapter, this process—facilitated by a grant over a two-year period—was essential as faculty members transitioned from curiosity and skepticism toward deeper engagement, agency, and ultimately leadership. As English faculty across the U.S. contemplate different and still-unfolding policy reforms, we recommend they seek—as soon as possible—opportunities for study, discussion with colleagues, engagement with administrators and institutional researchers, exploration of efforts in other places, experimentation, and documentation.

- **Read the research, and conduct your own.** At the center of the process that unfolded at this college, especially early on, was the opportunity for small groups of faculty to engage in reading groups to learn together as they studied the extant research literature, reviewed available statewide and local data, and explored ways to document the changes they were proposing. Most significant, in our estimation, were faculty members' opportunities to attend CAP workshops and conferences, where they saw examples from other colleges that had already implemented co-requisite designs and used high school GPA for placement. Throughout this process, faculty must take seriously data on student success in advancing toward and completing their goals. At the same time, as explored elsewhere in this volume, other forms of inquiry, such as case studies of individual students' experiences and examination of student writing, are crucial for understanding how to support students individually and collectively.

- **Communicate and collaborate with colleagues.** The survey we conducted also indicated that English faculty members found it helpful to hear from their department colleagues who were deeply engaged in reviewing research and investigating models of reform. One survey respondent planned to rely on colleagues for support because of lack of time, given large teaching loads, to think deeply about what the reforms would mean for teaching. These time concerns are especially relevant for adjunct faculty, who often have even less time and fewer connections to those most knowledgeable about the reforms than full-time faculty members do. Therefore, we recommend that one of the first things faculty do is advocate for time and structures to allow the kind of knowledge-gathering, discussion, and collaboration crucial to making informed decisions about how to proceed in the current reform climate. As one of the faculty members responding to our survey put it, "Resistance may not always mean 'I don't want this' . . . it might mean 'I'm not ready for this' or 'I don't know enough about this.'"

As the dean pointed out, one of the features of the reform efforts at this college was faculty members' skill in working with colleagues who remained skeptical. We suggest inviting critical colleagues to collaborate and to address their concerns directly. In fact, at this college some of the faculty who joined the acceleration team did so because of their initial alarm regarding the proposed changes. We also suggest using multiple modalities to understand and speak about the reforms. Quantitative data alone tell certain kinds of stories, but again it is important to consider students' voices, experiences, and writing, as well as the experiences of faculty members themselves.

- **Advocate for time and resources for professional development.** Also necessary are systematic opportunities for extending the knowledge and competencies of English faculty relevant to program models, curriculum, and pedagogy for teaching students from a wider array of backgrounds in transfer-level composition courses. As the dean pointed out, especially important is development for faculty on issues of second language writing and working with students with disabilities. The efforts discussed in this chapter were sparked and facilitated by a grant that provided a coordinator and modest stipends for interested faculty to meet regularly to engage in the hard work of curricular and pedagogical reform. At a time of continued budget shortfalls, resources for faculty professional development are often almost nonexistent. Yet given that teaching is *the* mission of community colleges (Grubb, 1999), along with the major instructional shifts called for by reforms in California and many other states, support for faculty's learning and engagement around these issues must come to be seen as non-negotiable.

Rodriguez, Cuellar Mejia, and Johnson (2018) report that faculty professional development experiences appeared to support addressing equity issues at colleges that were "early implementers" of the kinds of reforms called for by AB 705, helping faculty to recognize and address their own biases, adopt culturally relevant pedagogy, learn how to engage with students' affective domain, and adopt other "equity-minded practices and policies" (p. 28). Of course, faculty should be compensated for professional development and working on structural reforms. This is especially important for adjuncts, many of whom have especially heavy workloads and serve students needing the most support.

Many of our recommendations for faculty members are consistent with those that emerged for colleges and administrators from the study of early implementers conducted by Rodriguez, Cuellar Mejia, and Johnson (2018): for example, the admonition for colleges to start sooner rather than later in addressing the law, the necessity of effective professional development, and the need for both quantitative and qualitative research on student success. Rodriguez, Cuellar Mejia, and Johnson also point out the need to keep the focus on student *support*. The law itself will ensure more equitable access to transfer-level courses, but what will need to be created are the "academic and non-academic support structures in place to improve the likelihood of success of all students, especially underrepresented students, and to reduce equity gaps" (p. 28). In the case of all these recommendations, it will be in the interest of faculty members themselves—and the students they serve—for faculty to position themselves as agents and leaders in the context of reform rather than as merely supporters, resisters, or critical responders to changes imposed by others.

$\mathcal{A}$CKNOWLEDGMENTS

We wish to acknowledge helpful suggestions from Heather Schlaman and Charles Clay Doyle on an earlier draft of this chapter.

$\mathcal{R}$EFERENCES

A.B. 705. Assembly. Reg. Session (C.A. 2017). (Enacted).

Adler-Kassner, L. (2017). 2017 CCCC chair's address: Because writing is never just writing. *College Composition and Communication, 69*(2), 317–340.

Bailey, T. R., Jaggars, S. S., & Jenkins, D. (2015). *Redesigning America's community colleges: A clearer path to student success.* Cambridge, MA: Harvard University Press.

Basic Skills Student Outcomes and Transformation (BSSOT) Program. (2018). Retrieved from http://extranet.cccco.edu/Divisions/AcademicAffairs/BasicSkillsEnglishasaSecondLanguage/StudentOutcome.aspx

Bunch, G. C., & Endris, A. K. (2012). Navigating "open access" community colleges: Matriculation policies and practices for U.S.-educated linguistic minority students. In Y. Kanno & L. Harklau (Eds.), *Linguistic minority students go to college: Preparation, access, and persistence* (pp. 165–183). New York: Routledge.

Bunch, G. C., Endris, A., Panayotova, D., Romero, M., & Llosa, L. (2011). *Mapping the terrain: Language testing and placement for US-Educated language minority students in California's community colleges.* Report prepared for the William and Flora Hewlett Foundation. Retrieved from http://www.escholarship.org/uc/item/31m3q6tb

Downing, S. (2017). *On course: Strategies for creating success in college and in life (8th ed.).* Boston: Cengage Learning.

Gay, G. (2000). *Culturally responsive teaching: Theory, research, and practice.* New York: Teachers College Press.

Grubb, W. N. (1999). *Honored but invisible: An inside look at teaching in community colleges.* New York: Routledge.

Grubb, W. N. (2013). *Basic skills education in community colleges: Inside and outside of classrooms.* New York: Routledge.

Guided Pathways Electronic Toolkit. (2016). Sacramento, CA: California Community Colleges Chancellor's Office. Retrieved from http://cccgp.cccco.edu/Guided-Pathways-Electronic-Toolkit

Hern, K., & Snell, M. (2013). *Toward a vision of accelerated curriculum and pedagogy: High challenge, high support classrooms for underprepared students.* Oakland, CA: LearningWorks.

Hope, L. L., & Stankasas, J. (2018). Assembly Bill (AB) 705 implementation. [Memorandum]. Sacramento, CA: Chancellor's Office, Academic Affairs Division. Retrieved from www.CaliforniaCommunityColleges.cccco.edu

Kibler, A. K., Bunch, G. C., & Endris, A. K. (2011). Community college practices for U.S.-educated language-minority students: A resource-oriented framework. *Bilingual Research Journal, 34*(2), 201–222.

Multiple Measures Assessment Project Research Team. (2014). *Multiple Measures for Assessment and Placement* [White paper]. Retrieved October 1, 2018 from Multiple Measures Work Group of the Common Assessment Initiative: http://rpgroup.org/Portals/0/Documents/Archive/MMAP/MMAP_WhitePaper_Final_September2014.pdf?ver=2019-11-03-190118-400

Rodriguez, O., Cuellar Mejia, M., & Johnson, H. (2018). *Remedial education reforms at California's Community Colleges: Early evidence on placement and curricular reforms.* San Francisco: Public Policy Institute of California.

Schoenbach, R., Greenleaf, C., & Murphy, L. (2012). *Reading for understanding: How reading apprenticeship improves disciplinary learning in secondary and college classrooms.* San Francisco: Jossey-Bass.

TYCA Research Committee. (2015). TYCA white paper on developmental education reforms. *Teaching English in the Two Year College, 42*(3), 227–243.

TYCA Research Committee. (2016). TYCA white paper on placement reform. *Teaching English in the Two-Year College, 44*(2), 135–157.

Warnke, A., & Higgins, K. (2018). A critical time for reform: Empowering interventions in a precarious landscape. *Teaching English in the Two-Year College, 45*(4), 361–384.

14

Combining Developmental Writing and First-Year Composition Classes: Faculty Perspectives on How Co-Requisite Teaching Affects Curriculum and Pedagogy

Heather B. Finn and Sharon Avni
BOROUGH OF MANHATTAN COMMUNITY COLLEGE (CUNY)

Community colleges are an integral part of the national conversation on improving educational access and success for minority and low-income household students. Though they serve almost half of the undergraduate population in the United States (American Association of Community Colleges, 2020), community colleges suffer from low retention and graduation rates, and these numbers are even lower for students who place into math and English developmental courses (Hodara & Jaggars, 2014). While nationally about 60 percent of students graduate from four-year colleges and universities within six years, only 38 percent of students graduate within four years from community colleges (Shapiro et al., 2018). This is a significant discrepancy, which is often attributed to the fact that almost half of all entering community college students take at least one remedial course in math and reading and/or writing, which slows down their progression (Scott-Clayton,

Crosta, & Belfield, 2014). One of the central challenges is that placing out of developmental courses and becoming eligible for credit-bearing courses requires students to pass a sequence of developmental writing and reading courses. The additional time and financial commitment required for these developmental courses pose significant barriers; studies show that only 44 percent of students placed in developmental reading completed the recommended sequence of courses within three years (Bailey, Jeong, & Cho, 2010). In response to low retention rates among students placed in developmental education, community colleges nationwide have started to implement co-requisite course structures that enable students to enroll in credit-bearing courses while fulfilling developmental education requirements. Research on these acceleration models has shown that these streamlined models reduce the number of exit points, thereby boosting the students' likelihood of completing developmental education as well as introductory college-level math and English courses (Cho et al., 2012). The policy of eliminating the developmental course sequence and combining developmental education with credit-bearing courses in English and math has dramatically changed the community college experience for students as well as faculty (Barhoum, 2017).

While there is a growing literature on the quantitative findings of co-requisite programs and specifically their effect on retention and passing rates (Jaggars, Edgecombe, & Stacey, 2014), there is scant scholarship that focuses on the pedagogical and curricular aspects of accelerated models in community colleges (Walker, 2015). This study set out to provide complementary qualitative data on English professors who teach co-requisite first-year composition (FYC) courses. It focused on these two research questions:

1. How do faculty members develop their curriculum and pedagogy to meet students' reading and writing needs in co-requisite writing classes?

2. What aspect(s) of reading and writing pedagogy do faculty find most effective and challenging as they help their students to develop as college readers and writers?

To address these questions, semi-structured interviews were conducted during Spring 2016 with all 11 faculty members at one college who teach sections of English 100, the co-requisite course combining developmental writing (English 99) with English 101, the traditional FYC course. The new course was initiated during Fall 2015, so the interviews took place during the second semester that the course was in progress. Focusing on how faculty members positioned themselves as policy interpreters in the local context of their classrooms, the findings reveal the benefits and challenges in these newly developed co-requisite courses. On one hand, English FYC faculty members widely embraced the rationale for the co-requisite model and saw it as an opportunity to have additional class time to meet with students. They also revealed a new appreciation of their lower-level writing students' needs in the regular FYC class. However, faculty struggled with meeting the demands and expectations of the FYC course, particularly with regards to working through more complex readings and serving students who required substantial writing support.

Theoretical Framework

Documenting the ways in which educators (re)interpret, negotiate, and resist educational policies in their classrooms (Menken & García, 2010), this research shows the important role that teachers play in making sense of top-down initiatives in the local context of their classroom (Liddicoat & Baldauf, 2008), especially at the postsecondary level (Finn & Avni, 2016). As a unique form of educational policy in both its scope and newness, co-requisite teaching makes specific demands on teachers, who in the past may have taught FYC courses or developmental writing as separate courses with different goals and expectations. As such, this study puts classroom teachers at the center of the analysis, highlighting their agency (Canagarajah, 2005) as well as their challenges (Diallo & Liddicoat, 2014; Pease-Alvarez, Samway, & Cifka-Herrera, 2010). Our theoretical focus on policy-in-practice enables us to capture what this new policy means for FYC teachers' understanding of FYC courses and how this model impacts decisions related to pedagogy, curriculum, and assessment.

Context

The context for this study is a large urban community college we call City Community College (CCC) located in the northeast of the United States. At the time of this research, faculty members at CCC were required to teach 27 credits per year, which translated to a 5-4 teaching load. In the English department, there were two sequential developmental non-credit bearing writing courses for six hours each, English 98 and 99. To fulfill the college requirements and receive an associate's degree, all students were required to place out of these developmental writing courses and complete English 101 (four hours a week) and English 201, Introduction to Literature. Placement into the initial writing course was based on a writing test, as well as whether the student was identified as an English language learner (EL) or a "native" English speaker. ELs were placed into developmental writing classes that were specifically designed for ESL students and housed in the ESL department at CCC. However, it is important to note that there was a diverse ethnic and multilingual population at CCC and that placement was determined by the results of one writing assessment. As a result, emergent bilinguals and other ELs were often placed in classes designed for students for whom English was their native language, where their specific linguistic needs were not always addressed.

In early 2014, several English department faculty learned of the success of the Accelerated Learning Program (ALP) at the Community College of Baltimore County and began to question whether the sequence at CCC could be shortened. To improve completion rates, they began to explore reforming courses in the English department so that students could move through the sequence more quickly. After researching acceleration efforts at other community colleges and working through the process of new course development in Fall 2015, they implemented the co-requisite course, English 100, that combined the highest level of developmental writing (English 99) and FYC (English 101) into a three-credit, six-hour course. Accordingly, this class differed from English 101 in several ways. First, English 100 had an additional two hours of instructional time. Second, at the time, evaluation was not based on multiple measures, and students had two high-stakes assessments in

English 100: They had to pass the university writing proficiency exam and the regular English 101 final, combining the exam requirements for both English 99 and English 101. Third, the original conception of the course was to set the class size to 18; however, class size caps were not adhered to and the new cap was set at 25 students. One designated student tutor who had successfully completed English 101 was made available to each section through the College Writing Center.

In recognizing the differences between the new co-requisite course and the traditional English 101 course, the English department invited a representative from the Community College of Baltimore County to run a two-day workshop about curriculum design, program benefits, and additional topics related to acceleration. This professional development was followed up with in-house workshops designed to share teaching strategies, problems, and solutions.

Once implemented in Fall 2015, 208 students were enrolled in English 100, followed by 374 in Spring 2016, the semester our study took place. Institutional data showed that in Fall 2015, 75 percent of students passed English 100; in Spring 2016, this number dropped to 55 percent and remained relatively consistent in the next two terms. (In Fall 2016, 58 percent of students passed, and in Spring 2017, 59 percent passed.) Over three terms between 2016 and 2017, among those who started in English 100, 42 percent took and passed English 201. On the other hand, only 29 percent of students who started in English 99 enrolled in and passed English 201 in the same three-term period.

Methods

We were interested in the ways in which accelerated models of instruction affected students who needed language and literacy development and wanted to explore how instructors address language development in the co-requisite model. We conducted individual semi-structured interviews in Spring 2016 with all 11 instructors in the CCC English department who were currently teaching or had previously taught English 100 in Fall 2015 (see Table 14.1). Of these 11 instructors, two were part-time, and the remaining nine were full-time professors with teach-

TABLE 14.1. Participants

Name	Approximate Years Teaching at City Community College	Full-Time or Part-Time	Highest Degree
Carly	21	FT	PhD
Debbie	15	FT	PhD
Dave	3.5	FT	MFA
Elizabeth	4	FT	MFA
Jennifer	9	FT	PhD
Jane	27	PT	MA
Jo	8	FT	PhD
Myra	1.5	PT	PhD
Patty	13	FT	PhD
Susan	16	FT	PhD
Zoe	27	FT	PhD

Note: Names are pseudonyms.

ing experience at CCC ranging from 8 to 27 years. All the interviewed faculty members had significant experience teaching developmental writing. Each interview followed a protocol of questions that were developed to probe teachers' perception of the course, their teaching practices, and any potential changes they had made in pedagogical or curricular decisions. During the interview, we asked teachers to share materials from their courses. The interviews were audio-recorded, transcribed, and then analyzed and coded thematically.

Findings

Reconceptualizing/Recalibrating Reading and Writing Instruction

One of the main themes to emerge had to do with teachers' need to (re)calibrate and (re)define what it means to be an English 101 student and what knowledge this entails. While the English 100 faculty members reported that they appreciated the additional time afforded to them in a six-hour class, they also recognized that the added time was not always enough to make the class comparable to a traditional FYC English 101 in terms of reading choices and other content covered. Teachers noted that students needed time to grapple with the material typically used in an English 101 section and did not display the same academic reading proficiencies. Instructors therefore had to reconceptualize the curriculum in English 100 to meet their students' reading needs. As Carly explained: "Even though we're saying it's a 101, it's not. Maybe towards the end of the semester, they become 101 students, but you know, it takes a while to get there. It's not like you are really starting off with 101 students."

Carly points out a primary way in which instructors in English 100 needed to differentiate their curriculum and pedagogy in 100 as compared to 101. When asked about some of the specific differences between English 101 and English 100, teachers spoke about a difference in quality and quantity, even though students were still required to meet the English 101 learning outcomes. Susan, for example, noted that in 101 there were more readings, and the readings were more difficult. She elaborated: "We started doing a section on language and we did Rodriguez and Amy Tan [two authors commonly read in English 101] and, we just jump right in in the 101 class. A lot of them are having difficulty getting the important ideas out of the very simple, short readings." As Susan described, many students in 100 struggled with the complexity of the readings typically assigned at the beginning of English 101, so she, like many other faculty interviewed, needed to adjust the curriculum accordingly. Since there was additional time in the 100 section, she focused on fewer readings and spent time continuously reviewing material.

Like Susan, Patty felt that students needed additional reading support, particularly with locating the main idea and understanding the purpose of texts. She indicated that in a future co-requisite class, she would revise her curriculum to start with readings that were shorter and more accessible, and she would walk students through the academic reading process step-by-step: "You know, asking students to point out the main idea, what's the supporting evidence. I should have known to do that, I think, but I would certainly point out to colleagues that they may find that it's really important to devote some sessions to that."

As previously noted, faculty teaching English 100 attended a training session prior to teaching the course; however, once in the classroom, new questions and concerns arose. Patty's comment reveals that she had made an assumption that the students would have the knowledge and skills for reading the academic texts she used in her other FYC sections, but that she had to go back to the "basics." In general, her comment reflects many of the other faculty's sense that it was not only academic writing that she needed to develop, but also academic reading skills.

Debbie, a professor who had been teaching both developmental writing and English composition for 15 years, felt that students in 100 needed to start out with different material than in a 101 section, perhaps because of her extensive experience as an instructor of developmental writing:

> I don't start with that [101] level of difficulty. I like to start with an excerpt from the autobiography of Malcolm X. Malcolm X learning to read, where he teaches himself to read in prison, which always works really well. Even there, you know, it's not as complex as some of the later works.

Dave echoed Patty and Debbie's point about scaffolding the material more in 100; however, he didn't feel that students couldn't handle the 101 readings from the beginning; instead, he believed that the extra time allotted to the class should be used to focus more carefully on the reading. He explained: "I find that the English 101 stuff should be introduced much earlier on, but with a lot more time dedicated to understanding what these writers are actually saying, translating what they say into our own words. The process."

In other words, faculty were highly aware that there was a need to cover the 101 material at a slower pace and in greater depth, focusing on the process of reading and comprehending, rather than simply interpreting. Faculty members, therefore, could not spend as much time on interpreting and analyzing the literary texts they were reading with their students, which was the focus of their English 101 classes.

Not all faculty members felt the need to slow the pace of their readings to adapt to English 100. One faculty member, Elizabeth, felt that the students in her section were especially strong and were able to comprehend the readings more than the students in her 101 section:

> [I]n my section, I'm really pleased with them. To be honest, the last week before break, we were doing 101 final prep. Man, they caught on to the ideas quicker than my 101s. I'm teaching two 101s and then 100 this semester, and if I had to rate their level of understanding of the two 101 readings, I think I would probably place the 100 slightly higher.

Elizabeth's quote illustrates the variability between sections, the level of student preparedness within each, and the necessity for faculty to adapt their teaching and curriculum to the students within the class.

While some students did not struggle with issues like reading comprehension, the majority of faculty reported that in addition to slowing the pace of readings, they had to spend additional time focusing on students' writing skills—time that was not typically spent in a section of 101. Jo said, "The writing itself, even though they tried, I have to say that they need more time." When we inquired about which aspect of the writing required more time, she said that the students were not lacking ideas, but rather struggled with mechanical issues and vocabulary. Similarly, Zoe noted that the students' writing skills were not yet at a 101 level, and they were still struggling with areas like grammar, style, and syntax. Not all of her students had the comparative proficiencies in writing and speaking, and some students, though labeled as "native" English speakers, displayed "severe grammar problems." She explained why this posed a particular challenge by saying: "With students who write correct sentences, you could explain to them in a really short amount of time how to structure an essay and how to develop ideas, but grammar and syntax take time." Zoe's comment reflects an awareness that because of its complexity, learning to write academically requires time, and unlike the acquisition of other types of discrete skills, cannot always be rushed.

Finally, teachers spoke about the unintended effect that teaching 100 had on their views on their 101 teaching. Teachers clearly noticed a difference, at least from the get-go, between English 100 and English 101 students in both reading and writing. However, the lessons faculty learned about teaching co-requisite courses had a positive ripple effect. Susan pointed out that she found that the weaker students in 101 would benefit from a more scaffolded approach to teaching readings and that she thought she could apply her new appreciation of teaching reading to her regular English 101 classes. She described her approach:

> Pulling out the ideas out of the readings, comparing the different readings—just like really mapping it out. What does this one say? How does this one agree or disagree? Then, you know, separating the writing out of their own point of view, writing out their reason. I do scaffolding like that in 101 too, but we don't spend so much time on it; it's not so explicit.

She also noted that she is trying to use the time in 101 to talk to her students "more precisely about the different parts of an essay." All in all, Susan seemed to suggest that she would think differently about teaching 101 and be more explicit about the reading and writing processes, in addition to a focus on the prose, themes, and content of her assignments. Overall, these examples underscore the instructors' nimbleness to adapt to the varying students' levels in their classrooms and to continually reflect and reassess their expectations of the course material for FYC in light of their students' needs and abilities.

Reconceptualizing Goals and Assessment

The second theme to emerge had to do with teachers' questioning their goals and what their expectations were of students who completed their class. Susan noted that the prior goals in developmental writing centered on gaining comfort and confidence with writing, yet in English 100, much of this focus disappeared. She explained:

> In English 99, a lot of the goal for that class can also be building confidence, building enjoyment in writing, feeling comfortable writing, doing a lot of low-stakes work, doing descriptive work, engaging their senses in their writing, doing narrative writing and

seeing their writing get better over the course of the semester without being graded and evaluated. So that by the end of the semester there's often a lot of confidence built. What I have found that has been one of the hardest things about 100, is that there is no time for that. Then to be evaluating them in the same way that I was evaluating my 101 students, which, because they were not doing as well as the 101 students, I felt like had the opposite effect of, like, destroying their confidence and saying, you know, instead of that building up that I experience in developmental levels, that having to show them everything that they need to improve in their essays at that point, which were definitely far weaker than my 101 students.

Here Susan describes how she struggled with evaluating her students; whereas in developmental writing she felt that a primary focus was building confidence, when she assigned grades in 100, she worried that she was diminishing students' confidence about their writing skills. Thinking about her goals and expectations raised questions about how to assess and grade the students: Was it based on effort or quality of the writing they produced? She also pointed out the challenge of evaluating students' writing within the first month of class and the inevitable comparison between her 100 students and her 101 students:

I'm teaching two sections of 101, and I don't normally have to compare my developmental students to my 101s. It's like they're improving and building as developmental students and there's no obligation to look at their work as like, is it yet college-level work? But this time, I had to look at their work, you know, a month in, at the same time I'm looking at the first essays of my 101 students and I feel I'm obligated to sort of hold them to the same standards and, therefore, giving them low grades, and marking all these problems.

Other faculty also reported feeling challenged by meeting the same standards of assessment as in 101. Jane noted that she only had one student in her class who deserved an A and whom she felt was "really, really ready for 201"—the next course in the English sequence. She also realized that part of her concern stemmed from her own anxiety about the students' preparedness—not only academic, but also emotional—for the next level of English. She said:

> When I saw the 201 passages, I was like, this is too hard for them. Then, I took a step back and I really looked at the passages, I'm like, wait, these are easy passages. Again, I was just having this anxiety for them and it had nothing to do with the actual course itself because the material is easy. It's just I don't know how to get them emotionally ready.

Jo noted similar concerns about preparing students for 201. She explained that "combining these two, I think somehow they—I mean, okay, they learned what is 101, but in a very superficial way I would say, so they are not really well prepared for 201. I think they would rather take 101 one more time, but in order for them to do so, I have to fail them, right?"

Since English 201, Introduction to Literature, is a three-credit course that students need to receive their associate's degree, the "superficial" nature of what students have learned in 101 is cause for concern. As the CCC English 201 course description notes, "This is a course that builds upon skills introduced in English 101. In this course, literature is the field for the development of critical reading, critical thinking, independent research, and writing skills." Students in this course must engage deeply with literature, and if they are unprepared for this level of work and perform poorly in the class or are unable to pass, this could affect their ability to graduate in a timely manner. In reconceptualizing goals and assessment for English 100, instructors needed to balance a series of tensions, including lowering standards and teaching the course at a different level, building students' confidence in writing, preparing students for future English courses, and assigning grades that accurately reflect students' writing capabilities.

Implications: Effects on Teachers

This study raises a wide array of implications and spells out some concrete issues that prospective teachers of co-requisite FYC need to consider. First, the introduction of the co-requisite that combined the traditional first-year writing course with developmental support shaped the type of material that instructors chose. Rather than using the same level of readings as in other English 101 classes, co-requisite instructors looked for shorter and less complex readings and decelerated the rate in which they covered material. This choice was a reflection of their awareness that their students did not have the academic reading skills at the start of the semester to undertake more advanced material. This finding points to the need to think about co-requisite English writing classes as not only developing academic writing, but academic reading as well. Second, the co-requisite class also presented instructors with the need to dedicate time to the "nuts and bolts" of writing (i.e., grammar, spelling, sentence structure) rather than focusing on developing ideas and advancing an argument in the writing. Since many English 101 instructors come with backgrounds in literature or composition, this finding suggests that the definition of the FYC instructor needs to be broadened to include expertise in teaching the mechanics of writing and basic literacy. This necessity requires rethinking what it means to teach FYC and what skills FYC instructors need to be effective. Third, as the data reflect, this study also shows that teaching English 100 had a significant impact on how instructors see their role and their pedagogical practices, not only in English 100, but also in English 101. Instructors felt that teaching English 100 would have positive ripple effects that would change the way they thought about scaffolding texts, presenting ideas, and working with weaker students. At the same time, this finding suggests that there is potential for negative washback in the way higher-level English composition classes are taught. As the co-requisite model begins to replace stand-alone developmental writing courses, these classes may have consequences for curricular and pedagogical approaches in second-year composition courses.

Finally, this study points to the instructor as a local educational policy broker who must decide how to implement and navigate this new policy in the classroom. The diversity in the students' levels, along with the differences in the instructor's background suggests that there is no "one size fits all" approach to teaching co-requisite writing classes. Along with considering what readings to use, how to scaffold the readings, what aspects of writing to focus on, how many papers to assign, and how to assess students' writing efforts and products, instructors are navigating what it means to teach FYC and what constitutes the body of knowledge that this course entails. If some instructors in this study felt at times empowered by the opportunity to reflect on their teaching practices and valued the co-requisite structure for what it potentially offered in terms of their students' learning gains, others felt that the co-requisite policy left them trying to navigate a new set of principles and expectations for which FYC was not designed or intended. As such, this study raises critical questions about what it means to develop college readers and writers and how the new co-requisite structure necessitates an accounting of priorities, expectations, and value judgments, which may (or may not) align with instructors' perceptions or teaching practices.

References

American Association of Community Colleges. (2020). *2020 fact sheet.* https://www.aacc.nche.edu/wp=content/uploads/2020/03/AACC_Fast_Facts_2020_Final.pdf

Bailey, T., Jeong, D., & Cho, S. (2010). *Referral, enrollment, and completion in developmental education sequences in community colleges.* (CCRC Working Paper No. 53). New York: Columbia University, Teachers College, Community College Research Center.

Barhoum, S. (2017). The challenges of community college students in developmental writing and four ways to help. *Journal of Applied Research in the Community College, 24*(2), 47–56.

Canagarajah, A. S. (Ed.) (2005). *Reclaiming the local in language policy and practice.* Mahwah, NJ: Lawrence Erlbaum.

Cho, S., Kopko, E., Jenkins, D., & Jaggars, S. (2012). *New evidence of success for community college remedial English students: tracking the outcomes of students in the Accelerated Learning Program (ALP)* (CCRC Working Paper No. 53). New York: Columbia University, Teachers College, Community College Research Center.

Diallo, I., & Liddicoat, A. J. (2014). Planning language teaching: An argument for the place of pedagogy in language policy and planning. *International Journal of Pedagogies and Learning, 9*(2), 110–117.

Finn, H., & Avni, S. (2016) Negotiating academic literacy in community college developmental writing. *Current Issues in Language Planning, 17*(3-4), 369–384.

Hodara, M., & Jaggars, S. S. (2014). An examination of the impact of accelerating community college students' progression through developmental education. *Journal of Higher Education, 85*(2), 246–276.

Jaggars, S. S., Edgecombe, N., & Stacey, G. W. (2014). *What we know about accelerated developmental education.* New York: Columbia University, Teachers College, Community College Research Center.

Liddicoat, A. J., & Baldauf, R. B. (2008). Language planning in local contexts: Agents, contexts and interactions. In A. J. Liddicoat & R. B. Baldauf (Eds.), *Language planning in local contexts* (pp. 3–17). Clevedon, England: Multilingual Matters.

Menken, K., & García, O. (2010). *Negotiating language policies in schools: Educators as policymakers.* London: Routledge.

Pease-Alvarez, L., Samway, K. D., & Cifka-Herrera, C. (2010). Working within the system: Teachers of English learners negotiating a literacy instruction mandate. *Language Policy, 9*(4), 313–334.

Scott-Clayton, J., Crosta, P. M., & Belfield, C. R. (2014). Improving the targeting of treatment: Evidence from college remediation. *Educational Evaluation and Policy Analysis, 36*(3), 371–393.

Shapiro, D., Dundar, A., Huie, F., Wakhungu, P.K., Bhimdiwala, A., & Wilson, S. E. (2018, December). Completing college: A national view of student completion rates—Fall 2012 Cohort (Signature Report No. 16). Herndon, VA: National Student Clearinghouse Research Center.

Walker, M. (2015) Exploring faculty perceptions of the impact of accelerated developmental education courses on their pedagogy: a multidisciplinary study. *Research and Teaching in Developmental Education, 32*(1), 12–34.

15

Valuing Teacher Knowledge, Valuing Local Knowledge: FYC in Hawai'i Community Colleges

*M*eryl *S*iegal
LANEY COLLEGE

In 2018, with curricular changes to first-year composition (FYC) looming in California along with a concomitant push toward acceleration of students through FYC, I interviewed community college teachers in Honolulu to learn how Hawai'i community college faculty, in part because of their special position within the University of Hawai'i system, viewed their FYC programs and courses. There are seven community colleges in the state, and four are on the island of O'ahu; all the community colleges are part of the University of Hawai'i (UH) system alongside three four-year university campuses, which creates a unique professional environment for community college faculty. Faculty are given titles—assistant, associate, and (full) professor—and all faculty at the ten campuses statewide are in the same bargaining unit. Furthermore, faculty have access to a wider array professional and academic resources. In addition, connection to the larger UH system also affords community college English faculty access to their colleagues systemwide, including a more natural connection resulting in statewide intersegmental meetings focused on first-year composition with English faculty from UH campuses.

I interviewed 11 current FYC faculty from three different O'ahu community colleges across two departments, ESL and English, and one former faculty member. In this chapter, I focus on six faculty: Mike, Phillip, and Leilani taught at Campus 1, Cindy and Kay at Campus 2, and Tim at Campus 3. Faculty responded to my requests made through their department chairs and through professional contacts.

These interviews (see also Finn & Avni, this volume) constitute a case study of an institution and a department undergoing change. My intention was one that is rarely considered in educational research—to allow teachers the space to talk about what was on their minds and to share their expertise and professional acumen in ways that are usually not allowed or available to faculty. Indeed, in some states and institutions, faculty talking freely about educational policy and administrative mandates is equivalent to being seen as a traitor to the college or a malcontent and viewed negatively by administration and other faculty. Critical discussions about policy could result in job loss or less-than-desirable course assignments (Harklau, Batson, & McGovern, 2019).

With a focus on policy, faculty spoke about electronic textbook resources, student college readiness for FYC, changes in curriculum and placement, innovations in FYC curriculum, faculty-administration collaborations, and changing student demographics in FYC that affect FYC curriculum. Interviewees' names have been changed, and all information that might identify faculty and their colleges has been removed. The interviews were conducted while I was on sabbatical in Spring 2018 and offer insight into how faculty view and understand institutional change as it is happening. The interviews also show the complex ways in which changes do occur, yet they do not show the subsequent changes in actual student learning and achievement nor do they provide a take on the actual mechanics of instruction. Subsequent to the interviews, the Fall 2019 college websites showed some fine-tuning of placement processes, including in two cases, a pre-FYC writing class option. My hope is that the faculty who so generously gave their time to my project profited from the deep reflection afforded through the interview process (Adelman, 1993). This research study was approved by the University of Hawai'i Institutional Review Board. In quoted material, I have used "[xx]" to denote areas that could reveal the school of the interviewee; I have also used [brackets] to insert information said in the interview to make a particular quotation concise and coherent. In some of the interviews, [xx] stands for unclear language.

Going Through Changes

In Spring 2018 faculty spoke about the sweeping changes occurring in their writing departments. In each of the three schools I became familiar with, the FYC sequence had undergone different reforms. In 2011, Campus 2 was an early adopter in Hawaiʻi of the Accelerated Learning Program (ALP) (Adams et al., 2009). ALP is an innovative program created by Peter Adams, formerly a writing instructor at the Community College Baltimore County, who was a consultant for the community colleges in Hawaiʻi on implementation of his ALP model. Adams' program started out as optional for Baltimore County students: Students took a standardized placement exam, which they had the option to retake, and during the first week of school they took a diagnostic exam as a check to validate placement. Both ALP and non-ALP students were mixed in a regular FYC section, and the ALP students took a stand-alone support class. Adams' FYC sections in Baltimore enrolled about 20 students per writing class; about 7 to 10 in each class were also in the ALP support class. This model was adopted in Hawaiʻi.

In their 2009 paper, Adams et al. explain the success of ALP according to these eight tenets: (1) mainstreaming, which allows students to actually feel that they are in college; (2) small class size (a writing class of about 20 students, with a support class that is about half that number); (3) cohort learning (the students who are part of ALP develop relationships with each other); (4) contextual learning (the cohort group attends a support section that is directly relevant to the FYC class); (5) acceleration (therefore lessening the chance of students dropping out mid-stream in the pipeline toward college English); (6) heterogeneous grouping in the FYC course (in common parlance, we might call this inclusion education, such that students who previously were placed into a remedial class now are in classes with students who have mastered certain skills and the lower level students can be mentored or apprenticed to a higher skill level afforded in a heterogeneous environment); (7) "attention to behavior issues" (pp. 62–63; included here are skills such as calendar creation for keeping track of assignments); and (8) "attention to life problems" (p. 63; the focus is on making students aware of college support services to help them through life challenges).

Adams et al. (2009) provide not only charts that show improved student progress through FYC using the ALP model, but to supplement this data, students were surveyed about the fit of the classes they were placed in, and there was reporting from teachers who read student papers to compare ALP student work with students in remedial classes. This attention to detail is compelling, although like much of the accelerated movement's research, actual student writing artifacts were not included as part of the data nor were the course readings (or syllabi).

At Cindy's school, Campus 2, the ALP program was implemented with a FYC class of 12 students below the typical FYC placement level and 8 students at the regular level. The class met two times a week (for three units), and those who were below the regular placement level were required to attend a one unit support course two times a week with the same instructor. Cindy explained her program's placement policy: "When a student places one level below they are mainstreamed into college level writing through the ALP model." She noted that students who placed into developmental education, which she qualified as "students who would usually be a middle school reading level," could not take an English course at her school: "We do not offer courses for them." These students at the time of the interview were referred to Campus 3, a nearby community college that offered a FYC paired with a support class with 20 students per class for one level below and two levels below. Her understanding was that in Campus 3 classes, the lower levels were set up so that students meet four times a week (as compared to the regular FYC which meets two times a week), and there is "no differentiation in teaching." In other words, students in this model are following the same FYC "with more time and resources." Tim, a veteran faculty member teaching in this program at Campus 3, confirmed the program set-up and added that the courses one and two levels below regular FYC had embedded tutors as well as additional time afforded by meeting four times a week, the FYC on Mondays and Wednesdays and the support class on Tuesday and Thursdays. At the time of these interviews, data was gathered by the college on pass-fail rates but not on the actual differentiation of instruction for different

FYC or student writing artifacts, let alone researching longitudinally how students fare in their writing while in college and beyond. In the current race toward accelerating the time students spend in the English sequence with a focus on racial and ethnic equity demographics, in-depth research into what occurs in the new, reformed classroom is rare.

At Campus 1, ALP had recently been implemented, yet, according to Mike and Leilani, without fully vetting how the ALP program was working out, still more English department changes were implemented resulting in the loss of developmental and remedial English classes. Mike explained:

> We have the ALP model which is a stand-alone freshman comp course followed by a [xx], a development section. That cohort generally works [whatever way the instructor wants], I run mine as a technical section [working on things such as in-paper citations and grammar]... the college wants to know is this working? ...It's a fairly new program and we are still trying to see if it is working, but they are already talking about getting rid of it. Then we have English [xxx], which is the one that condenses all those five [developmental and remedial] courses into one course, so you have to be placed into it. So we're still trying to figure out if that works. I think what will happen is everything will be condensed into one freshman comp course that everyone takes and we don't do dev ed any more. I don't think we should get rid of dev ed. I think some of our students definitely need it.

What struck Mike was the swiftness of further curricular changes in the English department after the implementation of the changes in the ALP program that the faculty desired and liked. Indeed, Mike's colleague Leilani noted similarly that ALP is an accelerated program and wondered why further cuts were needed: "We have [xxx], the ALP accelerated learning program that was pretty much copied from Baltimore County Community College, so we have those [accelerated] classes." The further cuts in class offerings were not, according to the interviewees, decided upon or instigated by faculty. In response to a question I asked about changes in the student body, Leilani noted that the student body is the same, so she was wondering why the curriculum needed to be changed once again:

> [I haven't seen many changes in the student body], so what happened is that admin required us to get rid of our dev ed courses so we have students in our English 100 who shouldn't be there and are never going to make it. They're just not going to pass, they need the lower level classes and they're just not going to get them.

Leilani then mentioned that she had even consulted with a counselor about a student she was concerned about in her class. She believed the student needed a lower-level class that had been removed from her English department's program. I found in all my interviews that teachers were concerned about students and their pedagogy, a concern that can often translate into a job that does not end when the faculty member goes home; trying to create pedagogy that works within new administrative mandates called "reform" that do not take into account teacher classroom expertise not only contributes to teacher frustration and burnout, but also engenders a particular kind of structural violence (Farmer et al., 2006) in the students' educational experience. Farmer et al. (2006) define structural violence as a "way of describing social arrangements that put individuals and populations in harm's way. ...The arrangements are *structural* because they are embedded in the political and economic organization of our social world; they are *violent* because they cause injury to people. ...With few exceptions, clinicians are not trained to understand such social forces, nor are we trained to alter them" (p. 1686). The way education occurs at the community college level for some populations might be propagating a kind of structural violence. Structural violence might be exacerbated by accelerating individual students into classroom academic tracks, or beyond accelerating, reifying academic trajectories over hands-on work such as welding or carpentry; furthermore, the "deacceleration" of students in classes that have large underprepared populations is also type of structural violence. Importantly, the ease of acceleration discourages real structural change such as student driven paid internships; creative venues for student learning and personhood development; student driven inquiry projects that could substitute for course work; project based learning where students have time to fully and joyfully participate; housing that is clean, calm and affordable for students and their families; affordable healthy food; free and accessible health care including mental health. The community college in part seems fossilized under neoliberal approaches to reform and bureaucratic and systematic corruption that values pathways and consistency rather than human development and real power and personhood (Bailey, Jaggars, & Jenkins, 2015). Importantly, "Structural violence is often embedded in longstanding 'ubiquitous social structures, normalized by stable institutions and regular experience'. . . . Because they seem so ordinary in our ways of understanding the world, they appear almost invisible" (Farmer et al., 2006, p. 1686). As for Leilani's student, clearly the difficulty the student was having in the class troubled her. Leilani, a teacher at the school for more than 15 years, also noted the confusion surrounding student placement in English classes at that time: "Oh, the other problem we have is that admin got rid of the placement exam so we don't really know how students get placed in our classes." From Leilani's perspective, the elusive placement procedure is jeopardizing student learning and teacher efficacy.

Leilani also noted that the school had already implemented ALP, which she thought was an effective program (she had been part of a training cohort for the ALP program), but her concern was the removal of all the developmental education courses. She was puzzled as to why the administration would want to try a new program in the midst of evaluating the efficacy of the ALP curricular change. The curricular changes that were mandated by the administration did not include faculty consultation or consensus. Another concerning factor for Leilani was her students who could not accelerate. She raised a question that has not yet been addressed in the community college literature: What happens to the students who fail FYC once or more than once?

Concern for Students and Content

Faculty realized that some students had a tough time in the accelerated courses, and they also realized that course curriculum needed to be modified. Mike explained how the curricular changes affected his pedagogy:

> We have condensed a lot of the courses—[he lists five courses that have been cut from the program]—and those courses were geared towards helping students at a certain level gain the skills that they needed to advance to the next level and so forth; but now with this big push toward acceleration we have condensed a lot of those courses, and so in a course that might have had a student population where every student in that course had learning disabilities [and] needed to be [supported individually by the teacher], by the appropriate content and teaching methodology, those students are now in the same class as the standalone freshman comp students. In other words we have a broader spectrum of proficiency levels and learning styles, and so in the past I used to be able to give course content that was a bit more rigorous and challenging, but I have had to use content that is a bit more broadly accessible is probably a good way to put it. Um, the students who are marginally proficient to those students who are very proficient. I don't want to say that I have dumbed down the course, I have just had to alter certain things, a lot of the readings, and the lectures and things of that sort. So um, yeah, it's altered the way I have taught the course.

Mike was creating a new FYC curriculum because the FYC curriculum and methods he had previously found to be successful could not entirely work with the current range of students he was teaching. He suggested it was the loss of the developmental courses that precipitated his change in strategy for his FYC course. Later in the interview, when I asked what he wished the school could do, Mike suggested that professional development for teaching a broader range of students including ESOL and students with learning disabilities would be helpful. This was echoed by other instructors as well. Mike noted that he was not trained to teach the broader group of students, nor was he trained to teach the ESOL students he now found in his FYC who needed more basic grammar than what he usually taught at that level. Importantly, Mike believed that he had not "dumbed down" his FYC.

With the new student population in their FYC classes, teachers were hard-pressed to deliver FYC curriculum. They were tasked with implementing the changes, but they had not been a part of the decision making, and some remained skeptical of the new mandates. More serious is their worry that the support classes might not be enough to support students through the high bar of FYC writing education. Might the forced academic jump to FYC turn students off to the bigger benefits that a two-year college education could bring and further delay students in deciding on and moving forward with their college and career goals? Faculty feel the need to maintain course integrity and make sure that the standards (student learning outcomes) they have for student achievement can be upheld in FYC and achieved by the students in the classes. Mike ended his interview talking about something that had not come up in the interview previously, a "proficiency gap":

> We haven't done anything to close that proficiency gap that we are seeing because of the condensation of the course. Everybody is still spread out in terms of proficiency. I think that is creating a lot of problems for other instructors… I think some instructors are preparing their students well and others aren't.

At this point in the interview, Mike noted the importance of student services in serving the current FYC students properly and appropriately. He later talked about the way the changes had occurred. He said that data was collected "outside of us, for funding purposes." His understanding was that "administrators are doing all [that] with the numbers we don't see much of that. Yes, I would like to see (this data). I would be curious to just know what our students are going on to major in, what schools they go to, whether they graduate, even what other writing courses they are going to, I would like to know that." He reiterated that "what used to be five courses is now one course, that is working in some ways but is failing in others."

Although not as caught up in the changes as Mike and Leilani, Phillip, the longest-serving teacher I interviewed, took a long view. He noted that in 1997, many developmental classes were dropped. In terms of the current turmoil Philip responded directly: "How can I say it? For the [administrators] the thing is graduation and completion rates." For Phillip the push toward acceleration is turning his community college classes at Campus 1 into an "adult school."

According to the faculty I spoke with, new placement rules were decided by the administration during Spring 2018. Throughout the University of Hawai'i system, the placement system was changing. Cindy admitted that faculty were "just trying to understand these changes." The test that had previously been used for placement was discontinued, and she told me how multiple measures were used that could include the SAT, ACT, or high school GPA. Her understanding was that out of these different kinds of measures, the highest score was noted and used for placement. Leilani also mentioned a need for the new placement system to be adjusted:

> Unfortunately this semester I keep telling people my ALP [class] is backwards because a lot of the students who are in the developmental don't need to be there and a lot of the guys who are not developmental do need to be there, [in xxx], but they're not going to get the help and attention they need because they're placed in the wrong place. Faculty do not know how the students got placed. It's a mystery.

One further FYC issue faculty were puzzled about is the breadth of the student population in FYC. In Hawai'i, as in California, career and technical education (CTE) students take the same FYC as first-year students who are preparing to transfer to a four-year school. Leilani had designed her curriculum focused on areas of social justice in the spring, starting with Martin Luther King, Jr. Day, asking students to consider the Hawaiian correlates to King's social justice work (including King's visit to Hawai'i), and ending with an inquiry-based research paper on a subject that students chose with her guidance. For Leilani, the balance between the art and science of research, including devices for keeping information clear and accessible to the reader (i.e., Works Cited lists and in-text citations), seemed at times superfluous to what, might be most useful and appropriate writing and reading for first-year CTE students (see Jensen, Stieger, and Zulim, Chapter 10, this volume, and Arrizon, Chapter 18, this volume, for more about CTE and STEM writing courses): "They don't need it most of them, they are never going to use it, but they are forced to take it, so for them—a lot of them are in over their heads too. It's crazy and the faculty has really lost control over curriculum decisions, placement… ." As for her day-to-day curriculum, Leilani reminded me that she allots time for basic reading instruction in her classes, noting that the college no longer has a reading class; she was concerned about the underpreparedness of the students and the fact that there were students placed in FYC who did not belong there because their skills were not at an appropriate level where instruction could actually support them to achieve college-level work. Indeed, the majority of the interviewees were concerned about students with low reading levels.

Importantly, and not surprisingly, among faculty, there are different opinions about what is the best system for FYC. Whereas faculty in Colleges 1 and 2 thought it important to have developmental English education classes and a clear placement system, Tim's views differed from his colleagues' regarding placement and the necessity of accelerated FYC for all students: "I still don't understand why it's the business of community colleges to not let college students take college classes. I don't understand it." At Tim's college, Campus 3, all students entered into some kind of FYC: the offerings include the regular two-day-a-week class; a class that meets double that time, four days a week, designed for students who might be one level below FYC; or a class that meets four days a week and is two levels below the regular FYC. His goal in teaching FYC was to give students the idea that writing "isn't as hard as people made it out to be." He would like to see an expanded tutoring system at his school as well as professionally trained tutors rather than peers. Regarding the current broader range of FYC students, Tim believed this range was a part of teaching in a community college: "You know in every class you have one student you know will not pass. I don't think our system addressed those students as properly as they should. But it doesn't seem fair to punish people who could be successful." Clearly, faculty throughout the community college system were divided as to whether the new changes were pedagogically appropriate, and this divide suggests a need for better, substantive research to understand the new reforms through a more comprehensive lens.

Changes in FYC Require Campus Support

With the reduction in remedial and developmental classes, conceptual frameworks like K–12 inclusion models might need to be appropriated for the FYC. However, whereas in K–12 there is often an implicit and/ or explicit mandate for all students to move through the grades with supporting services that allow them to pass, that has not been the case in the community colleges, as traditionally community colleges have recognized the complexity of the lives of adults who are attending a two-year school, and schools were funded on the numbers of students attending. Now, in many states, college funding is also partially contingent on students passing and getting through courses and programs. In California the model is called the "student centered funding formula" (California Community College Chancellors Office, 2020). Based on research from projects such as the California Basic Skills Initiative (Illowsky, 2008) showing the efficacy of student services such as academic counseling and financial aid resources that result in better student persistence and retention rates, the new models of acceleration require and build in campus resources and support. All the syllabi I received from faculty included a list of the student support services on campus. For example, a faculty member included the campus' Makaʻala program in her syllabus, alerting the students to the idea that she might refer them to the program if she believed they needed it: "*Makaʻala* means 'eyes that are awake,' and reminds us that it is the responsibility of everyone involved—instructors, support services AND students—to be alert, watchful and vigilant and to attend to students' success with 'wide-open eyes.'"

Many of the teachers stressed the importance of support for students outside the classroom. Mike said, "Having students know they are part of a larger supportive community is important for their success and for our success as college instructors too." Similarly, Cindy noted the bigger picture that faculty need to consider in FYC:

> It is not just teaching students English … it is also about teaching them how to think and how to interact with others—it's also about acknowledging the difficulties of life because for many students this is a totally new environment for them. They may be the first in their family to go to college, they may be an immigrant student, they may be a second language student. They may be a working mom, so it's acknowledging the humanity in the room. I think about that I am not here to just make sure you enroll in your subsequent course but that you're a human being in my classroom and I am acknowledging all of you, and I will do whatever I can to help—within my realm within the services the campus can provide.

Phillip did not necessarily feel the demographics were changing; however, he said he did see a marked lack of social engagement between students: "It's very hard to get students to do small group work. In the workplace, big writing projects are community projects. In the real world most writing projects are group projects." He viewed his students as "academically good" but lacking in what he termed "college readiness skills" including taking notes, coming to class on time, being "civil to fellow students," and using mature social interaction skills. He noted this could be due to the advent of frequent cell phone use. Other interviewees echoed his concerns.

Cindy and Kay both believed that mental health issues seemed more prevalent among students and required more college resources. Cindy explained: "[Mental health issues are] definitely something my students will openly tell me that they are dealing with. 'Miss, I have high levels of anxiety and I am unable to come to class all the time.' [Students are] much more transparent about those issues... ." She noted that being aware of these issues had led her to "be more cautious of [my] speech and [xxx] how I present information." Kay, a six-year veteran and one of the newest teachers among my interviewees, felt she did not have enough knowledge of how to work with students who had mental health issues or learning disabilities and wanted more training in those areas. All faculty noted that the services on campus were unable to do much for students who struggled with undiagnosed learning disabilities. What wasn't said is that it is left to the individual teacher in the classroom to figure out, step by step, how to provide individualized support for struggling students.

Although some faculty were perplexed about the changes in the developmental education class cuts and said that they had not seen data to support class changes, others believed that students leaving the college before they enter FYC were the cause. Leilani called this a case of "false cause fallacy, i.e. correlation is not causality," and explained further:

> So they decided students were dropping out of dev ed without ever getting any data as to why students drop out. Why do students drop out? We know, taking care of *tutu* [grandmother], taking care of others, they have to make a living, because the cost of living is so high here, they move somewhere else, occasionally it's because they get deployed. And some of them just come, decide this is not the time in their life they want to do this, and go work for a while, and that's a wonderful thing. I think for people who need to stop going to school for awhile, get a job, see what it's like out there and then come back to college, I think it's fabulous.

Indeed, several faculty echoed the various responsibilities students at the community college juggle. Family is usually an extended family, and work is a big commitment for many students. Will accelerating their time in the community college really provide students with the skills they need to succeed once they graduate? How will we know?

Keeping Curriculum Front and Center

Curriculum is the heart of faculty's lives at the college. Interviewees were clear on their course vision, student expectations, and upper-division college course writing expectations. Student learning outcomes were acknowledged and assessed, and faculty were passionate about the teaching and learning happening in their classrooms (see Appendix 15A).

Two of the teachers, Cindy and Kay, taught a curriculum unique to Hawai'i. Both had been trained in 'Āina-Based Learning, a type of place-based curriculum (Center for Place-Based Learning and Community Engagement, n.d.) that has at its core a Hawaiian indigenous cultural perspective on community and puts the indigenous perspective at the center of the curriculum:

> 'Āina-based education is grounded in teaching and learning through 'āina, which encompasses the land, ocean, air, and all living things. Through 'āina-based approaches, learners can deepen their relationship with the natural environment, cultivate connections within their communities, and build critical skills that can be applied to real-world issues. This experienced-based learning and knowledge sharing offers students the opportunity to engage in holistic, place-based solutions that can address 21st century social, economic, and environmental challenges. 'Āina-based education can help to instill a sense of kūleana (responsibility) to mālama (care for) people, place, and planet in learners of all ages. (State of Hawai'i, 2020, para. 1)

Cindy's curriculum, through the 'āina perspective, innovated a way for students to be active learners, critical thinkers, and writers; she focused on learning through doing, and as with Leilani and Mike, research and information literacy were important:

> The teaching of information literacy, the ability to read, and understand and discern online textual material in addition to what is increasingly becoming a struggle is the research skills and the reading required in college. That's the heavier lifting of getting students ready for four year.

Her curriculum focus included genre awareness, research, and information literacy.

> We have to teach genre awareness, research, information literacy,
> in one 16-week class and we don't get to spread it over two semes-
> ters and still completing 20 pages of highly polished prose. It is a
> very high stakes course. Success rates are not awesome. We have
> tried as faculty to make this a two semester class.

Other faculty echoed Cindy's vision of a FYC class that was two semesters long.

Within the context of the ʻāina curriculum, Cindy widened the window of what FYC could be: "Just last fall I embraced a video project
where I actually had students go out into the community and interview
people for a project we were working on. That was attached to a group
research project that students were working on together. They went
and interviewed the public relations manager at the humane society...
and then they interviewed someone doing climate change and beach
clean up projects." She noted that through these projects the classroom
has become more "dynamic." She added that "project-based assignments and service learning has definitely creeped into the classroom
in different levels" in part because of the institutionalization of service
learning and sustainability on her campus. She created writing projects
connected to service learning projects close to campus at historic sites;
students have worked on signage and other kinds of written communication connected to these sites. The research component of that project
focused on public safety in historic natural sites. Kay also focused on
place-based curriculum in her ESL classrooms viewing the study of the
local area as a good way to help international students learn about the
island and become more comfortable in Hawaiʻi.

It is important to note that the efforts of these faculty to create
thoughtful FYC curriculum tied to the wider community and to college-
level programs was initiated before the massive administrative push to
completely remove developmental education. The innovative curriculum focused on broad campus initiatives, including the expansion of
service learning throughout the school and focusing on the local envi-

ronment through project-based learning. It might be safe to say that both Kay and Cindy knew that their students could be successful in the curricular projects they created (and that their curricular innovations were supported by on-campus service learning and sustainability projects); the added importance to the community would engage students across the finish line, so to speak, creating writing that is meaningful, interesting, and appropriate for FYC college-level students. The broader ʻāina curriculum, developed through statewide initiatives, is an example of what intersegmental approaches can create when faculty are treated as professionals and partners, not as mere implementers of curricular reforms created without faculty leading the initiative, and without faculty fully participating and understanding the curriculum implications to lead student excitement and learning, not mere "success."

Reform for Whom?

The faculty I interviewed approached their jobs professionally, thoughtfully, and with apparent delight when thrust into a new situation that they believed they were neither prepared for professionally nor entirely comfortable with. In Campus 2 we saw that remedial students were not accommodated and were advised to attend Campus 3, where their levels were supported as they accelerated through FYC. In Campus 2, some faculty also acknowledged that the methods and materials for the classes they were teaching were different from their previous FYC classes, and because of the change in the student demographics, they felt unprepared to teach at the lower level required for the new system. The faculty presented in this chapter know the expectations of FYC, yet with the new mandate to teach lower-level students inclusively in FYC, they see students struggle with reading and grammar. Faculty know that their campuses provide resources for students, and they know the limitations of these resources. Furthermore, the decisions made to change the structure of FYC were interpreted differently throughout the different campuses, and the rationales behind the restructuring differed at the three campuses. For example, while Adams' ALP program has clear principles for how FYC classes are constituted with at-level and remedial students (with a separate support class for remedial students), on many campuses the accelerated classes with support are created solely for those who need support. Teachers reported struggling to maintain a FYC curriculum despite the extra time given for support.

Finally, the teachers' narratives suggest that not only does research on FYC classes need to be more robust, focusing on instruction, reading, and student writing and comparing these aspects of FYC with classes outside of the community college (because we know that students will be transferring and need to be competitive once they transfer), but they suggest that in changing program structures without adequate support for teachers and students, and without a fully funded research program, campuses could be adding to structural violence (Farmer et al., 2006) for their students and their faculty. By pushing students through programs they are not ready for nor do they want, students could feel stressed and leave the class not prepared for the challenges that lie ahead. For the students who are already prepared for a robust FYC, a FYC course that incorporates remediation and is based on remediation models of education students could, as Finn and Avni suggest in Chapter 14 of this volume, actually "deaccelerate" students; in other words, the classes could be a repeat of what some students have succeeded at in high school and then would not provide them with what they need to be successful in upper-division classes and their college and career trajectory.

As for faculty, more research is needed to understand the emotional work that faculty perform, especially in regards to pushing students through programs when the students might not be competent nor want to follow a particular pathway; the added stress students encounter could cause more faculty burnout and compassion fatigue. Increasingly, faculty speak about administrators across the higher education spectrum who tend to blame faculty for a lack of skilled approaches to dealing with student underpreparedness (rather than consider that there is poor administrative planning, or the state legislators made a big mistake, or that the K–12 system is not preparing students for college work, or that the socio-economic situation of students living in the community has fallen so fast in the face of lightening speed gentrification that education has become a luxury rather than a priority or right). As seen in the interviews, faculty have started to internalize this narrative into blaming themselves in a never-ending cycle to speed up the community college trajectory. Might it be that the "get 'em in, get 'em through, get 'em out" proposals are accurate for planning course sequences, but not for actual teaching and student learning? Is actual instructional observation research or long-term ethnographic research needed to supplement or replace the current reliance on statistical data used to measure the efficiency (and some argue the efficacy as well) of the new accelerated FYC programs (cf. Grubb, 2013)?

In the new world of accelerated FYC, faculty are teaching students who have struggled with learning; remedial instruction is not limited to the support section, but throughout the FYC curriculum faculty adjust their pedagogy to the broader array of student learning needs. Teachers noted the time they needed to spend on teaching basic grammar and reading, and in some cases, they believed they were not prepared to teach at such a low level. The internalization of the narrative "not prepared" or "don't know how" is the beginning of the normalization of a system more concerned with paradigms of time and money rather than of education. A whole system can become complicit in getting the students through rather than focusing on what the students need to transfer to more challenging course work at a possibly more challenging school. Because of the added time needed to create curriculum for students struggling with the fundamentals of grammar or reading, time spent to create meaningful and innovative curriculum including technological innovations will be lessened. Faculty are being asked to capitulate to a system that might not be serving the students it was set up to serve. And acceleration is exactly a kind of structural violence within an already stressed wider political, social, and economic system. It is imperative that teachers' expertise in curriculum, as demonstrated by the Hawai'i teachers, be supported. Wise curriculum planning and change using the expertise of faculty and the innovative models that faculty are confident work, might actually increase the capacity of students to move through the community college system toward a four-year degree and challenging career trajectory.

Teachers need to be part of the decision-making process and must be part of all research when it comes to curricular changes. Faculty voices need to be listened to and protected within a larger narrative of student success and curriculum progress. Just as there is a faculty senate with a cabinet of President, Vice President, Treasurer, and other offices in the college dedicated to faculty input, there must be an office dedicated to faculty research input, especially when it comes to curricular matters and funding priorities. Although unionized, faculty are not mere service providers; they are trained professionals who have worked hard to get their positions at the community college. They are schooled through several degrees, their teaching and other professional experience, and the extra training and professional development they engage in throughout their careers. By ignoring faculty voices on student learning and curriculum, community colleges minimize faculty professionalism and faculty perspectives and could endanger their school's success.

I end with two final faculty perspectives on the complexity of faculty work at the community college that most administrators or legislators might not be privy to.

> I do email students [when they are absent]. I call them, you know. I try to help them—I even give them my home phone number. I encourage them to stay in touch, um, I try, but there's just so much I can do, if they're not willing to do the work, or they cannot get here. A lot of our students are wickedly stressed. I mean, it's just unbelievable. Sometimes I go home and cry. Like the student who comes in with black eyes. Can I get you something? Can I take you to somebody? And you know... (Phillip pauses here for a few seconds, and locks eyes with me acknowledging that students' lives are more complicated than we can ever imagine)

> I work all the time. I do a lot of one-on-one [about two hours of office hours a day] with my students. I start meeting with students at 8 am. I teach 9 to 2 without break. 2:00 to 3:00 I meet with students. I come home and work all night and work all weekend. I reach out to my colleagues a lot. I do a lot of groundwork. I ask them, can you work with my students? We have TRIO—counselors who work with students with learning disabilities. ...I have even asked to have counselors come to my class. I do whatever it takes. I try not to beat myself up over it. This student is not learning, but I don't know what to do. (Kay)

Acknowledgments

I want to sincerely thank all of the individuals who participated in the interviews for my project and helped me during my sabbatical in Hawai'i. To each of you, mahalo nui loa. You have enriched my life in ways that you will never know.

References

Adams, P., Gearhart, S., Miller, R., & Roberts, A. (2009). The accelerated learning program: Throwing open the gates. *Journal of Basic Writing, 28*(2), 50–69.

Adelman, C. (1993). Kurt Lewin and the origins of action research. *Educational Action Research, 1*(1), 7-24. doi: 10.1080/0965079930010102

Bailey, T.R., Jaggars, S.S. & Jenkins, D. (2015). *Redesigning America's community colleges: A clearer path to student success.* Cambridge, MA. Harvard University Press.

California Community Colleges Chancellor's Office. (2020). Student centered funding formula. Retrieved from https://www.cccco.edu/About-Us/Chancellors-Office/Divisions/College-Finance-and-Facilities-Planning/Student-Centered-Funding-Formula

Center for Place Based Learning and Community Engagement. What is place-based education? (n.d.). Retrieved from https://promiseofplace.org/what-is-pbe/what-is-place-based-education

Farmer, P., Nizeye, B., Stulac, S., & Keshavjee, S., (2006). Structural violence and clinical medicine. *PLoS Medicine, 3*(10), 1686–1691. doi: 10.1371/journal.pmed.0030449.

Grubb, W. N. (with Gabriner, R.). (2013). *Basic skills education in community colleges: Inside and outside of classrooms.* New York: Routledge.

Harklau, L., Batson, K., & McGovern, K. (2019, March). *Eliminating college ESL courses, services, & programs: Teacher perspectives.* Paper presented at the American Association of Applied Linguistics annual conference, Atlanta, Georgia.

Illowsky, B. (2008). The California basic skills initiative. *New Directions for Community Colleges, 144*, 83–91.

State of Hawai'i. (2020). 'Āina-Based Education & Community Engagement. Retrieved from https://dashboard.hawaii.gov/stat/goals/5xhf-begg/nmui-ua2k/vy3r-ycc2

APPENDIX 15A
Student Learning Outcomes (SLOs) for FYC at Three Hawai'i Community Colleges

Campus 1

SLO 1: Use a multi-step writing process that includes drafting, editing, and proofreading while making use of written and oral feedback.

SLO 2: Write compositions, including an in-class essay on an assigned topic, that are appropriate to a particular audience and purpose. Texts will have a main point and supporting ideas developed with specific and logically oriented details.

SLO 3: Compose complex and well-reasoned texts that incorporate source material.

Skill 1: Locate, assess, and use academically appropriate source material.

Skill 2: Use and combine sources without plagiarizing.

Skill 3: Give credit to others when using their words and ideas in writing.

SLO 4: Apply to writing the rules and conventions of grammar, word choice, punctuation and spelling.

SLO 5: Demonstrate effective use of study skills and college success strategies.

Campus 2

○ Employ a writing process which includes gathering information and exploring ideas, developing and supporting a point of view or thesis, organizing, revising, editing, and proofreading.

○ Produce different forms of college-level writing, such as narrative, analytical, and persuasive essays, whose content, organization, diction, and style are effectively adapted to various writing situations, purposes, audiences, and subjects.

○ Analyze and evaluate the logic, evidence, and strategies of an argument (written and/or presented in a visual or digital medium).

○ Analyze and interpret a literary work (nonfiction, fiction, poetry, or drama) or other textual material.

○ Find and evaluate information from a library, from the Internet, or from other sources; synthesize relevant findings in his/her own writing without plagiarizing.

○ Work effectively with fellow students and the instructor in providing and receiving written and verbal feedback on assigned work.

○ Write a coherent in-class response to an assigned question or topic

Campus 3

○ Demonstrate clear, logical, and inventive thinking through writing.

○ Gather and evaluate information purposefully from electronic and print sources.

○ Produce writing whose form, organization, syntax, diction, style, and tone are appropriate for college writing.

○ Write a research paper that supports a thesis, integrates expert opinions from various sources, and documents sources appropriately.

○ Revise, edit, and proofread for correctness, clarity, and effectiveness.

16

Institutional Research (IR) and Remediation Reform: A Contextualized Exploration for Faculty

Terrence Willett
CABRILLO COLLEGE

Mallory Newell
DE ANZA COLLEGE

Craig Hayward
BAKERSFIELD COLLEGE

Editors' Note: As we developed our vision for this volume, our priorities focused on broadening the scope of pedagogies and ways of understanding FYC. We wanted to provide community college FYC instructors with new ways of thinking about pedagogy not only from the perspective of faculty innovators, but also from the perspective of a new wave of researchers who are influencing CC policy and FYC curriculum. We believe that for English faculty to be most effective in the current campus political and funding climate, an introduction to institutional research is necessary. Good research can help FYC teachers be more effective in their classrooms and help colleges fulfill their educational missions. Questionable research, especially research done without faculty involvement, can severely devastate an English department, possibly leading to class cuts, problems with achieving good student learning outcomes, and a demoralized faculty.

In 2005, Meryl had the privilege of being part of a multi-college pedagogy and research program, "Strengthening Precollegiate Education in Community Colleges" (SPECC), sponsored by the Carnegie Foundation. Working with institutional and faculty researchers, participants formed faculty inquiry groups both to analyze data focused on student success (such as pass rates and retention rates) in their classrooms and throughout their departments and to reflect as a group on teaching and learning. Through the work of several entities including foundations, researchers, and SPECC faculty grantees, efforts for California community college remedial education reform grew, leading Katie Hern and Myra Snell to form the California Acceleration Project (CAP). In part, CAP's efforts were supported by the research ethos of the RP Group, a non-profit that was "formed in 1992 in order to advocate for and support the use of data and evidence to illuminate effective policy and practice within our state's community colleges" (www.rpgroup.org). Math, ESOL, and FYC faculty have worked with RP Group-affiliated researchers, and the RP Group's "Multiple Measures Assessment Project" (MMAP) is often cited in California's decision to forgo formal English placement testing, allowing students who in the past might have been placed into a remedial or developmental class direct access to FYC; this curricular designation was legislated through California's State Assembly Bill AB705.

Consideration of the importance of data for educational policy initiatives which directly affect classroom curriculum and teacher efficacy is also driven by fiscal imperatives. These policy and financial issues are not what most FYC teachers had in mind when they decided to become community college English faculty. Nevertheless, they are now essential concepts that all college faculty should understand as they envision their work in the larger context of their campuses and college systems. We have therefore invited researchers from the RP Group, Terrence Willett, Mallory Newell, and Craig Hayward, to elucidate the work of institutional researchers and the way they can support FYC faculty. We hope this chapter provides an introduction into the ways that faculty can work hand-in-hand with institutional researchers.

A Brief History of IR in California

In California community colleges, the expansion of institutional research (IR) offices has paralleled efforts to expand moral and fiscal accountability with clear goals and measurable objectives at the college, district, or system level. Established in 1907, California's community colleges grew out of the K–12 structure and modelled K–12 administrative control via elected local boards. In 1960, California created a three-tier master educational system that included the notion of transfer from community colleges into four-year degree programs; the University of California was the primary academic research institution, the California State Universities focused on graduate (professional and teacher education) and undergraduate education, and the community colleges were seen as having a broader reach including academic (the first two years of higher education) and vocational instruction (California State Department of Education, 1960). The state legislature created a community college system office in 1967 separate from the California Department of Education (CCCCO, 2004). The Seymour-Campbell Matriculation Act of 1986 created regulations for assessment validation that prompted the first in a series of accountability-related incentives for colleges to establish institutional research offices. In 1998, the legislature established the Partnership for Excellence (PFE) program (Education Trailer Bill, 1998), the next wave of accountability funding used in part to hire a new generation of institutional researchers to establish new IR offices or augment existing ones. For example, two of the authors of this chapter were first hired on PFE money to expand existing offices and then went to found offices at colleges without IR capacity. While the primary goal was to assist faculty, administrators, and staff to increase prescribed student outcomes such as degree attainment and transfer, IR offices also ensured compliance with regulations for placement testing. Establishing prerequisites as well as evaluating support services and addressing a variety of research-based inquiries were also part of the work tasked to IR.

A consequence of numerous colleges having IR offices is that college employees typically have an office they can turn to for assistance in deciphering and implementing policy and obtaining basic facts to serve as a basis for common understanding throughout the college. It is not uncommon for IR personnel to become "thought partners" as faculty and others develop proposals for new initiatives. Many researchers have community college teaching experience, which enhances the value of their perspectives. Acting as both a soundboard and data and regulatory authority, IR professionals can help provide early feedback to faculty about what is allowable, what is feasible, what is likely to work well based on prior research, and what funding sources may be applicable. Over time the IR role has expanded, and offices once overseen by directors are now typically overseen by deans and associate vice presidents. Some IR offices also have an affiliated grants office that can aid proposal development for private and government funding. This expansion has often included a change in roles from IR to "institutional effectiveness" or IE. Rooted in accreditation and accountability, this use of the term IE perhaps began in 1984 via updated standards by the Commission on Colleges (COC) of the Southern Association of Colleges and Schools (SACS) (Head, 2011). The phrase appears repeatedly in the Accrediting Commission for Community and Junior Colleges (ACCJC, 2014) standards and can be considered an umbrella term that covers student learning assessment, accountability, and institutional research (Head, 2011). For faculty, this means their IR/IE thought partners have developed a broader scope of understanding of regulations and standards, college operations, and student learning and so should be more effective in providing advice and assistance. At the same time, IR offices have grown in their responsibilities for mandatory reporting and ensuring that the college receives its regular allocations in addition to new grant resources.

What are some examples of areas where IR and faculty have worked together to make positive change in community colleges?

It is likely that the bulk of the examples of IR and faculty working together to improve the colleges are undocumented ephemeral instances of collaboration. From IR responding to a question about student demographics and success rates to faculty helping IR understand critical aspects of the classroom experience and advances in pedagogy, this routine dialogue improves information flow and grounds college operations. There are also formal collaborative examples including grant proposal development, writing institutional self-evaluation reports for accreditation, evaluating curricular and support innovations, and validating prerequisites and placement systems.

Whether a state grant like the recent Basic Skills Student Outcomes and Transformation (BSSOT) effort or a federal Title V or National Science Foundation (NSF) grant, these proposal efforts typically require extensive input from faculty to determine the details of a proposed innovation or project for students. IR provides the background information on the college as well as key data to support the fundamental problem statement for a grant proposal. This may be low throughput rates (e.g., the percent of a cohort of students completing transfer-level English within one year), skills mastery via student learning outcome (SLO) assessments, or equity gaps in program participation (e.g., women in science) or completion (e.g., difference in transfer rates among ethnicity groups). The dialogue among faculty, IR, and the grant writer around defining the aspects of college accountability or student achievement that the grant is designed to improve can be the most dynamic and interesting, especially when areas thought to be problematic turn out not to be as bad as perceived and unexpected areas of concern arise. Faculty implementation plans, including pedagogical changes, are also developed with IR input while grant writing to ensure the evaluation and reporting requirements of the grant can be met. Once the grant is awarded, there is then the ongoing relationship between the project faculty and IR to conduct formative assessment to ensure fidelity of implementation.

Of course, innovations can occur outside of a grant context and do not always require evaluation. It can be rewarding for both faculty and IR to partner on determining the efficacy of a new idea. In the early 2000s when working at Gavilan College, Terrence Willett attended a Learning Community symposium led by Vincent Tinto, a leader in student dropout research and learning communities, along with English department faculty. Colleagues in the English department were very excited to develop learning communities at the college. Upon their return, they worked together with other colleagues to determine all aspects of implementation including which courses and instructors to pair, how to schedule the courses and program the student information system to handle linked sections, developed surveys for the students, interviewed faculty on their experiences, and reviewed success and persistence outcomes. It turned out there was no impact on student success rates (earning a grade of C or better) for learning communities students. However, these students were more likely to enroll in the subsequent semester (persistence), which is consistent with classic work on student engagement and persistence (e.g., Astin, 1977; Tinto, 1993). Because of the trust and mutual respect developed between the English department and IR, when these findings were researched and presented, English faculty were open to understanding the results. The experiences of sharing common understandings and researching the efficacy of the school's learning communities helped to reshape the college's expectations about the effect of learning communities on student persistence and success.

A statewide example of faculty-IR collaboration is found in the California Partnership for Achieving Student Success (Cal-PASS). Two key components of this effort are data sharing among K–12 and postsecondary institutions and the resulting inquiry from intersegmental faculty. Linking the data to examine transitions among education segments, for example, high school and community college, served as a starting place for discussions among faculty at neighboring institutions. These discussions were structured through professional learning councils (PLC) with a moderator and assigned research staff to collect and address follow-up research questions.

The faculty helped IR by validating the classification of courses, which improved data quality, while IR provided faculty with data on how students fared in the transition from high school to college. A common finding when examining the high school to college transition was that the majority of students were repeating coursework already taken in high school or otherwise not progressing directly into college-level work. The early CalPASS PLCs (during approximately 2005 to 2010) compared course objectives and texts to attempt to better align curricula and develop shared projects to improve student transition.

English faculty PLCs began with the starting assumption that completion of 12th grade English should prepare students for first-year composition (FYC). However, they did not necessarily assume the college's remedial courses were analogous to high school grade-level classes. One area of misalignment they found was that high school standards tended to be literature based while those for college writing were more expository. Although K–12 instructors were grounded in the state standards and college teachers were rooted to the college composition outline to ensure it met graduation and articulation requirements, they were able to find areas of alignment. One effort in the San Diego area had K–12 teachers and college English faculty engage in an English Curriculum Alignment Project (ECAP) (Valdez & Marshall, 2013). This effort was coupled with a policy shift to allow students earning a grade of B or better in 12th grade English at the local high school direct entry into FYC. Using the CalPASS data system these faculty had helped refine, students were tracked from high school to college to assess their achievement. Pilot students had success rates in FYC at least as high as comparison students who placed using the college assessment test, with 84 percent of the pilot students and 70 percent of comparison students earning a C or better (CalPASS report, www.calpassplug.org). This pilot informed subsequent discussions of alignment with high schools and placement policies that now are framed against new California regulations (AB 705 placement reforms, discussed later in this chapter).

A more challenging collaboration for faculty and IR professionals centers around assessment and placement. Placement validation for incoming students can be inherently antagonistic, as IR has the role of following validation guidelines and ensuring compliance with assessment regulations, which can seemingly or actually encroach upon faculty's role in providing primary guidance on "standards or policies regarding student preparation and success" as a "10+1" academic matter (title 5 §53200 (c)). In addition, as English departments can be among the largest on campus, there is sometimes potential for disagreements within a department about how to handle placement issues irrespective of the input from IR and student services. At the college level, once again the virtues of trust and respect support compliance and Title 5's original intent of open access while honoring faculty concerns about ensuring that students entering courses such as FYC have sufficient preparation to be successful rather than frustrated.

Recent placement reform efforts have been built on collaborations between faculty and IR. For example, the steering committee for the Common Assessment Initiative (CAI) included Academic Senate faculty from many disciplines and college IR representatives as well as a team of researchers from the Multiple Measures Assessment Project (MMAP). The CAI was intended to provide a common platform and set of assessment tests free to all colleges in the system to increase placement accuracy and create placement portability as students moved among California community colleges. The steering committee of the CAI and the state Academic Senate in particular served as peer reviewers for the MMAP research. MMAP researchers presented findings to the steering committee in person and via email and phone conversations and responded to questions and concerns on methods; they then revised and resubmitted their report to the committee. In addition, local research offices using the openly published MMAP methods and analysis code would also provide feedback on their replications to further improve the analysis and the documentation of methods.

This collaborative and iterative research process has resulted in numerous research questions, validation efforts, and discomfort with the implications of the key findings that placement tests were underplacing students, especially students of color and women, and that high school achievement data have greater predictive validity than placement instruments, particularly in math and English courses. These findings to date have not only held true at the statewide aggregated level but also at the local high school and college level. Once the CAI was abandoned and the new legislation of AB 705 adopted in 2017 that required use of high school data in placement, a new collaboration was formed at the state level with the AB 705 implementation committee consisting of Academic Senate representatives, MMAP researchers, and student services personnel. This continued the iterative peer review process with committee members asking detailed questions on methods and requesting additional analyses to both verify main findings but also answer followup questions about specific subgroups. Some areas of additional scrutiny included examining local variation to attempt to find colleges with patterns that contradicted state averages and focusing on students with the lowest high school GPAs to see if any group benefited from remedial sequences more than from direct access to college-level courses. While local variation was present, no college examined had a pattern opposite the state-level findings that would lead to a different state policy. Even with the lowest-performing high school students, the MMAP team was unable to find any group that had higher completion rates of FYC or college-level math after going through a remedial sequence as compared to direct access to transfer level. These types of findings from the iterative peer review process challenged the assumptions of local variability and the effectiveness of remedial courses in preparing students for transfer-level courses including FYC. This not only had implications for placement processes but also caused another faculty-IR collaboration, the California Acceleration Project (CAP), to rethink their strategy on acceleration of basic skills and focus on concurrent supports rather than pre-transfer remediation. These efforts relied, in part, on the necessary tension among academics in the faculty and IR ranks with different perspectives to determine common understandings and agree on how to respond to new information. For example, there is the "tyranny of the average," where a new IR report can suggest policy reforms that should help more students on average, such as direct access to FYC with support, while faculty must work directly with the students who do not fit the average and struggle under the new policy. It can be difficult to watch an individual student struggle even if one knows intellectually that a reform policy will help more students succeed overall. It behooves IR personnel to remember this difference between the average versus the individual and honor the experiences of classroom faculty and their students as they work to integrate policy reform with daily practice.

How can faculty partner with IR to make sure that their concerns for data are heard and followed up by IR?

Most colleges tend to have both formal and informal processes by which faculty can request data and research from IR. The formal process may consist of a research request form or using a chain-of-command approach to bring their question to their department chair who can bring it to their dean then to the Vice President of Instruction to the President and then to the IR office (assuming they report to the President). Research requests could range from enrollment trends to rates of progression through curriculum sequences to disaggregation of success rates by ethnicity. Substantial changes in courses or supports also can lead to requests for evaluation to determine if student achievement has improved.

The informal process results from engaging directly with IR personnel such as before or after a meeting, via chance encounters in the hallway, or inviting IR staff to coffee. While IR staff have mandatory tasks and competing priorities, an engaged and curious faculty member's inquiry is often a welcomed reprieve from required routine reporting. However, IR staff may be cautious if a question has political or compensation-related implications and may ask that a broader circle of people be brought into the inquiry to provide a balanced perspective on the request. Getting research requests prioritized is discussed later in this chapter.

How can faculty work with IR to comply with changes in educational policy and funding requirements but at the same time not give up their pedagogical missions? What do faculty need to know?

Ideally there would be no conflict among educational and public policy, funding requirements, and effective pedagogy. However, there can be both perceived and actual conflicts. The current major policy change around intake and assessment with the passage of AB 705 that disallows California community colleges from blocking students from enrolling in the first transfer-level course in the English and math sequences "unless placement research that includes consideration of high school grade point average and coursework shows that those students are highly unlikely to succeed in transfer-level coursework in English and mathematics" without remedial coursework (Introduction, para. 3, provides an interesting case study). This legislation in part was driven by findings on both the positive effects of shortening remedial sequences, or acceleration (Hayward & Willett, 2014), and the strong predictive utility of high school grades over standardized tests known as "multiple measures" in assessment (Bahr et al., 2019). In addition to high school performance, other measures of student capacity include "credit for prior learning" such as skills learned in military service not associated with a certificate or degree. There are no uniform policies for granting credit in these instances, but it may be an emerging area of inquiry. Institutional researchers on both of these projects worked with a group of faculty to determine the research design and determine the implications of findings. With acceleration, the research team was brought in by members of the California Acceleration Project (CAP) to evaluate their innovations with new basic skills pedagogy and shortened sequences. This innovation was by no means broadly accepted, but when the results indicated that acceleration had "large and robust effects" (Hayward & Willett, 2014) that resulted in much higher FYC and transfer-level math completion rates, faculty were able to engage in discussions about effective pedagogy and rethink traditional classroom techniques.

On the heels of that finding, a team of institutional researchers worked under the auspices of the Common Assessment Initiative with Academic Senate peer review to explore the use of high school data as a multiple measure. That research indicated educators had been underestimating students' ability to succeed by using point-in-time low-stakes standardized tests and unnecessarily preventing students, especially students of color and women, from access to transfer-level coursework. Moreover, subsequent research to support the implementation of AB 705 could not find a group of students with high school transcripts who were more likely to complete transfer level coursework if they engaged in remedial coursework first (MMAP, 2018). This has been a challenging finding as the California community college as a system has had to grapple with the fact that the assessment systems were a form of unintentional institutional racism. Faculty across the state are again partnering with institutional researchers to test new pedagogical formats such as co-requisite "just in time" remediation. This type of remediation differs from traditional remediation that typically consisted of requiring a student to take one or more remedial courses prior to enrolling in a college-level course. Just in time remediation allows a student to enter into a college-level course and receive remediation during the term based on only specific areas of need. For example, a student enrolled in FYC might need extra help with transitions or more complex sentence constructions and can receive assistance in these areas in a co-requisite support course, tutoring, or other means. Testing new approaches like these can be fraught if there is not sufficient trust and scholarly openness to new information. Researchers must establish their credibility and be open to challenges to their methods and faculty must be responsible peer reviewers while also being receptive to disappointing results. In the best circumstances this cycle of trust, verifying assumptions, implementing reforms, and evaluating results can bring great benefits for students.

With respect to funding, one fundamental aspect of most public education systems is that there is a minimum viable class size on average. The typical college cannot afford to run large numbers of sections with fewer than 15 or 20 students. With increased expectations for faculty to provide holistic support to address non-academic issues (finances, housing, and food insecurity, etc.), larger classes can be efficient revenue generators in the short term, but if students are not sufficiently supported, they may be more likely to "stop out," or discontinue their enrollment at the college for one or more terms. Placing additional burdens on classroom faculty without support from student services could also increase the risk of faculty burn out. Increasingly, partnerships between classroom faculty and student services can effectively lower the teacher to student ratio as specialists aid students to find financial support and social services.

What does it mean to "speak IR"? How can a faculty member get their requests prioritized? How can IR and faculty agree on what positive change is?

Every profession has its culture and associated specialized language. The more one can understand the culture and use the language of a provider in a profession, the more likely they are to get what they want. Institutional researchers are trained to infer the intent of a research inquiry, ask many clarifying questions, and provide a report that provides answers to anticipated questions. Taken too far, this attempt to "mind read" and predict follow-up questions can miss the original intent, but the better the IR analyst knows you and your interests and the more you can use the language of IR, the more likely these additional analyses will be useful. Speaking IR includes knowing the definitions of specialty words such as:

Success: earning a grade of C or better in a course.

Completion: not earning a grade of W in a course or not dropping after census.

Retention: being enrolled in a subsequent term.

Basic Skills: a non-transferable course with a CB08 value of B (CB refers to the Course Basic table for the Chancellor's Office Management Information System (COMIS)).

All of these words have colloquial meanings as well and so can cause confusion if an analyst is unclear on whether the everyday or technical definition is intended. Also be prepared to provide specific timeframes of interest (e.g., Fall 2015 to Fall 2018 or the last five complete academic years), understanding that there is typically a time delay between the completion of a term and when the data have been vetted for use by IR.

Getting a request prioritized will vary greatly on the capacity of the IR office at that moment. The office may be short staffed or have a set of high-priority mandatory reports that could delay or table a request. Some tips to increase the priority of a request include: (1) asking a question well before a deadline and (2) having the request sponsored by a department, task force, committee, grant effort, or leadership (e.g., academic senate president, vice president of instruction, etc.). Engaging with IR well before a deadline will get the request in the queue and will allow time for dialogue on the request, including clarifying definitions, reviewing a draft report, and requesting revisions or follow-up items. Getting your item sponsored through a governance or leadership entity or connected to a funded project conveys that the request is of utility to more than a single person and will be used more broadly for improvement. These actions also aid relationship-building with IR. Having an early initial discussion of your research ideas over coffee or lunch can be a great way connect with IR professionals and get you answers when you need them.

Allowing time for these exchanges will also help develop a common understanding of positive change. Faculty can be rightly focused on pedagogy while IR professionals can highlight compliance or technical correctness of an analytical approach. Here again the "tyranny of the average," where perspectives are shaped by the most common occurrences while overlooking rare situations, can result in an IR report leading to policies that will help students on average but fail to address special needs. The MMAP research found that, in general, students with a high school GPA above 2.6 could likely be successful in FYC. However, that does not mean that all individual students are sufficiently prepared or have the capacity to succeed without substantial assistance either financial, social, or otherwise. Policies such as AB 705 were based on research showing what should work for most, but there still exists the need to attend to the needs of individuals.

How can faculty insight into qualitative data be inserted into IR priorities?

There is a quasi-faux distinction between quantitative and qualitative data that is a topic of great interest to IR practitioners. The terms *quantitative data* or *quantitative research* are often associated with vast arrays of numbers analyzed by multivariate regression, machine learning algorithms, or other arcane techniques. The output of these analyses can be likened to the reading of tea leaves or the entrails of a sacrificial lamb by the initiated. With inscrutability can come mistrust.

However, in education one of the key pieces of data are grades earned or conferred in a class by a student. A grade, strictly speaking, is an ordered categorical variable placing a student into a hierarchy of performance as defined by the instructor. In practice, grades are converted to numeric grade points and grade point averages, seemingly turning qualitative evaluations into quantitative data. Grades can also be thought of in categories: passing or failing. IR analysts often create binary success indicators, where a C or better is coded as a 1 and other grades as 0, which are often used in IR to calculate success rates. A successful completion typically means a student can progress to the next course in the sequence or can count that class for graduation or transfer. Once again, a category or qualitative measure has been converted into a number suitable for quantitative analyses.

Other data typically considered qualitative can range from anecdotes of students' overcoming adversity or failing to be responsible with assignments to data gleaned from focus groups or surveys of students, faculty, or staff. Often these data are summarized using quantitative measures such as the percentage of students indicating satisfaction with a course or the number of times tutoring services were mentioned in focus groups. Within a focus group, for example, qualitative researchers can spend vast amounts of time and effort coding interviews to determine themes by the frequency with which key terms are used and the quality and intensity of associated adjectives. For example, one can quantify the number of times tutoring services were mentioned and the percent of the time the comments were positive, critical, neutral, or mixed. These numeric summaries can then have quantitative techniques applied to their analysis. So while there is a distinction between quantitative and qualitative research methods, it is more of a continuum of analysis than a strict set of antipodal approaches.

Faculty insight is key to the effective use of research, often in the context of interpreting both how data were generated and how to usefully interpret analytical outputs. Interpreting grade points or success data necessitates knowing whether or not there is a norming of grades (i.e., faculty in a department agreeing on a common set of grading criteria) or a substantial pedagogical change during the study period or other influencing factor that only faculty would know. Further, having faculty, staff, and/or administrators involved in the development of research questions generally increases the relevance and utility of the work done. One approach to inclusion is inviting a faculty requestor to act as a member of the research team who defines the research question up front, gathers important contextual information, and interprets results to develop conclusions and recommendations. There could be concern about the ability of the teacher-researcher to maintain objectivity and independence in the process (Hammersley, 2002; Hodgkinson, 1957). This is a valid concern but not limited to just the inclusion of practitioners, and IR personnel can help to maintain fidelity. What is gained by including faculty in the research process is the development of research questions that are more likely to be perceived as useful and actionable by faculty. The faculty participant also gains more knowledge of the research process and can help with critical questions during the analysis phase to result in a more thorough and complete research product.

References

AB-705 Seymour-Campbell Student Success Act of 2012: Matriculation: assessment. (2017–2018). Retrieved from https://leginfo.legislature.ca.gov/faces/home.xhtml

The Accrediting Commission for Community and Junior Colleges. (2014). *ACCJC Standards June 2014.* Novato, CA. Retrieved from https://accjc.org/eligibility-requirements-standards-policies/

Astin, A. W. (1977). *Preventing students from dropping out.* San Francisco: Jossey-Bass.

Bahr, P.B., Fagioli, L.P., Hetts, J., Hayward, C., Willett, T., Lamoree, D., Newell, M.A., Sorey, K., & Baker, R.B. (2019). Improving placement accuracy in California's community colleges using multiple measures of high school achievement. *Community College Review, 47*(2), 178–211. doi: 10.1177/0091552119840705

California Community Colleges Chancellor's Office (CCCCO). (2004). *An aspiration for excellence: Review of the system office for the California community colleges.* Sacramento: California Community Colleges Chancellor's Office. Retrieved from www.cccco.edu

California State Department of Education. (1960). *A master plan for higher education in California, 1960–1975.* Sacramento: California State Department of Education. Retrieved from https://www.ucop.edu/acadinit/mastplan/MasterPlan1960.pdf

Education Trailer Bill to the Budget Act of 1998, California Senate Bill 1564 (Schiff) Chapter 330 (1998). Retrieved from http://www.leginfo.ca.gov/pub/97-98/bill/sen/sb_1551-1600/sb_1564_bill_19980821_chaptered.pdf

Hammersley, M. (2002, 12–14 September). *Action research: A contradiction in terms?* Presentation at the Annual Conference of the British Educational Research Association, University of Exeter, England.

Hayward, C., & Willett, T. (2014). *Curricular redesign and gatekeeper completion: A multicollege evaluation of the California Acceleration Project.* San Rafael: The Research and Planning Group for California Community Colleges.

Head, R. B. (2011). The evolution of institutional effectiveness in the community college. *New Directions for Community Colleges,* 5–11. doi: 10.1002/cc.432

Hodgkinson, H. L. (1957). Action research: A critique. *The Journal of Educational Sociology, 31*(4), 137–153. doi: 10.2307/2264741

MMAP Research Team. (2018). *AB 705 Success rates estimates technical paper: Estimating success rates for students placed directly into transfer-level English and math courses.* San Rafael, CA: The Research and Planning Group for California Community Colleges. Retrieved from https://rpgroup.org/RP-Projects/All-Projects/Multiple-Measures/Publications

Seymour-Campbell Matriculation Act of 1986, Cal. EDC § 78210-78218 (1986). https://law.justia.com/codes/california/2005/edc/78210-78218.html

Tinto, V. (1993). *Leaving college: Rethinking the causes and cures of student attrition* (2nd ed.). Chicago: University of Chicago Press.

Valdez, S. & Marshall, D. (2013). Working across the segments: High schools and the college completion agenda. *New Directions for Community Colleges,* (164), 47–55.

Conclusion:
Listening to Teachers

Betsy Gilliland
UNIVERSITY OF HAWAI'I MĀNOA

Meryl Siegal
LANEY COLLEGE

As we wrap up this volume, we want to return to some of the themes that initially inspired the book project as well as those that are raised in the chapters. These issues continue to be a concern for community college FYC teachers and their colleagues in other departments and at other institutions, and we do not pretend to have solved them with this book. Nevertheless, we value the contributions the authors of these chapters have made in raising the bar for what is possible in community college FYC nationwide. Their work proposes a new vision and understanding of FYC in community colleges.

One central issue that resonates throughout the book is a concern with equity—commonly defined as fair, rather than equal, treatment that allows all students access to learning experiences and opportunities for success. Equity for poor and ethno-racially minoritized students is one of the primary driving forces behind the multiple community college reform movements that have radically restructured FYC courses nationwide. The contributors have described ways that community college FYC programs enable access to and success in college for high school students living in rural Utah (Chapter 9) and middle class South Korean students who would otherwise not have a chance to study abroad or perhaps even attend college at all (Chapter 12). Teachers' approaches facilitate students' opportunities to feel comfortable in the writing classroom through building human relationships with their teachers (Chapter 6) and to learn the threshold concepts in writing ("concepts critical for continued learning and participation in an area or community of practice"; Adler-Kassner & Wardle, 2015, p. 2) necessary for continuing success in college (Chapter 4). Equity is also the driving force behind contract grading, an anti-racist practice that gives students agency in setting their own goals for learning in a course (Chapter 5).

Connected to equity is the importance of providing support and scaffolding so students can achieve learning goals from wherever they start out. These can be socio-cognitive, learning through observation, imitation, and modeling (Chapter 3), or from meta-level discussions of the ways that reading (Chapter 2) or writing (Chapter 4) happen in the context of FYC. Appropriate scaffolding can also support learners with disabilities to understand the structures of academic texts and create their own (Chapter 7).

Community college FYC courses have the potential to engage students through connecting with what the students themselves find inspiring. Courses designed for specific programs or learning communities at a college, such as Career Technical Education (Chapter 10) or a STEM Academy (Chapter 8), can transform the experience of FYC from feeling unconnected to students' reasons for attending college, to being meaningful and supporting the students toward completing their career goals. Individual instructors can also help students develop identities as successful college writers through carefully designed journal prompts (Chapter 1).

In addition to these practical concepts, these chapters bring our attention to the bigger picture around community college FYC programs. We see how analysis of national-level data can reveal ways that community college English learners engage with their college communities and persist in their studies, actions that FYC teachers can encourage to help their students access college resources and maximize their learning (Chapter 11). At the college or system level, Institutional Research Offices can provide teachers with information about their students' experiences and persistence while also supporting teachers wishing to conduct their own research into student learning (Chapter 16). When states or institutions propose major changes to placement or curriculum, teacher perspectives sometimes get lost in higher-level policymaking. Carefully designed reform processes may be able to engage teachers in feeling like they have some input (Chapter 13), although other teachers report feeling like their concerns were not heard and reforms pushed them to change their teaching in ways with which they were not necessarily comfortable (Chapter 14). Similarly, listening to teacher voices can reveal how important decisions at the curricular level do not necessarily include faculty, and teachers' stories can also point out important differences in how teachers (compared with administrators or legislators) view student (and teacher) success (Chapter 15).

Looking at the extent of work presented in these chapters we also wonder: What connects these courses? What makes a FYC course? What *is* FYC? The chapters give us a wide-ranging answer to these questions:

- ❍ FYC is a requirement to get a two-year degree or transfer to a four-year university.
- ❍ FYC scaffolds learning for students.
- ❍ FYC includes attention to teaching reading.
- ❍ FYC prioritizes faculty interacting individually with students rather than just lecturing.
- ❍ FYC develops students' identities as writers.
- ❍ FYC envisions writing as communication rather than exercise.
- ❍ FYC presents writing as reflection and as a process.
- ❍ FYC supports students' agency and self-efficacy toward their goals.
- ❍ FYC teaches students to do research and use sources.
- ❍ FYC develops critical-thinking skills.
- ❍ FYC fosters students' notions of belonging to a larger writing community.
- ❍ FYC engages students socially and pedagogically.
- ❍ FYC fosters students' humanity and dignity.

Taken together, these chapters reveal the breadth and depth of student experience in community college FYC courses, as well as the care that individual teachers take in developing programs and courses to address their students' needs. Because this volume came into being through individual chapter proposals, as well as invitations we issued to other authors, the book does not by any means cover all the pedagogical or policy concerns surrounding community college writing instruction.

What Do We Still Need to Know?

Focusing on the Students

Much recent policy has focused on the findings of "big data" that suggest that community college students who are placed in below transfer-level coursework are less likely to complete an associate's degree or transfer, compared with their peers placed directly into FYC (Mejia, Rodriguez, & Johnson, 2019). Poor, ethno-racially minoritized students of color have been disproportionately placed in remedial classes, and many find themselves unable to pass, while others end up taking multiple terms to finally reach FYC (Mejia, Rodriguez, & Johnson, 2016). Findings such as these throughout the U.S. have been used to justify many recent reforms that affect FYC programs, including California's AB 705, as well as national pushes for accelerated programs and co-requisite (rather than pre-requisite) support courses. However, the data is usually not disaggregated for specific learning disabilities, for example, a factor that might, in contrast, support more developmental education. Nor can the statistics of grades and completion rates capture the individual realities of students' home and work lives, qualitative factors that affect their performance in the classroom. A recent survey, for example, found that 19 percent of California community college students reported experiencing homelessness (Goldrick-Rab et al., 2019). Yet it is not yet clear how being unhomed or housing-insecure affects classroom practice, retention, and success rates. Further evidence is also needed to document how well curricular reforms or specialized support classes are able to narrow the equity gaps that have long denied students of color opportunities to succeed in FYC (Sims & Conaway, 2019).

In addition to rethinking basic pedagogical givens such as what language is in general and what language is or is not considered "standard" in FYC classes, we return to the issues that motivated a volume on pedagogy and policy in community college FYC classrooms and that has ostensibly opened the door to school administrators and state legislators toward reconfiguring FYC: the so-called "achievement gap," "opportunity gap," and "obligation gap." These "gaps" are seen by many scholars, however, as framed in racist views of students of color. Antiracist pedagogy and critical race theory applied to FYC have changed the rubrics, teacher's assignments, and the way we view literacy and achievement. With a focus on the achievement gap, Bettina Love (2019) writes: "Dark students and their families are sharecroppers, never able to make up the cost or close the gap because they are learning in a state of perpetual debt with no relief in sight" (p. 92). As faculty are asked to re-envision classrooms from an abolitionist perspective, putting forth paths for the classroom to become sites of social action, collaborative student-teacher social justice work, and social change within a classroom and school environment, as well as creative spaces to grow joy— how do these new perspectives change the FYC classroom? Is the call to action larger than FYC pedagogy? How do teachers work collaboratively with legislatures, administrators, and other faculty members to change the very structures that are oppressive in what Love and others see as a "sharecropper" system?

These concerns raise a larger question: Students come to community colleges for different purposes and not all intend to transfer to a four-year university, so *should they all be in the same transfer-level FYC?* With the elimination of remedial and developmental courses, students placed into a single section of FYC may include English language learners, students with severe disabilities, students pursuing vocational certificates, and students intending to transfer to academically intensive four-year universities. Patthey-Chavez, Dillon, and Thomas-Spiegel (2005) suggest that students whose stated goal was to transfer were more likely to succeed in reaching and completing transfer-level composition than students whose goals were to earn a vocational certificate or improve their basic skills. In addition, we have seen over the last few decades how reduced state and federal funding for adult education (McCarthy & McCann, 2014) has led to greater numbers of adult immigrants turning to community colleges to improve their English language proficiency due to lack of access to non-academic ESOL courses elsewhere; placing these students in FYC seems counter to their goals or interests. Furthermore, there is not sufficient data to explain why students actually do drop out. Do all pedagogies work equally well for all learners, or should instruction be differentiated? Of those students who do transfer, how do they fare in university writing requirements? Does the heavily scaffolded nature of the new FYC (which might not include as much depth as previously) actually *de*-accelerate students? If equity is not achieved in the new FYC, what are the college administrators and city and state governments doing to change the structural impediments towards equity?

We began our discussion understanding that the intensive focus on FYC grew out of generalized frustration with the number of remedial and developmental courses community college students were taking to reach college-level writing courses. We believe the better question that should be asked is whether FYC is appropriate for every student. Why not develop classes that provide community college students with direct access to literacy in their fields of study, especially in career and technical education? These concerns suggest we need more research into students' individual experiences as they progress through and beyond the composition course sequence. What forms of writing do graduates do in the workplace after they have received their degrees? How well has FYC prepared them for these writing expectations?

Student experiences also factor into other areas of community college FYC programs that we believe require further investigation. One is the role of culturally grounded learning communities such as Umoja (supporting African American students in California community colleges) and Puente (supporting educationally underserved students with transfer goals). How do writing courses in these learning communities support students' learning in ways that regular FYC courses do not? And how do these students do when they transfer?

Further investigation is also needed into how culturally affirming and specifically anti-racist approaches to FYC feature into community college students' experiences. How does actively supporting students' translanguaging with their home languages and dialects support students' engagement and learning in FYC? How does an explicit acknowledgement of linguistic injustice and validation of Black language ("This Ain't Another Statement!", 2020) foster students' writing and sense of belonging in the classroom?

Campus-level writing support beyond FYC is another area in need of more research. How does having a writing-across-the-curriculum (WAC) program affect what is taught in the FYC courses? In what ways do FYC teachers and content teachers interact? What is the role of tutoring in a college writing program, and how are these programs structured to support students? How does tutoring interact with teacher expectations? Does it matter whether tutors are peers (fellow undergraduates who have recently completed FYC themselves) or professionals? How many embedded tutors are necessary, and what kinds of training do they need? When students with particular disabilities are required to have note-takers, should the note-taker be trained? Should there be a note-taker in every FYC class?

Community college students come from all populations of our nation, meaning that many bring life experiences into the classroom that can affect their learning and participation. With better, disaggregated data, we could follow up on the needs of specific student populations. Homelessness and hunger are common concerns for students (Goldrick-Rab et al., 2019). Community colleges now recognize the importance of special centers for students such as military veterans and others who have experienced trauma or other life challenges. What effects does trauma-informed teaching have on students' learning to write? What other pedagogical approaches can help *all* students build their writing proficiency?

Composition Teaching for Transfer

While these chapters offer myriad ideas for supporting community college writers, we believe there is still room for much more discussion of pedagogy issues in FYC. One hot topic (raised by our anonymous reviewers) is the five-paragraph essay, a structure that has permeated both high school and college writing curriculum to the extent that many teachers feel like it has always been there (Caplan, 2019). Caplan argues that it is a relatively recent invention, first introduced in the 1950s and reified in writing textbooks ever since. Formulaic writing (in the form of the five-paragraph essay) is often used by teachers who feel like students are overwhelmed by college writing and need more structure, but as Caplan (2019) and Tardy (2019) point out, focusing solely on the form ignores the situated nature of writing where communicative purposes and audience expectations should determine the structure as well as the content and language choices of the text. While the focus on structure is often justified as a scaffold for students, with the idea that the scaffold can be taken away, too often students do not learn how to think about their writing process or figure out what the rhetorical situation is and how to shape a writing task to meet that situation (Tardy, 2019). We wonder, therefore, what the status of the five-paragraph essay is in community college FYC courses. How many programs still promote structure over genre? What other rhetorical approaches are being used? How is digital rhetoric being taken up?

Other pedagogical topics that merit further discussion include issues of language (including translingual writing and translanguaging), academic (dis)honesty and plagiarism, and response to writing. How can community college FYC courses build on the discussions of multilingualism and culturally informed teaching that seek to bridge concerns with teaching students how to use academic language (Matsuda, 2014) with efforts to bring students' individual voices and languages into academically valued texts (Canagarajah, 2015; Inoue, 2019)? How do we teach citation and referencing to students with very different perspectives on what counts as plagiarism and textual ownership? In what ways can teachers balance their heavy teaching load and large class sizes with effective and individualized commentary on students' texts?

The global COVID-19 pandemic has pushed higher education into online formats worldwide, bringing issues of technology in the classroom and the curriculum to the forefront. Even before the pandemic, online courses were burgeoning, with some institutions pushing instructors to develop hybrid and fully online courses that can be taught partially or entirely asynchronously. While these formats may offer access to students with non-traditional schedules or family responsibilities, we wonder what is lost in the movement away from face-to-face, synchronous writing instruction. For example, while hybrid classes might work for a mature returning student who has time constraints, new high school graduates might need the support of more than once-a-week meetings to stay on track. Recent research has noted that when weaker students take online classes, they fare worse than their counterparts in face-to-face classes, although better prepared students do equally well (Barshay, 2019). What effects does online FYC have on student learning in accelerated classes? How can FYC teachers maximize students' learning to write in an online course? What classroom technologies allow for greater student interaction or greater student efficacy in FYC? What technologies instead create greater distraction? What do FYC teachers think about the difference between teaching face-to-face compared with online and hybrid courses?

Finally, many of the chapters have raised the recent issue of state- or systemwide reforms pushing "acceleration" and placement of all students into FYC on enrollment at a college. Potentially at the expense of time to focus on teaching writing, FYC teachers are increasingly taking on content previously covered in developmental courses, such as "orientation to college" topics. Researchers have argued that courses such as a summer bridge program, first-year experience, and other kinds of college readiness courses are needed to support students in their first-year of college (Grubb, 2013). We therefore question why such college orientation should be taking place within FYC. We are concerned that these reforms have been enacted based on limited knowledge of what was happening at the classroom level in years prior to the changes. It is important to collect observational and qualitative data on the on-the-ground practices occurring in both the courses being cut—those sometimes labeled *remedial* or *developmental*—and in the new FYC courses that combine students who would otherwise have started in a developmental course. What is actually happening in the classrooms? How are these reforms influencing classroom teaching? How can FYC teachers prevent struggling students from slipping through the cracks?

Teacher Support and Professionalization

The third area where we see a large hole in the current knowledge base is support of community college FYC instructors. Faculty burnout, for example, is rarely discussed at the community college, even though it appears as a frequent topic in published scholarship. A recent survey conducted by the TYCA Workload Task Force (2020) reported that 54 percent of respondents taught 28 or more credit hours per term, with 41 percent teaching beyond their contractual load "to earn more money." Respondents said that their workload was most affected by class sizes, number of sections taught, number of different courses taught, and "student readiness for courses in relation to placement methods." Willett, Newell, and Hayward (this volume) note that burnout is another potential effect of new reforms, especially in regard to more diverse, and perhaps under-prepared, students in FYC classes with high administration-mandated enrollments. It may also help to separate *burnout*—defined as "physical or emotional exhaustion related to prolonged stress or frustration" (Berry, 2016, p. 8)—from *compassion fatigue*, "an extreme state of tension and preoccupation with the suffering of those being helped to the degree that it can create a secondary traumatic stress for the helper" (Compassion Fatigue Awareness Project, 2017). Burnout may happen more often for faculty frustrated by trying and failing to get things done at their institution, whereas compassion fatigue may affect those faculty who focus on supporting individual students with diverse and pressing socio-emotional problems as well as struggles with classroom materials.

Related to issues of burnout are those of hiring practices. One concern with hiring is that community college composition faculty are still predominantly white (TYCA Workload Task Force, 2020). As in U.S. elementary and secondary schools, this means that teachers' ethnicity does not reflect the diversity of community colleges' student bodies (AACC, 2020). A further concern is that community college FYC courses are regularly taught by part-time faculty, many of whom are "freeway flyers" commuting between multiple campuses. Overall, 58 percent of community college classes were taught by part-time faculty members (CCCSE, 2014), although the proportion of part-time writing instructors may be higher. Recent research has found that community college students in gateway courses (including FYC) taught by part-time instructors were less likely to continue to the next course in a sequence (Ran & Sanders, 2019). Ran and Sanders suggest that these outcomes may be due in part to part-time instructors' limited access to and knowledge of campus resources and facilities, which in turn may limit the guidance they are able to provide students.

These concerns may become greater as colleges remove preparatory courses: "Many of the challenges faced by part-time faculty highlighted in this study are likely to be amplified during the implementation of co-requisite courses" (Ran & Sanders, 2019, p. 28). Depending on the department and college, part-time faculty may or may not be included in departmental discussions. Indeed, with greater influence from outside funding sources, who participates in pedagogical reform is often those faculty who have the time, or whose time is bought by funding through outside grants. The issue of "participation" among community college faculty and how that affects pedagogy and English department policy calls for more research.

The issues raised here and throughout the book should be part of a national-level conversation, but in many locations, community college teachers have few meetings within their own departments that foster collegial discussions about pedagogy, curriculum, assessment, or students, and rarely opportunities (or funding) to travel to conferences where they could discuss interests and concerns with colleagues at other colleges in their state and across the country. All faculty should be compensated for collaborative work and supported in working with departmental FYC curriculum changes. Furthermore, all faculty should be provided ongoing, carefully constructed professional development relevant to their contexts and work. There also need to be ongoing departmentwide efforts to discuss how certain methods or approaches work within individual colleges. Their voices are similarly scant in the research being done within their colleges and across states, although we believe strongly that teachers' embodied understanding of their students and their writing should inform institutional research and program development. Campus IR offices could become more of a resource for teachers, used to support their pedagogy and curriculum development. Teachers can also contribute to the data collected by IR offices about their students' learning experiences and lives beyond the college campus. This qualitative, interpretive knowledge can reveal much more than holistic grades ever can.

These concerns with FYC teachers' status relate to an ongoing discussion of the (de)professionalization of English teachers. Too often, community college faculty are not consulted when curriculum and enrollment policies are implemented by administrators and legislators. Who makes the decisions about curriculum—administrators and legislators with limited understanding of education, or faculty with graduate-level knowledge of their subject areas and how to teach that content? What does accountability mean to teachers? To whom should FYC teachers be accountable—their students or the system? It seems unfair to rate instructor quality by how many students they get through a class rather than what students actually learn. Another key question of accountability is class size. How does that translate to schools where, to fulfill particular funding formulas, classes must be filled with a minimum number of students (a concept known as *productivity*) before they can be run? In an FYC program that has recently been "reformed," will classes also need to seat a minimum number of students, and what should that number be and who will decide? The ALP model as originally designed by Peter Adams (discussed in Chapter 15) apparently is intended for ten students in an accelerated support class and who are included in a total of no more than 20 in the full FYC class. What are the differences in instruction in this model versus one where 20 or more students are enrolled in the FYC support class? How are FYC instructors affected when more students are packed into a classroom? What about when classes are cut for not meeting minimum enrollments? We believe that all these decisions should be made with the participation of the instructors whose work will be affected; we further believe that instructors should be treated as the professionals they are, with job security, benefits, and promotion opportunities. How can we foster a culture of innovation within a community college system where all teachers feel empowered to contribute? How can colleges and states support writing teacher professional development, both in-service and pre-service?

Call to Action

We issue a call to action for the future of FYC at the community college. We believe that many of the concerns we have raised can be best addressed by *listening to the teachers.* Why is listening to teachers important? They are the ones in the classroom with access to individual students, knowing the stories that are not revealed in big data. They see what happens on a daily basis as societal changes intersect with campus policies and students' lives. As described in Chapter 13, when a department makes a concerted effort to bring faculty together, teachers can contribute to revising curriculum and feel like their voices are valued. We must change the way community colleges attend to faculty concerns.

One major way that teachers' voices can contribute to the future of community college policy and practice is through integrating faculty in institutional research more consistently. We believe with so much riding on IR, teachers need to be a bigger part of the IR team and part of discussions with IR. We need to have more research where teachers are partners. That said, we also recognize the demands on a college IR office in this era of accountability based on big data. We also wonder if it is appropriate to measure accountability solely on big data analysis. Teachers and administrators should be very wary of new policies and proposals that are not looking at how teachers can be partners in the research that occurs. This is especially important if the researchers come into their classrooms. There must be a long-term commitment from researchers, and *teachers* must be part of that commitment in terms of funding and learning. Institutions should recognize the research that teachers do, possibly with promotions, new credentials, or merit pay.

In closing, we want to thank everyone who contributed to this volume. We recognize that not only are community college teachers under considerable burdens, but they may also be hesitant to voice their experiences and perceptions. We still have long way to go, and we need to be activists to maintain community college teachers' voices.

REFERENCES

Adler-Kassner, L., & Wardle, E. (2015). Naming what we know: The project of this book. In L. Adler-Kassner & E. Wardle (Eds.). *Naming what we know: Threshold concepts of writing studies* (pp. 1–12). Logan: Utah State University Press.

American Association of Community Colleges (AACC). (2020). Fast facts. Retrieved from https://www.aacc.nche.edu/research-trends/fast-facts/

Barshay, J. (2019, February 4). Weakest students more likely to take online college classes but do worse in them. *The Hechinger Report.* Retrieved from hechingerreport.org

Berry, J.W. (2016). *Burnout, autonomy, and job satisfaction in full-time public community college faculty members: A regional survey and analysis.* PhD Diss., University of North Dakota.

Canagarajah, S. (2015). Clarifying the relationship between translingual practice and L2 writing: Addressing learner identities. *Applied Linguistics Review, 6*(4), 415–440. doi:10.1515/applirev-2015-0020

Caplan, N. (2019). Have we always taught the five-paragraph essay? In N. Caplan & A. Johns (Eds.), *Changing practices for the L2 writing classroom* (pp. 2–23). Ann Arbor: University of Michigan Press.

Center for Community College Student Engagement (CCCSE). (2014). Contingent commitments: Bringing part-time faculty into focus. Retrieved from http://www.ccsse.org/docs/PTF_Special_Report.pdf

Compassion Fatigue Awareness Project. (2017). Did you know? Retrieved from www.compassionfatigue.org

Goldrick-Rab, S., Baker-Smith, C., Coca, V., & Looker, E. (2019) *California community colleges #RealCollege survey.* Philadelphia: The Hope Center.

Grubb, W.N. (with Gabriner, R.). (2013). *Basic skills education in community colleges.* New York: Routledge.

Inoue, A.B. (2019). How do we language so people stop killing each other, or what do we do about White language supremacy? *College Composition and Communication, 71*(2), 352–369.

Love, B. (2019). *We want to do more than survive: Abolitionist teaching and the pursuit of educational freedom.* Boston: Beacon Press.

Matsuda, P. K. (2014). The lure of translingual writing. *PMLA, 129*(3), 478–483. doi:10.1632/pmla.2014.129.3.478

McCarthy, M.A., & McCann, A. (2014, February 27). Adult education data show signs of declining investment [blog post]. Retrieved from www.newamerica. org

Mejia, M.C., Rodriguez, O., & Johnson, H. (2016). *Preparing students for success in California's community colleges.* San Francisco: Public Policy Institute of California.

Mejia, M.C., Rodriguez, O., & Johnson, H. (2019). *What happens when colleges broaden access to transfer courses? Evidence from California's community colleges.* San Francisco: Public Policy Institute of California.

Patthey-Chavez, G. G., Dillon, P. H., & Thomas-Spiegel, J. (2005). How far do they get? Tracking students with different academic literacies through community college remediation. *Teaching English at the Two Year College, 32*(3), 261–277.

Ran, F.X., & Sanders, J. (2019). Early academic outcomes for students of part-time faculty at community colleges: How and why does instructors' employment status influence student success? [CCRC Working Paper No. 112]. New York: Community College Research Center, Columbia University. Retrieved from https://ccrc.tc.columbia.edu/publications/early-outcomes-students-part-time-faculty.html

Sims, J., & Conaway, T. (2019). Student equity plan executive summary 2019. San Mateo, CA: College of San Mateo. Retrieved from https://collegeofsanmateo. edu/ipc/docs/2018-2019/CSM_SEP_Finaldraft_5_13_19.pdf

Tardy, C. (2019). Is the five-paragraph essay a genre? In N. Caplan & A. Johns (Eds.), *Changing practices for the L2 writing classroom* (pp. 24–41). Ann Arbor: University of Michigan Press.

This ain't another statement! This is a demand for Black linguistic justice! (2020). Conference on College Composition and Communication. Retrieved from https://cccc.ncte.org/cccc/demand-for-black-linguistic-justice

TYCA Workload Task Force. (2020, March 25). Preliminary results from a national survey [Conference presentation]. TYCA Annual Conference, Milwaukee, WI. https://cccc.ncte.org/share-tyca-2020/ (conference canceled).

Questions for Reflection and Review

1: Negotiating Writing Identities Online and in Person: The Growth of Metacognition and Writing Awareness in FYC

1. What level of agency or control of your own learning have you had in your academic experience? How does your history of learning agency affect how you view student agency in the classes you teach?

2. How does viewing identity formation as a developmental process contribute to how you design reflective practice for your students?

3. What kind of experience have you had with reflective journaling? How does this experience contribute to your approach to teaching your students how to write reflectively?

2: They Are Reading from Screens, But (How) Are They Reading from Screens?

1. Do you read differently when you are reading on a screen versus reading printed text? How might you characterize those differences?

2. How do you navigate the challenges—both in the classroom and outside it—of working with your students on their critical reading skills when their readings are accessed on screens rather than in print?

3. How might you better leverage the advantages of screen reading?

3: The Socio-Cognitive Approach in Academic ESL Composition Classes

1. Why might students gain more insight to the composition process if they "discover" academic conventions such as cohesion rather than being taught them? How might you change the way you present information in your classroom?

2. Creating support groups for academic writers has both benefits and drawbacks. This chapter presents some benefits. What are some potential drawbacks and how could you mitigate them?

3. Asking students to analyze and think about their own drafts, edits, and errors requires a high level of metacognition that may be challenging to both students and instructors. Do you feel it is worth the time and effort to do so? Why/why not?

4: Using "Writing about Writing" Pedagogy with L2 and Developmental Readers and Writers at the Community College

1. What books and articles have impacted your own thinking about composing, reading, and language? How might these sources be adapted or excerpted for use in your composition classroom?

2. What are the threshold concepts that inform your approach to composition instruction? How have you made those concepts explicit for yourself and your students in your classroom, materials, assignments, and feedback practices?

3. If you assigned writing-about-writing texts, what scaffolding would you need to provide for your students? How might that scaffolding be formatted and delivered (via annotated texts, group reading, online support, or something else)?

5: Contract Grading as Anti-Racist Praxis in the Community College Context

1. What do you see as the challenges of contract grading in your context?

2. What aspects of contract grading can you see yourself implementing? How might you prepare students to succeed in what might be an unfamiliar assessment process?

3. How do issues of equity relate to issues of writing assessment? How do subtle forms of racism or systemic racism impact the teaching and assessment of writing?

4. What limitations or challenges does traditional grading bring to the writing classroom? How do you see contract grading helping you address or change these dynamics?

6: First-Year Composition: Building Relationships to Teach Emerging Writers

1. What are some significant obstacles students face in FYC courses at a community college? How can we best help students surmount them?

2. What does the instructor-student relationship look like in FYC courses at a community college? What are potential drawbacks to this relationship for both instructor and student? Potential advantages for both instructor and student?

3. What is the connotation of "emerging writer"? How can we apply our understanding of its connotation to the context of working with students in FYC courses at a community college?

7: Supporting English Learners with Disabilities in College Composition Courses

1. *Remember that ELs with disabilities are highly diverse and while they may need additional support with meeting the academic demands of writing, they may also have great strengths such as their abilities to connect with people, their specific interests and hobbies, and their multilingual and multicultural perspectives, to name a few.* With this in mind, what are some of the specific challenges that students may face with writing, and what supports are best aligned to those challenges? How can teachers help students to leverage their strengths as a foundation or stepping stone to develop their writing?

2. Think about what you are already doing to teach writing. Are there aspects of Self-Regulated Strategy Development that you are already incorporating? How can you expand on what you are already doing to integrate all of the key elements of SRSD into your current curriculum and materials? In addition, how can you plan to embed specific language development and instruction into this framework?

3. How might you adjust your implementation of strategies to meet the diverse needs of your students in writing? In what ways could you share with colleagues and other writing teachers to discuss your implementation, successes, and challenges, as well as support each other to adapt and adjust your instruction to effectively meet the needs of your language learners with disabilities?

8: Teaching Writing in a STEM Learning Community: The Heart and Science of Communication

1. Do you have any experiences coordinating courses for learning communities? What are the benefits and challenges—or what do you imagine are the benefits and challenges—for students who participate in these cohorts? How might teachers mitigate the challenges faced by students in learning communities?

2. How do the classroom activities and assignments described in this chapter help students build their metacognitive awareness of themselves as college writers?

3. What are other strategies and resources help bridge the worlds of STEM and college composition courses?

9: Motivating Students from Afar: Teaching English in a Live Broadcast Concurrent Enrollment Program

1. Since distance education is becoming more common in higher education, how might we better engage with students using technology? How might we as educators prepare ourselves to teach more effectively given the challenges of using technology?

2. What political, geographical, financial, and cultural factors influence the way concurrent enrollment programs might be structured in your area?

3. What challenges do you see in implementing concurrent enrollment at your college? How might you address these challenges?

10: Contextualized FYC Courses for Career Technical Education

1. Students in composition courses linked to vocational education excel when they can use both visual and kinesthetic learning styles to accomplish rhetorical tasks such as writing for an audience. What assignments might you have that can be modified to take into account different learning styles such as visual and kinesthetic? How might you modify other assignments to ensure equity for students who bring different learning styles into the composition class?

2. What other assignments would be a good fit for CTE courses like English 107 and 108, where students need to learn workplace writing as well as traditional FYC genres?

3. How might you design a FYC class to fit into one of your school's career and technical education sequences that would also be articulated with the FYC courses at four-year schools?

11: Heterogeneity among Community College English Learners: Who Are Our ELs in FYC and How Do They Compare?

1. What experiences and training do your CCEL students bring to your classroom? How do you integrate CCEL students' perspectives into your classroom?

2. How is your CCEL student population similar to or different from the national CCEL profile presented in this chapter?

3. What, if any, supports does your college provide to bolster CCEL students' academic engagement? What do you think might be most helpful for your CCEL students?

12: Avoiding the "Cliffs": Korean International Community College Students and Rhetorical Flexibility

1. What factors should teachers consider when working with international students in FYC and other community college classes? In what ways might international students be different from and similar to domestic second language students?

2. Without the institutional access afforded by FYC, many of the Korean international students in this study would not have been able to attend four-year universities. In what other ways might community college coursework benefit international students?

3. In addition to the approach to teaching FYC described in this chapter, what else could community college FYC programs and instructors do to support international students whose goal is to transfer to four-year institutions?

13: First-Year Composition Faculty in a Changing Community College Policy Landscape: Engagement, Agency, and Leadership in the Midst of Reform

1. What forms of institutional change have occurred recently in your institution? What were the reasons for the changes and how was the change initiated? To what extent were instructional faculty involved with the change process? How would you characterize the successes and challenges that your institution faced during this process?

2. How might you leverage data and research to inform decision-making within your department?

3. What professional development do you and your colleagues need to engage in as agents of change and to work collaboratively and collegially?

4. What models of faculty collaboration are you familiar with at your campus? Are those models effective? In what way? What kinds of considerations are necessary at your campus to create collegial and effective faculty collaboration?

14: Combining Developmental Writing and First-Year Composition Classes: Faculty Perspectives on How Co-Requisite Teaching Affects Curriculum and Pedagogy

1. What types of professional development are needed to assist FYC instructors to better identify and address the diverse needs of their students in co-requisite courses?

2. In what ways might new learning structures such as co-requisite courses affect the curricular and assessment practices of FYC courses and future English courses?

3. How can FYC instructors meet the needs of English language learners and other students in need of greater support in reading and writing in a co-requisite model of instruction?

15: Valuing Teacher Knowledge, Valuing Local Knowledge: FYC in Hawai'i Community Colleges

1. In what ways can a community college teacher work with students who are not prepared for the rigors of college or FYC in a heterogeneous classroom situation?

2. In what ways can a community college teacher ensure that students who wish to transfer to a four-year college are challenged and supported sufficiently in a classroom that may also include underprepared students and students who desire not to transfer?

3. Kay and Cindy considered the environment in which they teach and their visions for their courses when creating their curriculum. How would you create a curriculum that focuses on your vision? What kinds of resources would you need? Who would be your helpers and who would be your advisors in creating the curriculum? How would that curriculum fit with your student learning outcomes and assessment processes? Would these need to change?

16: IR and Remediation Reform: A Contextualized Exploration for Faculty

1. What line of inquiry about your teaching experience could IR help you explore and why? How would you go about approaching your IR office?

2. How could a partnership between an English department and IR influence the strategic direction of your college? Can you identify your college's strategic direction? Your department's strategic direction? Thinking about both or one of those, what kinds of research might you do to influence these directions?

3. What kinds of placement into FYC composition does your college do? How successful is that placement, and how do you know it is successful or not? What kinds of research do you currently do (if you don't do any, what kinds of research might you consider planning with your IR?) that could inform how students are placed in FYC?

Glossary

10 + 1: Reference to California Assembly Bill 1725 Chapter 973 passed in 1998 that provided for faculty participation in governance and said that community college governing boards should rely primarily on faculty input for ten distinct academic areas, such as curriculum development, plus any additional items agreed upon by a local academic senate and governing board.

Andragogy: The methods and practices for teaching adults.

Anti-racism: A stance that recognizes the complexity and ubiquity of racism in contemporary society. It opens the possibility of confronting racism without claiming to be outside of the structures and beliefs of a racist society. For more on this topic, see Ijeoma Olou's *So You Want to Talk About Race* (2019) and Ibram X. Kendi's *How to Be an Antiracist* (2019).

Articulation: Used in higher education to denote the process by which one institution matches its courses (through coursework, assessment, etc.) to another institution to create a way to assess the sameness of courses and allow students to change colleges and not need to repeat the same course.

Baseline: In statistics, the starting measurement of a set of variables, factors, or characteristics against which results from future models that account for other characteristics are compared.

Community College English Learner (CCEL): Community college students who speak a language other than English at home and who are still developing English language proficiency necessary for full participation in academic activities. Callahan, Hartman, and Yu (Chapter 11) identify CCELs as the subset of bi-/multilingual community college students in the CCSSE dataset who had completed, or were currently taking, one or more of the following courses: ESL, Developmental Reading, and Developmental Writing.

Community College Survey of Student Engagement (CCSSE): A large-scale survey administered annually to more than 400,000 students in more than 700 community colleges nationwide since 2014. The CCSSE collects information about how students engage while enrolled at community colleges and how those institutions can work to improve student engagement and, ultimately, student retention, achievement, and attainment. More information about the CCSSE can be found at: http://www.ccsse.org/

Content Analysis: A research technique used to analyze text looking for thematic patterns that occur throughout the text as a way to examine qualitative data through a quantitative lens.

Contract Grading: Involves students negotiating the amount of labor they will complete to earn a course grade. It departs from more common assessment methods because students earn grades based on goals they set and/or the amount of labor they put into the class. Teachers can also set a limit on absences or require other criteria for grading that fit their values and contexts.

Control: In statistics, an individual or contextual background characteristic that must be accounted for, but is generally not a substantive factor of interest—for example, gender or prior schooling.

Co-requisite: A required support course for students who are co-enrolled in a credit-bearing course in accelerated models of developmental coursework.

Discourse: Defined by linguist James Gee (1989) as "a socially accepted association among ways of using language, of thinking, and of acting that can be used to identify oneself as a member of a socially meaningful group or 'social network'" (p. 18).

English for Speakers of Other Languages (ESOL): A program focused on developing proficiency in English as an additional language.

English Learner (EL): A designation for students whose first language is not English and whose English language proficiency is judged to be inadequate for full participation in academic work in English without special support.

Equity: A concept in social justice work that is often contrasted with *equality*. While equality aims for sameness, equity promotes fair and just outcomes rather than assuming similar starting points.

Exploratory Factor Analysis (EFA): A statistical method designed to identify the underlying relationships or structure of a group of variables.

Factor: A characteristic; see **variable, independent**.

Habitus: Qualities or dispositions of individuals that make them more likely to behave in certain ways over others. According to Thompson (1991), "The dispositions generate practices, perceptions and attitudes which are 'regular' without being consciously co-ordinated or governed by any 'rule'" (p. 12). Sociologist Pierre Bourdieu (1984) connected habitus to an individual's social class, as well as upbringing and education.

Identity: A conception of the self in relation to external social contexts. Adopting an identity is the discovery of the self as an actor in a new social context.

Intersegmental: Crossing institutional levels in an educational system (such as K–12, community college, and four-year universities).

Journaling: Regular, informal reflective writing, usually for oneself or in dialogue with a teacher. In the academic context, journaling can be a way to analytically explore procedural, declarative, and conditional knowledge.

Kindergarten through 12th Grade (K–12): Refers to the U.S. public education system serving the primary (elementary) and secondary grades.

Knowledge, Conditional: Includes the strategies for applying procedural and declarative knowledge in different contexts.

Knowledge, Declarative: Refers to facts that writers know. It involves the ability to describe and define writing terms such as rhetorical situation, audience, and genre.

Knowledge, Procedural: Refers to the process for accomplishing tasks.

Literate Behavior: Literate behaviors include the acts of reading and writing as well as strategies for approaching different kinds of reading and writing and valuing literacy as a way to understand the world.

Mean: In statistics, a measure of central tendency, also referred to as the *arithmetic average.*

Metacognition: The ability to think about one's own thinking processes and reflect on how one comes to understand new knowledge.

National Survey of Student Engagement (NSSE): A large-scale survey administered annually to approximately 300,000 students in more than 500 colleges and universities, the NSSE collects information about student demographics, academics, and engagement. More information about the NSSE can be found at: http://nsse.indiana.edu/html/about.cfm.

Number (N): In statistics, reported as either population or sample size.

Open Access: The idea that anyone can be admitted to a college. Open access colleges generally do not have application requirements such as a minimum GPA or test scores.

p-value: In statistics, the probability value that the null hypothesis is true or the likelihood that any differences between groups occurred by chance alone.

Parameter Estimate: The estimated change in an outcome associated with a one-unit change in the predictor variable, all other variables held constant; also called a coefficient.

Reflective Practice: Involves analyzing one's own behavior as a way of learning from experience and applying what one has learned to novel situations.

Regression: A statistical process designed to estimate relationships between variables.

Scaffolding: The process of providing supports that allow students to progress though interactions with the teacher, other students, or instructional materials from more basic skills to more advanced skills with increasing independence.

Self-efficacy: Belief in one's own ability to succeed.

Standard Deviation (SD): A measure used to quantify the amount of variation that occurs, on average, within a given dataset, around certain values. When measuring from the mean, one can expect roughly two-thirds (67 percent) of the population to fall within one SD, and 95 percent within 2 SD.

Stop Out: A student enrolled in college who discontinues enrolling for one or more terms. This is distinguished from the term *drop out*, which implies a permanent discontinuance. The term *stop out* allows for the possibility of re-enrollment at the same or different college at a later date.

Title 5: Refers to a section of law in the California Code of Regulations that govern education including the K–12 California Department of Education (Division 1) and California Community Colleges (Division 6).

Threshold Concept: An idea that serves as a framework for knowledge within a particular discipline. These concepts can initially cause difficulty for students, but once attained, they transform students' learning and allow them to synthesize disciplinary knowledge. The concepts serve as a threshold or gateway to knowledge and practice within a given discipline.

Test of English as a Foreign Language (TOEFL)®: A standardized test commonly used to determine prospective international students' English proficiency and college readiness.

Throughput Data: The number of students who successfully complete transfer-level English requirements. This data collection strategy shifts the focus away from individual students' success or failure in a particular course and instead illustrates the ways in which placing students lower in the English course trajectory makes it less likely that they will pass transfer-level English.

Transfer of Knowledge: The ability to use knowledge from one context in a new context.

Tyranny of the Average: Used by statisticians to describe how a central tendency alone does not account for the variability in a set of data. For example, using only the average shoe size to produce footwear would not account for those with smaller and larger than average feet. In a policy context, regulations often address the most common situations and can fail to account for special circumstances.

Variable: In statistics, a measurable or quantifiable characteristic.

Variable, Demographic: A subgroup of independent variables. A background characteristic (e.g., race, gender, age upon immigration) that may, for example, shape a student's academic outcomes.

Variable, Dependent: An outcome that depends on the various independent variables and their interaction therein.

Variable, Independent or Predictor: An experiential or contextual factor (e.g., prior educational experiences, credits completed to date, peer and mentor relationships) that, for example, may shape a student's academic outcomes.

Variable, Ordered Categorical (also called **Ordinal**): Variable categories that can be sorted into a particular order (e.g., low, medium, high) but that are not inherently spaced evenly (in contrast with numerical variables, which are evenly spaced).

ℛEFERENCES

Bourdieu, P. (1984). *Distinction: A social critique of the judgment of taste.* Cambridge, MA: Harvard University Press.

Gee, J. P. (1989). What is literacy? *Journal of Education, 171*(1), 18–25.

Kendi, I. X. (2019). *How to be an antiracist.* New York: One World.

Olou, I. (2019). *So you want to talk about race.* New York: Seal Press.

Thompson, J. B. (1991). Editor's introduction. In P. Bourdieu (Ed.), *Language and symbolic power* (pp. 1–31). Cambridge, MA: Harvard University Press.

Contributor Bios

Editors

Meryl Siegal is an English instructor at Laney College. She teaches courses in teacher education and applied linguistics internationally and in the San Francisco Bay Area. She is co-editor of two volumes on multilingual writers. Her areas of research include pragmatics, language learning, community college policy and pedagogy, and teacher education.

Betsy Gilliland is an associate professor in the Department of Second Language Studies at the University of Hawai'i, Mānoa, and teaches courses in language teacher education and second language writing. She leads a study abroad teaching practicum in Thailand and was a Fulbright Scholar at Universidad de Atacama in Chile. Her research examines adolescent second language writing and language teacher learning.

Authors

David A. Allred is a professor of English and Philosophy at Snow College in Utah, where he also serves as department chair. He teaches developmental, first-year, and research writing classes along with literature courses via face-to-face, online, and IVC classrooms.

Gonzalo Arrizon is a retention specialist in the STEM Center at Cañada College in California, as well as an adjunct English instructor. He holds a BA in English from UC–Berkeley, and an MA in English from UC–Santa Barbara. He is proud to have been a first-generation college student himself and enjoys building bridges between the sciences and the humanities.

Barbara A. Auris started her teaching career as a Peace Corps volunteer in Gabon, Central Africa. She then taught in South Africa after completing her master's degree in Applied Linguistics. She recently completed her doctorate in Higher Education and currently teaches and coordinates the ELL program at Montgomery County Community College in Pennsylvania.

Sharon Avni is an associate professor in the department of Academic Literacy and Linguistics at Borough of Manhattan Community College, City University of New York (CUNY). Her research interests include academic literacy development and emergent bilinguals and the teaching and learning of Hebrew in American educational contexts.

Ruth Benander is a professor in the Department of English and Communication at the University of Cincinnati Blue Ash College, where she teaches developmental, first-year, and second-year composition in addition to faculty development seminars. Her research interests include social justice in online learning, eportfolios in STEM education, and fostering intercultural awareness through experiential learning.

George C. Bunch is a professor of Education at the University of California, Santa Cruz. A former high school ESL teacher, he conducts research on policies, institutional practices, curriculum, pedagogy, and teacher preparation for English Learners in K–12 and community colleges. He holds a PhD in educational linguistics from Stanford University.

Rebecca M. Callahan is an associate professor of Educational Policy & Planning at the University of Texas–Austin. A former bilingual K–12 educator, her research examines immigrant adolescents' transition into young adulthood, with a focus on how language, education, and immigration policies intersect for these youth.

Ann Endris is the Title V Director at Cabrillo College. At the time she wrote the chapter in this volume, she was an adjunct faculty member and program director, and she has been involved in multiple efforts to transform the California Community College system to increase equity.

She earned an MA in Latin American Studies from the University of California, San Diego.

Heather B. Finn is an associate professor of ESL and linguistics at Borough of Manhattan Community College, City University of New York. Her research focuses on students' experiences in the second language writing classroom and the development of language and literacy within accelerated models of instruction.

Catherine E. Hartman is a postdoctoral research associate at the National Resource Center for The First-Year Experience and Students in Transition at the University of South Carolina. Her research focuses on community college student success, student transfer from community colleges to four-year schools, and the educational experiences of linguistically diverse students.

Craig Hayward is Dean of Institutional Effectiveness at Bakersfield College in California. He has contributed to statewide initiatives including the Program Pathways Mapper (2018), the Basic Skills Cohort Progress Tracker (2011), the Student Success Scorecard (2012), and the Transfer Velocity Cohort Report (2010). He is a member of the Multiple Measures Assessment Project (MMAP) research team.

Chandra Howard is an English Instructor at Modesto Junior College in California's Central Valley. She teaches pre-transfer accelerated writing courses and was on the development committee for piloting acceleration in the English Department. She is also the English instructor and department liaison for the college's Umoja program.

Erin B. Jensen is an associate professor of English at Belmont Abbey College. Previous to teaching at Belmont Abbey, she taught technical writing at Great Basin College. Her research focuses on first-year writing courses, digital and multimodal writing pedagogy, and technical writing.

Kylie A. Kenner is a doctoral candidate in Education at the University of California, Santa Cruz, where she researches support initiatives for community college students. She earned an MA in English Composition from San Francisco State University and has experience teaching FYC, rhetoric and inquiry, and college readiness courses.

Sarah Klotz is an assistant professor of English at the College of the Holy Cross. She taught for three years at Butte College in California. Her research focuses on Native American rhetorics and anti-racist writing pedagogies. She received the Conference on College Composition and Communication Emergent Researcher Award for her book *Writing Their Bodies: Restoring Rhetorical Relations at the Carlisle Indian Industrial School.*

Andrew Kranzman is an English Instructor at Modesto Junior College in California's Central Valley. He teaches pre-transfer accelerated writing courses, co-requisite writing courses, and British Literature courses. Andrew was on the committee that redesigned pre-transfer pathways in English, including a co-requisite pathway. Prior to MJC, he taught at Skyline College, Michigan State University, and San Quentin State Prison.

Michael Larkin is a lecturer with the College Writing Programs at the University of California, Berkeley, where he teaches composition and creative writing. He also curates UCB's Summer Reading List for New Students, which can be found at reading.berkeley.edu.

Miriam Moore is an assistant professor of English at the University of North Georgia. She holds a PhD in Linguistics from the University of South Carolina, and she taught FYC and ESL for twenty years at community colleges in New Jersey and Virginia. She is co-author of several developmental English textbooks.

Mallory Newell is Director of Institutional Research and Planning and teaches political science at De Anza College (California). She has served as project lead for the Multiple Measures Assessment Project (MMAP), which has assisted more than 90 California community colleges with implementing high school transcript–based multiple measures assessment. She received her EdD in Higher Education and Policy studies from Sacramento State University.

Kade Parry teaches composition and literature at Snow College in Utah, including first-year writing, research writing, and literature courses on myths and folktales, science fiction, and Gothic and supernatural. In addition to online and face-to-face teaching, Kade teaches live-broadcast IVC classes.

Brenda Refaei is an associate professor in the Department of English and Communication at the University of Cincinnati Blue Ash College, where she teaches developmental, first-year, and second-year composition. Her research interests include examining composition pedagogy, eportfolio pedagogy, and assessment process to better support equity and inclusion initiatives.

Jennifer Stieger is an English instructor at Great Basin College in Nevada and teaches technical writing to first-year Career Technical Education students. She co-designed the technical writing first-year writing sequence that is required for CTE students.

Caroline Torres teaches Second Language Teaching and TESOL to pre-service and in-service teachers and college-level writing to English learners at Kapiʻolani Community College in Hawaiʻi. She has taught English in Japan and Hawaiʻi. Research interests include ELs, ELs with disabilities, writing instruction, Universal Design for Learning, and place-based learning.

Kellyanne Ure teaches composition, literature, and philosophy courses at Snow College in Utah, including IVC concurrent enrollment composition courses, British literature, and world religion.

Carl Whithaus is a professor of Writing and Rhetoric at the University of California, Davis. He served as Director of the University Writing Program (UWP) from 2011–2018. He studies writing assessment, writing in the disciplines (particularly communication in the sciences and engineering), and digital culture.

Justin G. Whitney is a former community college student who is currently an assistant professor at Tennessee State University. He studies and teaches writing with particular interest in technical and professional writing, culture, and knowledge transfer.

Terrence Willett is Dean of Research, Planning, and Institutional Effectiveness at Cabrillo College (California) and previously Senior Researcher for the RP Group, Director of Research for Cal-PASS (an intersegmental data system), Director of Research for Gavilan College, and Research Technician for Cabrillo College. He also taught field biology at Gavilan College and tutored math and science at Cabrillo College.

Hongwei Yu serves as graduate faculty in the Department of Curriculum and Instruction at Texas State University (San Marcos). His research centers on student persistence and academic achievement, part-time faculty, and vertical transfer and student academic misconduct.

Whitney Zulim is an English Instructor at Great Basin College in Nevada. She earned her BS degree in Business Administration from the University of Nevada, Reno. Based on her experience with CTE students and faculty, she creates a learning environment that engages and motivates students to be prepared for various workplace communication situations.

Index